SET _84 – 48_   NO. _____

PROPERTY OF
ESTHERVILLE PUBLIC SCHOOLS

YOU WILL BE REQUIRED TO PAY FOR ANY DAMAGE THE BOOK MAY
RECEIVE WHILE IN YOUR POSSESSION OR FOR ITS FULL VALUE IF LOST

WHEN LOANED	CONDITION WHEN LOANE	TO WHOM LOANED	WHEN RETUR EU	CONDITION WHEN Re D	FINED

N-NEW; E-EXCELLENT; G-GOOD; F-FA ; P-POOR

COMPOSITION AND APPLIED GRAMMAR

THE WRITING PROCESS

10

Miles C. Olson

Gale Dugas Hulme

Daniel R. Kirby

Iris M. Tiedt

Allyn and Bacon, Inc.

Boston   Rockleigh, N.J.   Atlanta   Dallas   San Jose

London   Sydney   Toronto

The Writing Process—Books 7 through 12

Authors and Consultants

Miles C. Olson, Senior Author—Professor of English Education, University of Colorado at Boulder; Director, Colorado Writing Project.

Allen Berger, Consultant—Professor of Language Communications, University of Pittsburgh; Director, Pittsburgh Reading and Writing Consultants; Editor, *English Education.*

Nancy Tia Brown, Coauthor, Book 12—Project Director in Career Education and Gifted Education, Jefferson County Public Schools, Colorado; former high-school foreign languages teacher.

Warren E. Combs, Coauthor, Book 8—Writing Consultant, Clarke and DeKalb County Schools, Georgia.

Philip DiStefano, Coauthor, Book 11—Professor of English Education and Reading, University of Colorado at Boulder; Co-Director, Colorado Writing Project; Consultant, National Assessment of Educational Progress.

Michael G. Gessner—Research Associate, Center for the Study of Reading and Writing, University of Colorado at Boulder. Contributing Author, Book 11.

Gale Dugas Hulme, Coauthor, Books 7 and 10—Language Arts Consultant for Gwinnett County Public Schools, Lawrenceville, Georgia; former high-school English teacher and department chair.

Sandra Jones—Language Arts Supervisor for the Dougherty County Schools, Albany, Georgia. Contributing Author, Book 7.

Daniel R. Kirby, Coauthor, Books 7 and 10—Professor of English Education, University of Georgia at Athens.

Kathleen Kirby—Instructor, University of Georgia, Athens, Georgia. Contributing Author, Book 10.

Carol B. Kuykendall, Coauthor, Books 9 and 12—Executive Director, English Language Arts, Houston (Texas) Independent School District.

Cherie A. Lyons, Coauthor, Book 12—Project Director in Career Education, Jefferson County Public Schools, Colorado; former high-school English teacher.

Iris M. Tiedt, Coauthor, Book 10—Professor, San Jose State University (California); Director, South Bay Writing Project.

Acknowledgments for material quoted from other sources will be found on page 328 which is an extension of this page.

Senior Editor: Patricia A. Browne
Senior Designer: Beverly Fell
Preparation Services Coordinator: Martha E. Ballentine
Production and Art Services by Tonia Noell-Roberts

Library of Congress Catalog Card No. 81-68466
© **Copyright, 1982, by Allyn and Bacon, Inc.** All rights reserved. No part of the material protected by this copyright notice may be reproduced or utilized in any form or by any means, electronic or mechanical, including photocopying, recording, or by any information storage and retrieval system, without written permission from the copyright owner.

Printed in the United States of America
ISBN 0-205-07546-0

4   5   6   7   8   9   89   88   87   86   85   84

CONTENTS

Finding a Voice

Chapter 1

A New Way of Writing

What is your first reaction when a teacher says, "Now I want you to write a composition"? If you're like most high school students, your reaction is something less than unrestrained joy. For many students, school writing assignments are difficult at best and often outright drudgery. If you are fortunate enough to be among those who find school writing assignments enjoyable, congratulations.

What is it about writing school assignments that frustrates so many students? Are some assignments more rewarding than others? Have you ever written a teacher-assigned composition which pleased you? How can writing assignments become positive experiences?

Free Writing 1: School Writing

Take out a sheet of paper and start writing. On your paper, talk about your school writing experiences. Respond to the preceding questions or develop your own response. Keep writing for about ten minutes. Don't stop to correct your writing. Just express feelings about school writing assignments. Get your pen or pencil and start writing. Your teacher may ask you to share some highlights from free writing with class members.

Getting
It
Started

A Word About Free Writing

If you have never tried free writing, you may find it a strange experience at first. When you free write, you write as fast as you can, letting words and ideas tumble out of your mind onto the page. You try to keep writing until you have said your piece. You do not worry about the niceties of organization and mechanics. Free writing is a way of finding out what you know and feel. Free writing helps you to discover. You will do a number of free writings throughout this book. Some of them will blossom into more polished pieces of writing; others will just help you clarify your thinking. All free writing will be a part of the "learn to write by writing" philosophy of this book.

<hr />

Free-Writing Checklist

**Checking
It
Out**

Quickly reread your free writing aloud. Add missing words. Punctuate as necessary. Work for clarity.

<hr />

SPOTLIGHT

Teachers and Writing

It may surprise you to know that many English teachers are frustrated about teaching writing. The burden of reading and grading student writing is time consuming, and student compositions are sometimes dull and uninspiring. Teachers complain that some students are more interested in getting a grade than in learning to write. Teachers bemoan the general disinterest students show toward writing assignments. Ask your writing teacher to talk about the frustrations of teaching writing. Listen and ask questions.

If learning to write is such a difficult experience for teachers and students, why bother? Why torture yourself with this writing business, anyway? How important is it really to be able to write well? Will you use writing after you get out of school? Try compiling a quick list of the ways people use writing after high school. Your teacher may use your ideas to make a list on the board.

Look at that list on the board. Did anyone suggest that writing is a way of organizing thoughts? Often, as we write, our thoughts become clear to us. Many writers testify to the writing process as a clarifying and organizing activity. Writing to discover what you know and feel, writing to weigh both sides of an issue, writing to tell someone something which you cannot say in person are all valuable experiences which all too few people enjoy in adulthood.

This book has two important purposes. The first aim is to help you discover or rediscover the joy of writing well. The second purpose is to help you learn to use writing as a process of discovery to shape and clarify ideas and feelings.

School Writing

Some students say that they enjoy writing in journals and that they like to write for themselves in private; but when the teacher makes the assignment, they lose their enthusiasm. Have you ever written on your own without being told to do so? Do you have private writings which you share only with a close friend? Do you feel differently about those private writings than you do about school assignments? How does self-sponsored writing differ from school-sponsored writing?

Some students say that school assignments are less enjoyable because the teacher selects the topic, or because the teacher requires an outline, or because the teacher expects rigid adherance to a particular form. Students complain that school writing assignments are often limited to the five-paragraph theme. If you are not familiar with the five-paragraph theme, you soon will be. Many composition textbooks teach only that form. Basically the five-paragraph theme is a formula. The first paragraph introduces the paper. Each of the next three paragraphs makes a separate point about the topic. The final paragraph concludes the paper. The steps to writing such a paper are 1. limit your topic, 2. make an outline, 3. write your paper using the five-paragraph formula, 4. recopy it neatly. This five-paragraph theme written by a student will illustrate the formula for you.

Anyone who drives a car should be able to maintain it. There is a lot of satisfaction for drivers who own a car when they are able to maintain it themselves. There are three reasons for being able to maintain a car.

The first reason is to save money. If a driver doesn't keep oil and water in the car, the engine could be ruined. A complete overhaul would be needed if the engine was ruined, and that would cost a lot. Sometimes it is cheaper to junk the car and buy a new one than to repair it.

The second reason is so the car will run better. If a driver doesn't check the water level in the battery, the battery might be dead when he or she needed the car. If the driver lets the tires get too low, they might go flat, and he or she could be left without a car. If the spark plugs get bad, the car will use much more gas than it should and will not have much power.

Finally, a driver should be able to maintain a car so that he or she can learn something about mechanics. Anybody who drives a car needs to know about mechanics in order to figure out what's wrong if the car doesn't work right. Also, drivers who know about mechanics will be able to tell whether they are getting a bad deal from a mechanic.

Being able to perform routine maintenance on a car can save money, make the car run better and be more dependable, and teach the driver something about mechanics. All drivers should learn how to maintain their cars.

Jerry

Students report that this approach to school writing is sometimes frustrating and often does not result in their best writing. Many student writers find an outline enslaving and artificial. They find it difficult to write interesting and powerful pieces using such a formula.

In this book you will learn a process for writing clear, forceful school writing without resorting to the five-paragraph formula. Student writers can discover ideas and organizational strategies as they write. In some ways the process you will use in this book will be far more demanding than traditional theme writing is. As the writer, you will have to rely more on your own intuitions and judgments, but you will also be able to use more of your own resources to develop your writing assignments. You will work longer and more deliberately on each writing assignment, but you may be more pleased with the final product. If you are willing to give this process a chance, you should learn to discover topic ideas, develop writing strategies, draft effective pieces, and shape and revise drafts into polished pieces.

SPOTLIGHT

Transactional Writing

You are probably familiar with the traditional labels for classifying types of writing. For at least a hundred years or so, writing teachers have talked about four different kinds or modes of writing. Even your parents and older brothers and sisters can probably recite the list: description, narration, exposition, and argument. Briefly, description describes, narration tells, exposition explains, and argument persuades. The labels are precise and easy to define. They date back to a time when types of writing were also easier to classify. Contemporary writing is often difficult to label neatly within any one of the four types. Look at these four excerpts from a contemporary author and classify them using the traditional four modes:

Excerpt 1

> Freeman's son George is slender too. He stands about four inches taller than his father, and is a shade darker. In the summertime on the waterways of British Columbia, where George has lived from the time he was seventeen, the long days and the refracted sunlight tan him so darkly that he is taken for an Indian. He dresses entirely in wool, which stays warm when wet, and he is impatient with Northerners who don't dress that way. His taste, or his necessity, runs to long woolen underwear, baggy oft-patched wool trousers, ragged wool sweaters, and wool watch caps. He often goes barefoot. His hair is moderately long and it hangs scraggly in the rain. He is in his early twenties, and his beard is still sparse.

This is definitely descriptive, isn't it? The author gives us a sharply detailed picture of George Freeman.

Excerpt 2

> Between Mars and Jupiter lies a large gap where one or two planets, perhaps even three, are thought to have orbited. The planets collided, or suffered some other serious accident, for the gap is now filled with fragments. These are the asteroids. There are many thousands of them, of which sixteen hundred have been tracked, each in its private orbit around the sun. They appear through telescopes as starlike points of light, hence the name. Astronomers have learned a lot about asteroids by analyzing their light. Asteroids spin, and the variations in the sunlight they reflect reveal their shapes. The smaller asteroids are irregular, the larger ones spherical. On big asteroids, gravity is respectable—nearly that of the moon. The asteroid Ceres is 480 miles in diameter. Pallas is 300 miles wide, Vesta 240, Juno 120.

The author explains the origin and characteristics of asteroids. This is definitely exposition.

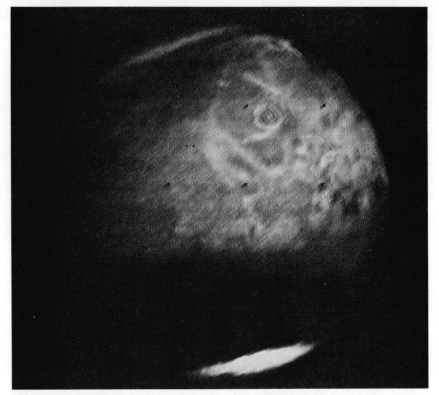

Photograph of Mars taken by the Mariner 7 spacecraft.

Excerpt 3

For the next two days he worked his way against the wind through Cordero Channel, then Wellbore Channel, and then past Whirlpool Rapids. When he reached Johnstone Strait, where the narrow passages open up, the wind changed. A strong southeaster blew up the strait. The wind ran against the tide, setting up big breaking waves. George raised his sails for the first time. "I was scared to death," he says. "I didn't know what my boat would do in these big waves. Everyone had told me I'd never survive some of those places." But everyone was wrong. The baidarka covered forty miles that morning. It was, George concedes, a great moment. "At that point, I knew I had a canoe to travel in. Until the sails worked, it was just a big kayak."

This is a short paragraph—a mini narrative—summarizing George's canoe trip.

Excerpt 4

> Mouse Woman believed that her personal metabolism required some animal protein with her meals. This, George thought, was superstition. It was all in her head. He himself ate some fish, a lot of rice, vegetables, and potatoes, and very little meat. Meat just sits in your stomach and clogs things up.

This is a compact anti-meat excerpt. It's also an argument of sorts.

These four passages come from a book entitled *The Starship and the Canoe*, a biography about a man and his son. The author, Kenneth Brower, uses all four modes of writing in the same work—sometimes even in the same paragraph. The author's intent is to create a biography as interesting and beautiful as any novel. He is not bound by the conventional modes, and his writing defies simple classification.

Many composition textbooks still use the labels you have just read about (page 7), and you may want to memorize them. However, this

writing text will use a new label for school writing: *transactional writing*. Any writing in which the author's primary intent is to "get something done" or to contact an audience directly, will be called transactional writing. Grocery lists, letters of inquiry, written instructions, critical reviews, persuasive pieces, position papers, written apologies, formal essays, and even Kenneth Brower's moving biography are all transactional writings. They all involve an author in an attempt to use writing as a verbal transaction. Writers may use descriptive detail, tell a story, explain a confusing concept, or try to convince the reader; but if the writer's primary purpose is to discuss something with another person, the writing is a transactional piece. The term *transactional* is more flexible than the traditional labels and is directly related to the writer's purpose. Most assigned school writing is transactional writing.

Discovering

The starting point for any effective piece of writing is inside your own head. Your experiences, memories, knowledge, intuitions, and feelings about any writing topic are your first and most important resource. Learning to discover what you already know and feel about a writing topic is the first step toward writing effective transactional pieces.

Most professional writers keep a notebook, a log book, a journal, or a day book. Whatever they call it, this book is the place for sorting out ideas, trying out strategies, and planning writing projects. You will learn to work more deliberately as a writer by using the writer's most important tool—the Writer's Notebook. Learn to use the Notebook to discover, to develop, and to draft pieces of writing.

There are only two basic rules about the Writer's Notebook—

1. It is yours—personalize it any way you wish. Keep all of your writings, notes, observations, and drafts in it. Your teacher will look at it occasionally to see what you are doing, perhaps even responding as a special reader.
2. Share it with others—your teacher will not require you to share, but you may be invited to do so. Writers learn much about writing by observing the process used by other writers. Your teacher may mark effective pieces in your Writer's Notebook and ask your permission to show it to other writers. While you practice and gain confidence as a writer, you will need response from a wider audience. Your classmates can help you make decisions and judgments about your writing; learn to look to them as a resource.

Free Writing 2: Looking Inside

Good writers have learned to trust their own intuitions. They write about things they have thought about or experienced. They have a "feel for" personal resources which can inform and entertain other people. You will begin every major writing assignment by looking inside your own head. All good writing begins there. With practice you can learn to find and select from all that chaos, just the right words and phrases for a piece of writing.

Take out paper and pencil and prepare to free write. Look inside yourself. What special knowledge and abilities do you have? What are some things you know more about than other people do? What are some things about yourself which make you proud? What are some hopes you have for the future? What are some things you plan to know more about? What do you spend most of your non-school time doing? Don't try to answer all of these questions in your free writing. If you get rolling on something, stay with it. Let your pencil follow your mind. Keep writing for at least ten minutes.

Getting It Down

Reread your free writing. Add any missing words, and forgotten punctuation. Reword any confusing parts, then file the free writing in your Writer's Notebook.

Checking It Out

Free Writing 3: Looking Outside

Good writers who trust their own intuition also check frequently with other people and try their ideas out on them. They test their own perceptions by comparing them with perceptions other people have. You can inform your own writing by using knowledgeable outsiders as consultants.

Get a reality check on Free Writing 2 by asking someone else about yourself. Choose a consultant who knows you well—maybe a close friend or a parent or relative. Choose someone whose opinion and judgment you respect, and set up an interview. Be sure to allow for at least a half hour of uninterrupted discussion.

Getting It Started

Take your Writer's Notebook and several pens or pencils to the interview. Put your consultant at ease by explaining that you want him or her to answer a few questions while you take notes.

The purpose of this interview is to get a second opinion about yourself. To get helpful information from your consultant, you need to have thought through a series of good leading questions, such as the following:

Sample Questions

1. What do you see as my strongest points? What are some things I do that you wish you could do?
2. Do I have any idiosyncrasies that make you laugh? Do I do anything that drives you crazy?
3. Where do you think I'll be in five years?
4. If you were describing me to someone who didn't know me, what are some things you would tell that person?
5. What's the first thing you think of when you hear my name? Why?

Questions such as these are designed to draw out your consultant and inform your perceptions of yourself. You may feel self-conscious asking a friend to talk about you. Relax, listen carefully, take notes, and enjoy the conversation.

SPOTLIGHT

In your next assignment you will rework your interview notes. This example from Becky's interview might help illustrate what you need to do.

BECKY: Do I do anything that drives other people crazy?

CONSULTANT: (laugh) Well this doesn't drive me crazy, but you are always fooling with your hair. You are always changing it. Sometimes you curl it; other times you have those two pony tails. Sometimes you part it in the middle, sometimes you have a bun. And that's not the worst of it—you always want to know what I think of it. "Do you like it better up or down?" "Do you think I should curl it?" "Should I pin it back?" Come to think of it that does drive me crazy.

Becky's free writing looked like this:

I drive my friends crazy worrying about my hair. My consultant says the worst of it is all my questions, "How does it look?" "Do you think I should curl it?" I guess I'm a hair person.

〜〜〜〜〜〜〜〜〜〜〜〜〜〜〜〜〜〜〜〜〜〜〜〜〜

Now, rework your notes into a piece of free writing. Try to capture your consultant's exact words. Also include some of your own reactions to what he or she told you. Don't worry about organization or mechanics. Just use your own words and those of your consultant.

Getting It Down

〜〜〜〜〜〜〜〜〜〜〜〜〜〜〜〜〜〜〜〜〜〜〜〜〜

Free Writing 4: Pulling it Together—A Personal Statement
You have now used two important sets of resources: inside resources—your own head, and outside resources—a consultant whose opinion you trust. Read your free writings aloud to a partner. Listen to the two pieces. Look for recurring themes in the two pieces. Can you find a focal point? What jumps out at you?

Getting It Started

〜〜〜〜〜〜〜〜〜〜〜〜〜〜〜〜〜〜〜〜〜〜〜〜〜

Draft a personal statement—a description of yourself to share with your classmates. Try to use both inside and outside free writings to construct an honest view of yourself which will inform your audience.

Experiment as you draft the piece. Try several different openings. Use your intuition as you write the draft. Follow your mind. If the piece takes off in a new direction, follow it.

Getting It Down

〜〜〜〜〜〜〜〜〜〜〜〜〜〜〜〜〜〜〜〜〜〜〜〜〜

~~~~~~

**Checking
It
Out**

Don't hurry your drafting. Read your free writings again, then share the draft with someone *as* you write it.

~~~~~~

**Getting
It
Right**

Tinker with your personal statement until you are satisfied that it is an accurate picture of you.

Your teacher may ask you to share the finished piece with the class or with a small group.

~~~~~~

SPOTLIGHT

Look at Matt's first draft of a personal statement:

First Draft: Personal Statement

I'm at least two very different people. My friends look to me as the answer-man. For some reason I'm expected to know everything. I even make up answers if I don't know them. I'm comfortable with this smart-kid image.

When I'm alone, however, I'm full of questions. Where am I going? What will my life be like in a few years? When I'm alone I don't feel like the smart kid any more.

Matt

Reader's Comments

Not a bad first try. I like the contrast between answer-man and question-man. I like the honest admission that you "make up" answers.

What does the piece need?
- Maybe a less conventional opening.
- More specifics. What are some questions people ask you?
- Where did you get this reputation as a smart kid?

Second Draft: You Probably Know Me as the Answer-Man

For some reason people expect me to know everything, from "Who won the Braves game last night?" to "When do snakes lose their skin?" I'm the answer-man. I feel an obligation to know these things.

I even make up answers if I don't know them. I guess this smart-kid image goes back to my fourth-grade teacher Mrs. Knapper. Whenever someone asked a question, "What's ESP stand for?" Mrs. Knapper would say "I'm not sure; Matt, do you know?" I remember heading for the encyclopedia that night so I could elaborate on extra sensory perception in class the next day.

The smart-kid image leaves me when I'm alone, however. I spend quiet time trying to picture where I'll be in five years or ten. I don't want to get locked into a routine job and a dull life. I want to make something happen. I want to change things. But how? Where? What do I do now, to get ready for an unknown future. I'm the question-man when I'm alone.

Matt

Reader's Comments

Much better! I like the opening—it speaks directly to the audience. I like the specific questions. I like the way the piece ends. Honest, personal, insightful—share it!

Chapter 2

A New Way of Thinking

Are you feeling any better about writing? A new way of writing is not an instant cure-all. Overcoming negative feelings about writing is a gradual process. If you will stay open to help, and work at this writing business, you will find a process for growing as a writer. If you want to write well but are still feeling gloomy about your writing, you're probably tripping over past experience. One of the first things you need to do is to develop new ways of thinking.

Old Way of Thinking: I Can't Write.
(or I don't write very well)

This is deadly! If you and writing are going to make a fresh start, you're going to have to try positive thinking. If a stranger asked you what you do, you'd probably reply, "I'm a student." You wouldn't wail, "I'm not a student. I make the worst grades in school." You don't have to wait until you're a great student to claim that status. "I'm a student" means you're trying.

How is all this connected to your new way of thinking? Contrary to popular belief, good writers aren't born that way. Just like you, most have to work at it. They practice. At some point they take a courageous, deep breath and say, "I'm a writer." They risk. They admit they're trying. More importantly, they withhold judgment about their abilities. Say to yourself, "I'm a writer; I'm willing to work at it."

New Way of Thinking: I Can Write.
(or I can be a better writer)

Unless a savage beast has wrenched off both your arms and stomped on your brain, you can write. How good a writer you become depends on how much you're willing to practice. Beginning today, start thinking of yourself as a writer.

Your new role as writer may feel a little strange at first. But thinking of yourself as a writer is simply a pact with yourself. It's a commitment to get serious about writing.

Becoming a good writer is possible, just as becoming a good skater or pole vaulter or sky diver is possible. You just have to get serious—serious, not humorless. Being serious doesn't mean you can't have any fun.

~~~~~~

Free Writing 1

Getting
It
Started

Think of something you're good at—something you're serious about. Maybe you're an excellent gymnast, a math whiz, or a card shark. Perhaps you're in the *Guinness Book of World Records* because you downed more hot dogs than anyone at a five-minute stretch, or you may hold the school's unofficial Biggest Flirt title. Maybe you're a great guitarist or a dancin' fool—no matter. Select one thing you do well and try a free writing.

Before you begin, consider these questions. When did you get interested? How did you get started? How serious are you about this activity? Is your interest a diversion or an addiction? Were you always good? Was it easy in the beginning? Did you ever want to give up? Is it easy or difficult now? What makes you good and those around you only so-so? How often did you practice in the beginning? How much do you practice now? How does being good at this activity make you feel?

~~~~~~

Getting
It
Down

Write for ten minutes without stopping. Answer one or several of the preceding questions in your Writer's Notebook, or put pen to paper and let your mind lead.

~~~~~~

Another Word About Free Writing

Free writing is a technique used by many good writers. You pour words down to discover what's inside your head. It's a way to get ideas flowing out of your head, down your arm, through your pen and onto paper. Let it happen. Don't try to control what comes out.

Free writing is a beginning, not an end. If you are looking for a polished piece, you're missing the point. Free writing is a way to get words out there for you to look at. It's a way to find out what you have to say. You can fix it up later. Remember, it's easier to work with something than it is to work with nothing. If you get stuck, just write around the hard parts. Keep your pen moving across the page for the full ten minutes.

Reread your free writing. Do you see anything you like? Circle that part. Then share your writing with a partner. Ask your partner to listen for the good parts, too. If you think the piece has possibilities, you may want to tinker with it some more. If you don't like it, file it in your Writer's Notebook. No piece of writing is ever wasted effort. You may come back to it later.

Checking It Out

Inside Out

It's hard to get fired up about writing if you don't know anything or care anything about the topic. A topic far removed from personal experience is usually a dead-end. Good writing grows from the inside out. That means it begins with writers' ideas and feelings about the people and experiences in their lives. Effective writers shape pieces from the inside out; they begin by discovering what they have to say first, then they develop their writing for outside audiences. The first drafts are for discovery. When the piece is being readied for an audience, usually several drafts later, writers concern themselves with matters such as word choice, spelling, and mechanics.

Effective writing begins with you. That means starting inside your head. In Chapter 1 you looked closely at yourself. In this chapter you will do the same with those around you.

People

Every day you come in contact with hundreds of people. You brush shoulders with people in your own school without so much as a nod.

Outside of school you pass others you barely notice. The media bring you in contact with even more each week. To protect yourself from sensory overload, you ignore most of these people.

Yet these people are a part of your experience. That makes them a potential source for writing. In some way they touch your life—but how?

Writers make connections between their experiences and their writing. How would you make connections between these people and your experience? How would you then discover an idea for writing? You could start by sorting these people into groups. One way might be to clump them together by occupation. There are bus drivers, teachers, school administrators, store clerks, and street cleaners drifting through your life. You could categorize them by physical appearance—the lean, the voluptuous, the stocky, the squat. Age groups might work. You certainly see children, young people, adults, and senior citizens daily. These connections still seem a little distant. The people are still far away.

Think the way a writer does. How can you bring these people into focus? Where are the links between your experience and the strangers you've kept at arm's length?

Old Way of Thinking:
School Writing Has to Be Impersonal.

If you overlooked your feelings about these people, you neglected one of your best sources of discovery. Powerful writing doesn't grow out of the impersonal. Think about the kinds of writing you like. Many students say they enjoy notes passed in class, personal letters, diaries or journals, and essays in which they can express their feelings. It's the same way with reading. Would you like to curl up with a government document? When you begin to trust your own instincts to start with personal experience, you begin to work the way a writer does.

New Way of Thinking:
Effective School Writing
Grows Out of the Personal.

It's a mistake to ignore feelings. Effective writing grows out of personal feelings, opinions, ideas, and experiences. Feelings are the key. Without feeling there is no involvement. It's difficult to generate enthusiasm as a writer if you are not interested in a writing idea. Without involvement, the piece is flat. With a new way of writing, you'll learn to adjust the intensity of your feelings according to the purpose of your writing and the needs of your readers.

Divorce feeling from writing and you produce artificial writing. A new way of writing keeps writing and feelings together. You may not be wild about every assignment, but you will have ideas that invite you to write.

~~~~~~

Here's your first invitation. It concerns your feelings about people. No one will tell you which people to write about. That's your decision as a writer. In this first invitation, you will have two topic options. You'll be in charge of generating ideas about both topics and you'll also decide on one idea for writing. You'll look inside your own head to discover which topic is more promising. Your topic choices are *People We Can Live Without* and *People We Support*. Before you make your decision, brainstorm with classmates for a list of people in both categories. Here's a quick review of brainstorming procedures.

Getting It Started

Brainstorming

Brainstorming is a way of shaking ideas out of your head. It works best when one person fields responses and records them on the chalkboard or some place all can see. If you've used this technique, you'll recognize these guidelines for effective brainstorming.

Accept everyone's ideas.
Encourage *all* kinds of ideas.
Piggy-back on each other's responses.
Try for quantity. Fill up the board if possible.

Have someone write these two categories on the board: *People We Can Live Without* and *People We Support*. Have the recorder leave plenty of room for responses from the class.

People We Can Live Without include those who rub you the wrong way. They are people who constantly complain they're going to fail, then make the only A; or people who claim to be your best friend, then steal your steady; or people next door who have a party and don't invite you. *People We Can Live Without* drive you up the wall.

People We Support are people you identify with. Others may ridicule them, but you understand them. They may be people you feel for; they could even be people much like you. Maybe

they're people who are shy or people who cry at sad movies or people who are dreamers.

Brainstorm for people in each group. Keep your thoughts flowing. Play off each other's responses. Don't stop until you've exhausted the list of people who spark your interest.

SPOTLIGHT

Once the board is filled, study the responses. Select the category you find most appealing. Then limit your attention to just one group of people to write about. Here's one student's choice.

People We Can Live Without   *People We Support*

People who
    brag all the time
    complain constantly
    abuse children
    break into lunch line and
        invite all their friends
        to join them
    play practical jokes
    laugh when nothing's
        funny
    use your locker as a trash
        heap
    use the public highways as
        their private garbage
        dump
    sing in the shower
    mumble under their breath
    answer every question with
        another question
    don't trust teen-agers
    think they're cute
    are rude or inconsiderate
    sit on their horns if you
        don't take off when the
        light turns green
    mow their lawns at 7 a.m.
        on your only day to
        sleep late
    take their half of the road
        out of the middle

People who
    are lonely
    have been wronged
    have been jilted
    are frightened
    wear braces
    are uncoordinated
    feel no one loves them
    have family members who
        are political hostages
    are political hostages
    are short
    don't have a car
    daydream
    fight for noble causes
    fight for what they believe
        in
    are good sports
    are funny
    are sick
    are terminally ill
    get blamed for things they
        didn't do
    are disorganized
    jog at 6 a.m.
    are hungry

                                Cindy

Old Way of Thinking: Getting Started Is Impossible.

Blue lines hover expectantly on white space. They wait for some
miracle. So do I. I put pen to paper again. A few halting phrases
stumble out. No good. I crumple another sheet hoping to squeeze
out a coherent thought.

    I try again. Icy fingers grip my gut. Beads of sweat pop out on
my forehead. Palms turn clammy. Stomach dances a light fandango.
Mind shuts down.

                                Cindy

For many students, getting started is the toughest part about writing. You often don't know exactly what you want to say when you put pen to paper. That's why mapping out your strategy early may feel strange. At some time in your school career you've probably resorted to writing an outline after you finished your paper. Deciding what you want to say too early can be a mistake. If you've ever felt uncomfortable committing yourself to a plan in the beginning, you have good instincts as a writer.

New Way of Thinking: With Discovery, Getting Started Is Possible

Writing is a complex process. For most kinds of writing, jumping from a blank sheet of paper to an end product, even in outline form, is unrealistic. Rigid planning denies one of the most powerful attractions in writing—discovery.

If outlining isn't the answer, what is? How do you get started? How do you discover what you know? There are ways of cutting down the anxiety of getting started. By using the discovery process you can get ideas onto paper quickly.

You've already begun to use one of your most important resources as a writer—the Writer's Notebook. The Writer's Notebook is your place to discover what you have to say. It is a place for practice and experimentation. Writing in your Notebook is a way of clearing your throat on paper.

Discovery is often a matter of unlocking the floodgate of ideas in your head. Once those ideas are on paper, it's much easier to think about selecting just the right words. Good writers begin with their own intuitions. Free writing is one way to tap these intuitions. It's a technique for discovery. The jot list is another.

The Jot List

You're familiar with lists that remind you of things. These include grocery lists, shopping lists, lists of things to do, and lists of errands or jobs to do around the house. You jot down items on these lists to help you remember not to forget. Jot lists for writing help you remember details you may want to include in your writing. Writing down one snippet of information often jogs your memory, and soon you're thinking of other things. A jot list helps you think by giving you a method for recording experiences and ideas. It's a tool to use in your process of discovery.

Looking Inside

Using your Writer's Notebook, begin your jot list. Concentrate on the category you've selected. Think about the people who are your focal point.

Good writing grows from the inside. It begins inside your own head. Start there. Search your memory for contact with the people who are your focal point. Recall vivid recollections. Sift through personal knowledge which may include reading and viewing. Record tidbits as they come to you. Jot down specific details. Note any biases, hang-ups, or unabashed interests you have in these people. Consider some of these questions to get you started, but don't let them limit your thinking.

Getting
It
Started

OPTION 1: People You Can Live Without

Who are these people? Do they share common characteristics? Can you recall your last run-in with these people? What happened? Do you have these encounters often? Specifically, what do these people do that irritates you? How does their behavior make you feel? How do you react? Do you think these people should change? Why? What would you suggest they do? Given the chance, what would you say to them?

If you don't get something going with your jot list, try another idea. Experiment until you have selected people you really have something to say about. Look at Cindy's jot list.

People I Can Live Without—People Who Break into Lunch Line
Every day people break into lunch line
Wait till teachers' backs are turned
They have different techniques:
    boldly walk up
    sneak
    push
    charm their way
    follow a teacher who's walking to the front
I'm hungry, too
They make me late to class
Sometimes I get detention
I was there first
I'm burned up because everyone lets them get by with it—including me.

Cindy

OPTION 2: People You Support

What are these people like? What about them touches you? How are you like these people? Have you been in a similar predicament? Do you consider these people underdogs? Explain. In what ways are these people different from you? How do others respond to them? How do you think others should react? Why? How do you react? What could these people do to help themselves or improve their situation? What words of encouragement do you have for these people?

Frank wasn't as lucky as Cindy. Ideas about his first choice, "People who have family members who are political hostages," didn't come easily. After struggling over his jot list, he realized he didn't know enough about the topic without doing further research. He found the topic "People Who Are Short" much closer to his own experience. Take a look at Frank's jot list.

People I Support—People Who Are Short

Males and females 5′ 3″ and under.

My height is 5′.

I've been called "Shrimp" for as long as I can remember.

I have to take a bodyguard everywhere I go.

I'm the shortest person in my family.

Some short people are *under* dogs. They definitely come under the armpits of most people.

Some short people (mostly female) are happy that way.

Usually but not always called "cute" by those who don't suffer from this affliction.

Others should keep their mouths shut because some short people (like me) are sensitive.

Advice: Wear lifts or learn to walk on stilts.

Don't worry if you're short, you'll get a lot of attention in life. Who wants to walk among the clouds anyway?

Remembrances of always wanting to be a basketball player.

Rejection by tall girls.

The good part—acceptance by Lori, 4′ 9″, my good-looking steady.

While your thoughts on the topic are fresh, free write. Read over your jot list. You don't have to use everything, but it's a good idea to mark those parts you want to include. Then just pour down your thoughts. At this point don't concern yourself with conventions of writing such as spelling and mechanics. This writing is strictly for you. Remember you're working this piece from the inside out. In your Writer's Notebook, write for at least ten minutes. Discover what you have to say.

**Getting
It
Down**

SPOTLIGHT

Cindy wrote this from her jot list:

Not that lunch is anything to get excited about. It's not. That's not the point. The point is this. I was there first. So were all the other people standing behind me.

It really burns me up. After sitting in class four periods in a row, I'm hungry. I stand in line for an eternity listening to mindless chatter from the freshmen in front of me and exaggerated stories of athletic prowess from seniors behind. That's enough to make anyone lose her appetite.

Suddenly, out of nowhere, this parade of line breakers appears. They come in all shapes and sizes but never fail to show.

Their behavior reminds me of animals. The sneaky kind. Some of them slink up. They actually think we're too stupid to notice them. Others push and shove. They just dare you to say anything. They're like a herd of buffalo except buffalo have more dignity. The ones I despise though are the charmers. They act as if they're your dearest friend or as if they've got something they're dying to tell you. As soon as you let those leeches near you, they try to weasel their way in front of you. Before you know it, they're worming their way on up the line.

I also resent their making me late for social studies. What really kills me is that nobody does anything about it. Something ought to be done.

Cindy

What do you think? Is Cindy writing from inside her own head? Explain. Can you hear Cindy talking? How would you describe Cindy's feelings about people who break into line? Have you ever felt this way?

Old Way of Thinking: School Writing Should Sound Phony.

> If one ponders on the use of formal language in one's academy, one sees the erroneous logic in such thinking. One knows that real writers flee from pretention.

What?! If you take a few minutes, you can probably decipher these sentences. But why should you have to try so hard? Good writing is straightforward. The best writing speaks to the reader directly and truthfully.

One problem with the previous piece of writing is the unnecessary, perhaps senseless, use of big words. Some students think they're giving teachers what they want by using padded language. Instead, their inflated writing is tiresome to teachers and themselves.

A second problem is the writer's use of the word "one." Who is the writer? Can you hear the writer's voice? Read the piece aloud. It sounds stilted rather than natural. Writer Ken Macrorie calls such writing "Engfish." Writer James E. Miller, Jr. calls it "prose in a grey flannel suit."

New Way of Thinking: Good Writing Is Honest.

When you use words that aren't your own, your writing sounds phony. The best writing is honest. By cloaking writing in formal language or disguising it behind jargon, you hide your voice as a writer. Use your own words in writing. They're best. Doing so will help you develop a distinct and recognizable voice—the hallmark of great writers.

Looking Outside

Your next step in the discovery process is to tap outer resources. Getting a second opinion is a way of enlarging your perspective. Talking to others frequently gives you a new slant on a topic. At times conversation with someone else brings out an angle you had overlooked or simply hadn't considered. Sometimes it will strengthen your convictions and lead you to develop certain points. Often it gives you a notion of how another person thinks.

**Checking
It
Out**

Good writers frequently check their intuitions against those of a respected consultant. Choose your consultant carefully. Look around the room and find someone whose opinion you value. Pull up a chair and interview that person. Prepare questions that encourage your consultant to share views. Open-ended ones work well. Use any of the questions you found helpful in compiling your jot list. Record your consultant's opinions in jot-list fashion.

When you have drawn out the ideas of your consultant, share your free writing. Get some help. Let your consultant help you find parts that have potential. Ask your consultant to point out parts that need to be developed.

Your writing will eventually be shared orally with your classmates. Since your consultant is a member of your potential audience, get his or her reaction. Who knows? Your consultant may have some suggestions for making the piece more effective.

SPOTLIGHT

Cindy talked to Juan. Here's their interview.

INTERVIEW WITH JUAN
TOPIC: PEOPLE WHO BREAK INTO LUNCH LINE

Cindy: Have you ever noticed anyone breaking into the lunch line?

Juan: Sure. It happens all the time.

Cindy: How do you feel about it?

Juan: It makes me mad, but you've got to admire their style.

Cindy: What do you mean? Tell me more.

Juan: You know, the way they pull it off. I get a kick out of the con artists. They've got finesse. Nice part about them is that all you've got to do is say "no" and they'll leave you alone.

Cindy: What about the bullies?

Juan: Ah, they're the easiest. Kid around with them a little or, better yet, pretend you're not going to like them any more. You've got to use a little psychology. They just want attention.

Cindy:	Do you think there's a way to stop people from breaking into line?
Juan:	Are you kidding? The minute we all decide we're fed up with it, they'll stop. Trouble is, nobody's brought this to our attention. It's a constant nuisance everyone accepts. If somebody did a little consciousness raising, maybe approached the problem with a little humor, you'd see a change.
Cindy:	Do you have any other thoughts about line breakers?
Juan:	Not really.
Cindy:	Would you look at my free writing and tell me what you think?
Juan:	Sure. (Juan reads Cindy's free writing—page 27—and hands it back.)
Cindy:	Now be honest. I need help.
Juan:	You sure do, but that has nothing to do with writing. (laughs) Just kidding. Okay, let me look at it with you. (They look at Cindy's free writing.) Okay, I like the flavor of it. A lot of people feel that way. This line-cutting really bothers you, doesn't it?
Cindy:	(sarcastically) How could you tell?
Juan:	As a matter of fact, I could tell because right here (points to second paragraph) you say, "It really burns me up." You *always* say that when you're mad. Sounds just like you. I like that. I also like the part about the animals.
Cindy:	You don't think it's too nasty?
Juan:	It's not nasty enough. You want to see a change; *you're* (points to Cindy) going to have to make it happen. Your problem is that you're too nice. You'll think of cuddly animals like pussycats and French poodles when you should be thinking of slimy swamp critters—like alligators, snakes, and lizards.

Notice the kind of help Cindy gets from Juan. He shows her the specific parts he likes—first. Then he encourages her to develop a section, the part about animals. Again, he makes specific suggestions concerning the types of creatures she should use.

A Word About Sharing

If you feel a little uncomfortable with sharing at first, don't be surprised. Sharing requires trust, and developing trust usually takes time.

Juan is gentle with his criticism. He jokes with Cindy to put her at ease and even gets her to laugh at herself. But he doesn't waste too much time playing around. You can tell that Juan is serious about writing. That's probably one of the reasons Cindy chose him as a consultant. He's also building the groundwork for trust.

Remember that being a writer is just part of your role. Your other role is that of consultant. Like Juan, encourage your friend to trust you. Like Juan, help your friend grow as a writer.

SPOTLIGHT

Pulling Together Inner and Outer Resources

Before you wander off to rewrite your paper, take a look at Cindy's efforts. By jotting down her ideas and by free writing, Cindy discovered what she knows about her topic, line breakers. Next she consulted Juan for outside help. Then Cindy marked specific points in her interview with Juan that she wanted to include in her paper.

Now Cindy is ready to rework her piece using Juan's advice and her latest feelings on line breakers. Her first inclination is to write a five-paragraph theme. Cindy feels confident using that form; she's had a lot of practice with it and has found it successful for school writing. For Cindy the five-paragraph formula is easy: write what you want to say (one paragraph); say it (three paragraphs); summarize what you just said (one paragraph). Here is Cindy's first response to the assignment: Rewrite your paper for your classmates.

COMPOSITION 210
September 6
Cindy

LINE CUTTERS

The purpose of this paper is to bring the tactics of lunch-line cutters to your attention. Too many students passively accept line cutting as a way of life. Although students are victimized by line cutters on a daily basis, few seem to notice. Students do not realize they are allowing the problem to continue by looking the other way. While all line cutters are irritating, three types are particularly disturbing. These are the bullies, the sneaks, and the charmers.

The first line cutters I would like to discuss are the bullies. Bullies push and shove their way to the front. They pick on those smaller than themselves. Often these cowards use threats or force to work their will. Bullies strike fear in the hearts of many by using intimidation.

A second group of line cutters is equally annoying. They are the sneaks. Sneaks think they are putting something over on someone. They pretend to be nonchalant, but all the while, they are looking for an opportunity to break into line. When sneaks think no one is looking, they slide ahead in the line. Sneaks depend on the inattentiveness of others.

The third group of bothersome line cutters includes the charmers. Charmers' ways are particularly provoking. These line breakers use popularity to achieve their end. Charmers often pretend to be friends. Once in line, however, charmers quickly lose interest in friendship. Instead they attempt to progress even farther up the line.

In summary I would like to say that lunch-line cutting is a serious problem in our school. On a daily basis students are victimized by inconsiderate line breakers. Such students include bullies, sneaks, and charmers. Too few students recognize the actions of these students as a real problem. I hope my paper has shed light on this menace.

What is the purpose of this paper? How many sentences are in the first paragraph? Locate the topic or main sentence in the middle three paragraphs. Count the number of sentences in each of these three paragraphs. Look at the last paragraph. How does it compare with the first paragraph? How well has Cindy followed the five-paragraph formula? Does Cindy's paper get you fired up about line breaking? Do you like her paper? Explain.

Preliminary Check

As soon as a draft of her five-paragraph theme is finished, Cindy shares it with Juan. Here are his reactions:

Juan: Not bad. It's well organized. Looks like a paper you'll get at least a "B" on.

Cindy: Juan, you don't sound enthusiastic. Come on. It won't hurt my feelings. What are you thinking?

Juan: Well, your paper is totally predictable. There are no surprises.

Cindy: Go on . . .

Juan: Umm, well, I'm not inspired to do anything about the problem. This paper is prim and proper; sounds as if you wrote it for an adult audience. You're trying to reach us— other students. Loosen up.

Do *you* like your paper?

Cindy decides to rewrite the paper as if it were a self-sponsored piece. Here's what she writes.

OPEN LETTER TO LINE LIZARDS

Dear Line Lizards:

To the slimy lot of you I would like to say: What makes you think you're special? Have your classes been any longer, any more boring than mine? Are you any hungrier, any more deserving of the cafeteria special, warmed-over peanut butter goulash? Just what makes you think you've got a right to acid indigestion before me?

Every day I watch you crawl out from under your rock. First come THE BULLDOZERS. The Bulldozers, gargantuan reptiles, lurch their way to the front threatening to rip out the heart of any who object. The lunch line shrinks back horrified; I begin a slow burn.

The next wave of lizards, THE SIDEWINDERS, lurks patiently in the shadows waiting for any sudden moves. Their victims, usually

unsuspecting freshmen or inattentive sophomores, lean forward to make a point in conversation. Stealthily, the Sidewinders slink to the empty spot. Before the naive innocents can step back in place, the Sidewinders have wormed their way to the next yawning crevice.

Just as I'm about to blow my top, a friend approaches, extends a smooth hand, offers a limp shake and scuttles in front of me. I notice he has a green complexion but assume he's merely sampled the culinary delights of the kitchen. He pulls along a female companion who suspiciously resembles a salamander. She flashes white teeth before snaking in behind. It dawns on me. These aren't my friends. These are THE DEADLY CHAMELEONS, LINE LIZARDS in disguise.

You reptilian monsters make my skin crawl! I'd like to see the lunch line stick out its collective foot and send you sprawling on your lizard faces, or pick you up by your scaly tails and sling you into the nearest swamp.

While you lunge, creep, and slide ahead, I wait in lunch line five extra minutes. That means warm goulash for the reptiles; cool glue for the Kid. Who do you think you are? Tomorrow it's hot goulash or the menu will read STEAMING FILET OF LIZARD!

Signed,

Ravished Lizard Luncher

What do you think of Cindy's use of humor? Is it effective? What do you think of the alias Cindy has chosen?

Compare this piece with Cindy's five-paragraph theme. Which is more imaginative? Which is more likely to capture her audience? Which do you prefer? Explain. Use your Writer's Notebook to answer.

Your Turn: Pulling It Together

When it comes to writing, most people find personal tone appealing. Pull your piece together now, keeping your audience in mind. The following points may be helpful:

Getting It Down

1. Reread your jot list and free writing. Note any parts you want to include in your final paper.
2. Review your interview notes. Mark any passage that looks promising.

3. If you're still unsure about where you're headed, try another free writing. Talk to yourself, weaving together your thoughts and the advice of your consultant.

4. Draft a piece for an outside audience or your classmates. Don't get trapped into thinking the five-paragraph theme is always best. Experiment with the open letter.

The Open Letter

Open letters are frequently heard on television editorial spots. Viewers send in letters expressing their opinions about a certain issue or group of people. Before they are read to television viewers, these letters are carefully selected to promote audience interest.

It may be helpful to compare the open letter to a more familiar form—the personal letter. Personal letters are a special and private form of communication. Open letters are powerful; they are a public form. Open letters keep you in touch with a larger audience, usually a group of people. Personal letters are generally read by one person only, while open letters may be read by anyone.

Open letters are especially good for expressing your viewpoint. You address a particular group of people directly, telling them how you feel. Open letters have the added appeal of allowing others to read over your shoulder. In this case address your letter *directly* to the people you have selected. Remember that all the students in your class will hear your letter, so keep them in mind. (Don't worry, these letters will be read anonymously, so go ahead and experiment fearlessly.)

SPOTLIGHT

Considering Your Draft

The Hook

A beginning that snags your readers' attention is called a hook. Try to hook your audience. Practice several hooks; experiment with different beginnings, trying each one on your consultant. Use the one that seems most effective. Here are three possibilities.

Quotes

Go over your interview notes. Did your consultant say anything that piques your interest? Cindy might start with something Juan said.

"The minute we all decide we're fed up with it, they'll (lunch line cutters) stop." Sophomore Juan Rominez is confident that students can put an end to the problem of line breaking.

OR

"Ah, they're (lunch line bullies) the easiest. Kid around with them a little or, better yet, pretend you're not going to like them any more. You've got to use a little psychology. They just want attention." This remark by a Number One High School sophomore represents the prevailing attitude of many students.

Another word about trust: Be sure you ask your consultant before using that person's name. Check with him or her to see that your quote is accurate.

Rhetorical Questions

Rhetorical questions are questions for which you don't really expect an answer. They're fun because they often give you the advantage. You pose questions your readers (or listeners) can't answer, leaving them sputtering.

You could experiment with *innocent questions*:

Who would believe that line breaking could happen in our school?

Or *loaded questions*:

If you cut into lunch line, you appear to be inconsiderate. You wouldn't like to be considered a jerk, would you?

Or questions carefully calculated to put your audience on the *defensive*:

What makes you think you're better than anyone else?

Anecdotes

Almost everyone enjoys a good story. Try beginning with a slice from your own experience. The experience Cindy mentioned in her free writing has possibilities if developed:

I stand in line listening to mindless chatter from freshmen in front of
me and exaggerated stories of athletic prowess from seniors behind.
It's enough to make anyone lose her appetite.

Humor is another possibility. Can you think of others? Experiment with
several hooks.

Some writers write their piece, then work on the hook last. Others
make it their first concern. See what works best for you.

Writer's Workbench

Strong Verbs

Good writers not only concern themselves with what they want to say but
with how they say it. They pay particular attention to verbs because verbs
communicate the action or lack of action in a sentence. The verb is the
heart of the sentence.

Line lizards (move) in front of me.

Move, the heart of the sentence, tells readers what action line lizards
take.

They (move)

In this sentence *move* is a weak verb. It's imprecise. Readers are left
wondering how line lizards *move*.

Practice using strong verbs in your writing. Strong verbs are precise;
they strengthen sentences. How do line lizards *move*? Think of strong
verbs to replace *move*. If you get stuck, look back at Cindy's open letter.

Line lizards ♡ in front of me.

How about *crawl, lurch, slink, scuttle*? These strong verbs create a picture
for readers. They accurately describe how line lizards move.

When you have written your draft, look at the heart of your
sentences. Do your verbs create strong pictures? Do they communicate
the message you intend? Do they strengthen your sentence?

In small groups or individually, brainstorm for strong verb possibilities for these sentences.

Line lizards   move   in front of me.
                    crawl
                    lurch
                    slink
                    scuttle
                    creep
                    worm
                    snake
                    glide
                    slide

1. The monitor (came) to the door.

2. A kid in the back (read) a book.

3. The teacher (walked) to the student's desk.

4. The culprit (got) out of her seat.

5. Meanwhile my friend (put) an apple on my desk.

Moving Out

Cindy's open letter is a polished piece, but it didn't start that way. With the help of her consultant Cindy reworked chunks of her paper to get the satirical effect she wanted. Since the papers are to be read aloud, she had her consultant read her paper out loud so that she could see how it sounded. As their final concern, Cindy and Juan painstakingly checked spelling and punctuation. They didn't want to chance having a reader trip over their careless mistakes, spoiling the effect of this humorous piece.

In the next chapters you'll have some direct help with the specifics of revision and proofing. ● For now, rely on a dictionary, the Handbook at the back of the book, and your own intuition. With your consultant's help take time to finalize your open letter.

Going Public

With one or several good readers serving as news commentator, the front of the classroom can become a news studio. The papers can be read as anonymous commentaries. (Your teacher may ask you to turn in a slip of paper with your real name below your alias. Your identity will be withheld unless you want to claim credit for your letter.)

Going public is exciting. As the papers are read, listen as a writer and as a part of the audience. Measure the impact of each letter as it is read. Note techniques you'd like to try. Watch your classmates' faces and listen to their comments as your paper is read. Their feedback will give you valuable information.

~~~~~~

Getting
It
Down

Evaluating Your Efforts

As soon as possible after the open letters are read, talk to yourself in your Writer's Notebook. Your teacher will give you credit for taking your piece through the process. You will be responsible for evaluating your efforts.

Consider your role as consultant. Were you a good listener? Did you give positive feedback and specific suggestions? Did you begin to establish your credibility as a consultant? How do you feel about the trust level between the writer and yourself?

Talk to yourself about a new way of writing. Comment on the jot list, free writing, and talking to your consultant. Were these resources helpful? How? Was it helpful to talk to someone else?

Think about your classmates' reactions to your paper. Did they like it? Did your hook capture their attention? Do you need to rework any sections? Did you achieve the effect you intended? Was it helpful to have feedback? Do you consider your paper successful? Are you pleased with it?

Looking Inside

Chapter 3

Changing

The first two chapters of this book have described new ways of looking at the process of writing. Some of the ideas and suggestions in this book contradict the conventional wisdom which says that writers first find out what they want to say, and then prepare an outline to direct their paper. On the contrary, good transactional writing grows first from the resources you have inside your own head. These next two chapters will work together to help you write a unique transactional piece entitled "On Growing Up." This chapter will take you through a series of explorations on the theme. Your writings will be personal, so you will share them with a friend or someone who knows you well. The purpose of this chapter is to help you gather some momentum for the more formal writing in Chapter 4.

Adolescence is a time of rapid and dramatic change. Your body grows quickly, and your responsibilities accumulate with a gerbil-like geometry. If you're like most other adolescents, your life is a bit like a roller-coaster —a good day—a bad day—happy times—sad times. This chapter will give you some opportunities to reflect on your life, to make some sense of the growing-up hassle, and ultimately to explore the phenomenon of adolescence.

The Pressure

Take a time out. For the next 15 minutes or so, jot down the pressures you feel in your life. What do you feel *most* pressured about? Are all pressures equal? Where do the pressures come from? School work? deadlines? job responsibilities? pressure to conform? pressure to be perfect? to be right? to be tough? to be good? How do you react to pressure?

Try jotting your thoughts just as they come to you—write for at least 15 minutes.

Getting
It
Started

You may wish to share your jottings with a close friend or you may prefer to keep them strictly private.

SPOTLIGHT

Look at this excerpt from a student's paper on a similar subject:

I'm supposed to take after my father, but I don't think I do. I look like him, but my values are different. He's always in there working, thinking up the angles. He admits it. He makes a lot of money and he gives us all we need, but he never stops and asks himself things. He doesn't wonder what it's all about. I've asked him that sometimes, and it's not that he's dumb or an arrogant Wall-Street type, who calls you kooky just because you want to do a little thinking, a little questioning. No, he'll go for a walk with you and tell you that he's the way he is, and you're different. "I'm a scratcher, that's what I am, son." He'll talk like that. "I come from poor people and I had to work my way through college and law school. I had no time to do anything, to ask any questions—I just worked." I've never known what I'm supposed to say when he talks like that. He's not trying to be mean but he looks at me and he wants me to understand all he's gone through in his life. Then, when I try to tell him what I'm going through, right now, he can't understand. I've even written him letters about how I feel. I figured that way I'd make myself clearer; and he'd have time to read over my words a few times, so he would maybe see what I'm trying to say. But it never works. We just can't get across to each other, it seems. I took a course in psychology last year, and the teacher said that was how it goes sometimes. But I knew that before I heard him say it, or read it in any book.

A lot of times I feel the way those Greek philosophers must have felt. I mean I'm looking at people and I feel I'm up on a mountain, far away. I'm not crazy, I know. I'm doing fine. It's just that I don't always feel in the best shape. I don't feel like pushing, pushing, like my dad does. I want to sit back and read and lie in the sun, or I want to go swimming, that's all—not worry about what I have to do, and where I'm going after college, and what I want to be. It's pretty sad, I'll tell you, thinking about the rat race people get themselves into and call it "happiness."

Marty

What kinds of pressures does this writer feel? What things does he question? What does he feel he needs from adults right now?

～～～～～～～～～～～～～～～～～～～～～～～～～

The Joys

Fortunately there is more to adolescence than pressure and uncertainty. There are good times, happy times—times when you feel in charge, confident, or peaceful. Now that you've spent some time exploring the pressures and frustrations, take time to contemplate the sources of joy and happiness in your life. Use the same jotting technique. Reflect on the best parts of your life. When do you feel happiest? When are you most relaxed? What things give you feelings of success? When are you most satisfied? Which people are best at cheering you up? Where do you go to enjoy life? What are the best things about being your age?

Jot or free write about the good things in your life. Keep writing and thinking for at least 20 minutes.

Getting
It
Started

～～～～～～～～～～～～～～～～～～～～～～～～～

Writer's Workbench 1

Showing Instead of Telling

I feel like
  an empty
soft-drink cup
    left
under the bleachers
after a game
            —Kurt

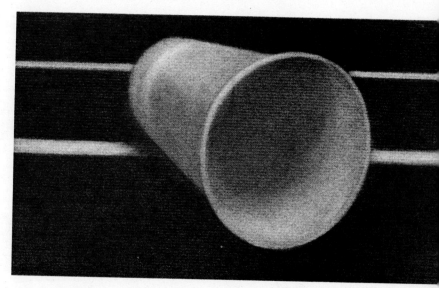

If you're like most teen-agers, you've experienced the emptiness this student describes. His words are simple yet compelling. They reach out to you. For a moment you, too, feel lonely.

If the poet had written, "I feel lonely," his words might go unnoticed. Instead he arrests your attention by making a comparison—a comparison between his feelings of loneliness and a discarded soft-drink cup. The result is clear, honest, surprising language.

Writers know that *showing* us how they feel is more effective than *telling* us how they feel. They often use comparisons to accomplish this. Comparisons paint a picture in the mind's eye. They also create a vivid image that shows the reader how the writer feels.

Writers try to create fresh comparisons. Striking comparisons surprise readers, often causing them to rediscover the familiar. Creating sharp images causes readers to view the everyday with an enlightened eye. Unexpected comparisons stretch the reader's imagination.

Creating such mind-stretchers is not as difficult as it may seem. The key is to *show* instead of *tell*. Look around you. Let your mind drift to images that capture the feeling. Experiment!

Examples:

I feel *lonely*.

I feel like . . .

a pair of faded jeans
a deserted concert hall
a lost child
paper's ragged edge

I feel *fragile*.
I feel like . . .
    a colt on newborn legs
    fall's last clinging leaf
    crystal exploding on a hardwood floor
    a paper plane tossed by the wind

I feel *happy*.
I feel like . . .
    a quarterback rifling a completion
    a crisp winter morning
    windchimes dancing in the breeze
    bright balloons floating free

In your Writer's Notebook jot down comparisons that capture the feelings of loneliness, fragility, and happiness for you. If none of the preceding phrases works for you, create your own comparisons. The best comparisons often reflect experiences shared by reader and writer.

Form small groups for brainstorming. Try creating fresh comparisons. Let your imagination create word pictures that show the feeling.

1. I feel *angry*.
   I feel like . . .
2. I feel *hopeful*.
   I feel like . . .
3. I feel *peaceful*.
   I feel like . . .
4. I feel *alienated*.
   I feel like . . .
5. I feel *sad*.
   I feel like . . .
6. I feel *carefree*.
   I feel like . . .

You probably remember that direct comparisons are called *similes*. *Similes* use the words *like* and *as*. Experiment with *similes* that use the word *as* to connect comparisons.

The following words reflect at least a portion of the teen-age condition. From this list, choose words that reflect feelings you experience. As a group, reach consensus on the feeling word to be placed in the first blank of each sentence. Then brainstorm at least three similes for each.

puzzling	joyful	free
predictable	sad	frenetic
unpredictable	disappointing	embarrassing
humorous	scary	frustrating
painful	serene	satisfying
exciting	reassuring	confusing

Example: Being 15 is as *painful* as . . .
                        a slap on a sunburned back
                        the screech of fingernails down a chalkboard
                        a scratch on a new album

1. Being 14 is as ___ as . . .
2. Being 15 is as ___ as . . .
3. Being 16 is as ___ as . . .
4. Being a teen-ager is as ___ as . . .
5. Being a sophomore is as ___ as . . .
6. Coping with adults is as ___ as . . .

Writers often use *figures of speech* like the ones you just created. *Figures of speech* are word pictures. Used judiciously, *figurative language* enhances writing.

Look at the poem on page 47. The writer's *simile* perhaps progressed like this.

I feel lonely.

I feel lonely, like an empty soft-drink cup left under the bleachers.

I feel ~~lonely~~, like an empty soft-drink cup left under the bleachers.

The poet could take his writing one step further.

Loneliness is an empty soft-drink cup left under the bleachers.

The preceding sentence is a figure of speech called a *metaphor*. The comparison is indirect yet powerful. In a metaphor one thing is called another, and the words *like* and *as* are omitted.

⁓⁓⁓⁓⁓⁓⁓⁓⁓⁓⁓⁓⁓⁓⁓⁓⁓⁓⁓⁓⁓⁓⁓⁓⁓⁓⁓⁓⁓

**Getting
It
Started**

For practice, toy with creating metaphors on adolescence. You may remain in your group, but make your metaphor an individual effort. Here are some options from which to choose.

Option 1:   Draft a free writing that begins: Adolescence is . . .

Option 2:   Draft a free writing that ends: Adolescence is . . .

Option 3:   Draft a jot-list poem using the sentence comple-
tions brainstormed by your group. Using your jot-list poem as
stimulus, create your own poem.

After you have written your first draft, try it out on a
consultant. Get advice on revision.

If you select metaphor option three, consider these suggestions, too.

Suggestion 1:   Rearrange lines for a specific effect. Adjust
metaphors as necessary. For instance, try listing negative
images at the beginning and positive images at the end. To
offer contrast, alternate positive and negative images of
adolescence. Delete metaphors that detract from the effect
you want to create.

Suggestion 2:   Focus on one image. Develop that single
metaphor in a revised poem.

SPOTLIGHT

Here is Gale's jot-list poem and revision.

First Draft—Jot-List Poem

> Adolescence Is
> a pair of faded jeans
> horses galloping into dusk
> a roller coaster ride
> first love
> the sun peeking around a cloud
> a patchwork quilt
> a butterfly emerging from its cocoon
> a colt on newborn legs
> a slap on a sunburned back
> a soft kiss
> a fleeting glance
> a practical joke
> the dawning of tomorrow
> childhood's curtsy

windchimes dancing in the breeze
hot-rod hearts
blonde hair spilling over sundrenched shoulders
serenity's moment
loony tunes
paper's ragged edge
four walls
a shared secret
midnight feelings
simple dreams

Gale

First Revision—(Using suggestion #1)

Adolescence Is

Adolescence Is
        childhood's practical joke
a roller coaster ride on the ragged edge
jean clad dreams gone loony tunes

Adolescence Is
        life's celebration
blonde hair dancin' in the breeze
hot-rod hearts and simple dreams

Adolescence Is
        Solemnity's stepchild

Gale

Compare this revision with the original. What metaphors are singled out? How have certain metaphors been reshaped? What effect do you think the poet is trying to create? Do you like the effect?

First Revision—(Using suggestion #2)

Adolescence

Hot-rod hearts play chicken

Racing down the ragged edge
                we zoom
Locked on a collision course

From the sidelines
Maturity laughs
             madly

As if her Secret
Could save
        us

Gale

How does the poet focus her writing? Point out how the poet develops the metaphor, "Adolescence is a hot-rod heart." Do you think this *extended metaphor* works in the poem? Of the three versions, which poem do you like best?

~~~~~~

**Getting
It
Started**

As a class, collect examples of figurative language in music. Peruse old albums for examples of similes and metaphors. Weave your findings together in a salute to rock and roll.

~~~~~~

Notes to Myself

**Getting
It
Down**

So far you've been scratching around in your Notebook jotting down the good, the bad, and the ugly. You've explored and reflected on sources of anxiety and sources of joy in your life. You've been engaging in introspective writing. Introspection is an inward examination in which the writer takes an inventory of thoughts and feelings. Many closet writers or people who write privately use introspective writing as a way to clear their minds, find answers, or unload frustrations.

Most people at one time or another talk to themselves. Just before a job interview you might give yourself a pep talk. "Be confident. Look her in the eyes. Don't fidget. You *can* get this job." Just before a band concert you try to calm yourself. "Don't get nervous. You've practiced this stuff for weeks. You know it cold. It's just another practice. Give it your best shot." After a losing game: "It's not the end of the world. You gave a good effort. Be a good loser."

This writing activity asks you to take a more objective view of yourself. Using the jottings you have made in your Writer's Notebook, set up a situation in which you can talk to yourself. Select a frustration, a pressure, or a happy situation you can talk over with yourself. Depending on your personality or your mood, you may want to laugh at yourself, preach to yourself, have a dialogue with yourself, or see yourself as an outsider sees you. Look at the Getting It Started on page 45 and the one on page 47, then select something worth talking about.

~~~~~~

SPOTLIGHT

If you need some ideas, read these student examples.

> Look Swartz . . . you've been moping around this house long
> enough. Your friends (the two you have left) are sick of your com-
> plaining. Your parents think you are first cousin to a dragon. Your
> school work is in a shambles. Mrs. Johnson (English, etc.) asked if
> you were having trouble at home. You haven't been excited about
> anything. Last Sunday you didn't even bother to watch the Falcons
> trounce the Eagles. Let's face it Swartz, you are a sick boy.
>
> What has become of the carefree lad with tousled hair? What
> has become of the confident young man with the quick retort? Most
> of your one-liners have become "poor me messages." Where has the
> happy, "he's so funny" guy gone?
>
> Look Swartz, the woman is not worth it. She told you to lighten
> up; to back off, to "not be so serious." "Let's slow down and be
> friends," she says after all those smiles and phone calls and notes in
> your locker. She doesn't know what she wants. She is scared, imma-
> ture, not ready for your kind of love. So look, don't begin to doubt
> yourself. It's her problem.
>
> Get a plan for rehabilitation—maybe the new girl in French
> class has possibilities. She thought your "Bonjour, mon ami" was
> cute. Or maybe it's time to swear off girls for awhile; make them
> miss you a little. Take yourself out of circulation. Start a fish
> aquarium or take up coin collecting or consider entering a monas-
> tery. Swartz, it makes no sense to mourn your life away after the
> most beautiful blue-eyed girl in the class. Get over it!
>
> Your more carefree self,
Dick Swartz

Dick Swartz takes a light-hearted approach to a frustrating misunder-
standing with a girl friend. How does he make fun of himself? Where else
does his humor show through? What do you think of the way he handles
the problem? Do you think he will "get over it"?

Self to Self

Self #1:   So you're in another one of those grey moods, huh,
Charley? What is it this time? No money— No friends! No
luck, or is it something serious?

Self #2:   I'm not sure. I feel kind of spacey—out of touch—a serious case of the blahs—school's a bore—I can't find a decent job. I'd like to develop a little financial independence.

Self #1:   Now wait a minute. Let's take your complaints one at a time. School is boring. That's where your friends are. That's where you're supposed to learn stuff. How much are you putting into school? Are you really trying to find the good there?

Self #2:   You want an honest answer? No, I'm not trying very hard. It seems like we do the same stuff over every year. I'm tired of answering the questions at the end of the chapter, and I'm tired of pop quizzes. There's not enough variety, not enough real challenge.

Self #1:   The teachers are to blame, huh? They're not motivating you.

Self #2:   Well no, most of my teachers try hard. They put in long days with big classes. I couldn't stand to spend every day with hundreds of teen-agers. Maybe school isn't supposed to be exciting or maybe I just don't care right now.

Self #1:   O.K. School's no help. What about a job? Have you looked . . . I mean knocked on a few doors? What about Bob's service station? He likes you. Maybe he needs a general flunky around there. What about the Burger Doodle? That place is always a mad house. I'll bet they need some warm bodies to pass out those grease burgers.

Self #2:   I sort of mentioned a job to Bob last fall. He didn't seem interested. I'd be embarrassed to work at Burger Doodle.

Self #1:   You do have your pride, don't you? Sounds to me as if you haven't really tried very hard. You don't get a job by "sort of mentioning." You come right out and tell old Bob what a good hand you would be around the place. I really think a job would give you a lift. Something new—a challenge and yes, a little money.

Self #2:   Think so, huh? Maybe I'll give it a try.

Charley constructs a dialogue with two selves. How successful is he in keeping the two distinct voices going? How would you contrast the two voices? What do you think of the advice Self #1 gives? What else could you tell Self #2 to help him over the grey mood?

Case Study #0999
Name: Linda McAdam
Age: 16
Occupation: Tenth Grade Student

Case study #0999, Linda McAdam, won the fourth annual speech
contest held in the Central City Auditorium this week. One judge
reported, "Ms. McAdam dazzled us with her self-assurance." Considering the subject's past history, her accomplishment can be described as a stunning achievement.

Update on Previous History

At the beginning of the year, subject suffered from an affliction
known alternately as stage fright, performance anxiety, and the knee-
knocking blues. Despite exhaustive preparation—memorizing lines

verbatim, practicing before her bedroom mirror, and trying out her speech on her closest confidant, Alex the cat—subject experienced uncontrollable panic before each speech. Reportedly, the subject once faked an illness to avoid facing her peers. In all fairness to the subject, she was, indeed, suffering from a pounding heart and a queazy stomach. Even her mother conceded that, "Even if Linda's Social Studies teacher had succeeded in unclenching Linda's fists, Linda's shaky voice would have given her away." (Not to mention the perspiration rings down to the subject's waist.)

Present Condition

It is believed that the subject is not yet out of danger. She herself admits, "I'm still a frightoholic." The subject keeps her condition in control by following six steps: 1. by admitting her fear, 2. by remembering that her audience is composed of ordinary people just like herself, 3. by positive thinking—telling herself she *will* do well, 4. by reminding herself that people in the audience like her, 5. by thoroughly preparing but *not* memorizing her speeches word-for-word, and 6. by rewarding herself for small successes.

Summary

The subject has made dramatic progress over the past seven months. Her most significant achievements are believing in herself and facing her problem head on.

Sometimes an objective view can put a problem in perspective. Notice how Linda steps outside herself and writes the account as if she were an uninvolved observer. Linda uses the third person "she" to keep her distance. She even refers to herself as "the subject." Occasionally, Linda laughs at herself. Do you think a sense of humor has helped Linda solve her problem? What is your prognosis for Linda's future as an orator?

The Many Selves of Me

Replacing the selves of childhood are the selves of adolescence. But who are they? What do they contribute to the complex being known as you? When do the selves show up? How do they announce their presence? In which selves do you take pride? Which selves need a little work? How many selves are you?

Jot List

Before you try a free writing, take time to marshal your resources. Using a jot list, list your selves. Include concrete examples that illustrate your selves.

Getting
It
Started

SPOTLIGHT

Now, look at Andrew's jot list.

Selves	*Illustrations*
Insecure	Around girls . . . they're all beautiful, poised, sure, and vicious.
Showy	Hot driver, fast dancer, big eater, three burgers.
Responsible	Take care of younger brother and sister, family garbage man.
Irresponsible	Forget to call when I'm late. Messy. Avoid stuff.
Aggressive	Yell at the driver who cuts me off.
Tender	Protect little animals and little kids and old ladies.
Competitive	Pinball wizard, grades. I'll take a B but not a C.
Lazy	My best trait. Watch sports on TV before anything else. Dirty clothes. Like to be waited on.
Wacky	Wise cracks, clowning, singing top-40 songs off key in the shower, open-house signs on lawn of my neighbor.
Vain	My hair—has to look just right, always sneak a peek at my reflection in store windows.

Free Writing the Selves

Once your jot list is in shape, use a free writing to develop the selves. You may want to introduce your selves or simply acknowledge their existence. In any form that seems right, talk through your many sides in the piece.

Getting
It
Down

SPOTLIGHT

The Many Selves of Me

Andrew's writing is one example of a selves piece.

It's crowded in here. There's an insecure mousy little guy who is afraid of girls. His throat tightens and his voice gets higher just talking to them. He thinks all girls are poised, mature, and vicious. There's a hot shot, cocky, showy guy who scratches off at stop lights, dances a bit too flamboyantly and amazes folks with his ability to consume hamburgers. There's a competitive guy who hates to lose at tennis, and can't stand to get a C on a test. There's an aggressive guy who yells at drivers who cut him off and a softy who protects little animals, lets dogs sleep on his bed, and takes the neighbor kids on hikes.

And of course there are a few selves that drive other people crazy. No. 1 irritant of an "everything in its place" mother is the lazy self who leaves dirty clothes around the house, grows green cultures in old milk glasses in his bedroom, plays rock music too loud on Saturday morning, and continually asks people to bring him things. "While you're up, Mom, bring me a . . ." No. 2 crowd pleaser is the wacko who sings top-40 songs off key in the shower, dances through a church committee meeting in the living room wearing his oldest clothes, and puts Open-House signs on his crotchety neighbor's lawn.

These colorful characters sometimes stumble over each other and sometimes war with each other. Sometimes they show up at the wrong time. Most people don't know all of them. I'm not sure I understand all of them. But I'm basically a happy person, and I am learning to live with this motley collection.

Andrew

Writer's Workbench 2

Revising Strategies

You've been struggling to develop a draft which makes a coherent statement about all those selves in you. If you are satisfied with that first draft, you have pulled off a minor miracle. Most first drafts of challenging writing assignments have that "worked on" look. You may need "the right word" here or there. The piece may ramble around without much direction. More often than not, both the beginning and ending need more work. Perhaps, worst of all, you may still not know exactly what it is you want to say. You have a few strikingly clear sentences scattered throughout the piece, and the rest is mush. Further work on the piece at this time may frustrate you, and ultimately condemn the writing to becoming just another assignment.

Revision Strategy #1   A Breather

You and your writing may need to take separate vacations. Put the piece away. Take a break for a day or two. How about plunging into that class novel or a news magazine? Get some exercise. Take a long walk by yourself or bike with a friend. Let the writing cool off. Let your subconscious work on the writing while you do something worthwhile.

Many good writers interrupt their composing with breaks away from their writing. They get some distance from their own words and also relieve the tension of writing. The reunion of writer and writing can often produce new insight and vision.

While you are away from your writing for a while, do this Workbench. It will help you review sentence-combining strategies you may have studied in earlier years, and it will give you some ideas for making your sentences stronger.

Creating Dependent Clauses

Each sentence-combining problem presents two or more sentences and a cue that tells you how to combine them into one larger sentence. The cue used in the following exercise is (when). Its purpose is to tell you how to combine the two sentences:

> Mary always feels better.
> Sandy has run her daily three miles.   (when)

The arrow tells you what to do. Simply move *when* to the beginning of the sentence and combine the two sentences. Your combined sentence should be

> Mary always feels better when Sandy has run her daily three miles.

The cue (after) operates in the same way.

> Sandy has run her daily three miles.   (after)
>
> Mary always feels better.   (,)

The result:

> After Sandy has run her daily three miles, Mary always feels better.

The word groups you have created as you added *when* and *after* to sentences are *dependent clauses*. When you add a *subordinating conjunction* like *when* or *after* to a sentence, it cannot stand alone as a sentence any longer. It must be joined to another sentence. ● See the Handbook, page H-67, for any needed review in this area.

Look at this example:
1. I bought a car.
2. I didn't have to walk or ride my bike any more.

Both word groups are sentences. But if the first word group is

> When I bought a car

it is no longer a sentence. It is a *dependent clause*. It must be attached to a sentence in order to make it complete. The resulting sentence could be

> When I bought a car, I didn't have to walk or ride my bike any more.

OR

> I didn't have to walk or ride my bike any more when I bought a car.

Now look at the use of the comma in the next example.
1. I got a job.   (When)

2. I bought some really nice clothes with my first check.   (,)

> The combined sentence is
> When I got a job, I bought some really nice clothes with my first check.

You should use a comma following a long introductory adverbial clause (that's what the *when* and *after* dependent clauses are). You should also use commas after introductory adverbial phrases (like *in the morning* in the sentence "In the morning, Neil must call the police"). Usually, you will use a comma after an introductory single-word adverb (like *however* in the sentence "However, Henry must call the police right now"). ● Check page H-17 in the Handbook for help in using commas after introductory adverbials.

The words (since), (because), (until), and other similar words operate the same as the (when) and (after) cues do.

Now do the following sentence-combining problems. You may do them in your Writer's Notebook or on a separate sheet of paper, whichever your teacher directs.

1. We installed a computer.   (Since)
    My checkbook always balances.   (,)
2. I had to miss basketball practice.
    I was ill.   (because)

3. We'll stay right here.
   The police come.   (until)
4. The clock strikes twelve.   (Until)
   We will continue to be afraid.   (,)
5. We have gone.   (After)
   You can let the photographers in.   (,)
6. Life is no fun.
   You get your driver's license.   (until)
7. I've been going steady.   (Since)
   Everybody seems to ask me for dates.   (,)
8. Our play tryouts had to be called off.
   We couldn't find anyone to play the lead.   (because)
9. Our basketball team has won all of its games this year.
   We have a 7'2" center.   (because)
10. Seven of Joe's friends showed up.   (When)
    The party got out of hand.   (,)

~~~~~~

**Checking
It
Out**

Revision Strategy #2   A Second Look

After you've given that first draft a much needed rest, read it aloud with fresh eyes. You are now more reader than writer. Exploit that objectivity. Assess the piece as though it were the work of someone else.

Look first at its strengths. Is the author's voice *strong, consistent, personal*? Are there *specific examples* to illustrate general statements? What do you like *best* about the writing?

Try summarizing the piece in a single sentence. Look back at the writing and mark any sections which sound out of place. These sections may need to be tied in more directly or they may need to be removed. If some parts of the writing sound as if they belong in a different writing assignment, take them out—even if they're wonderful. Don't throw any good material away. Keep it in your Writer's Notebook. These bits and pieces may fit into another writing or they may spark other ideas later.

What part of the writing needs the most work—the beginning, the ending, the details? Rework parts of your writing. Try several beginnings or endings. Brainstorm for more detail. Tinker with the writing the way a mechanic tunes a motorcycle.

Revision Strategy #3   Surprise

Once you are satisfied that your writing is structurally sound—

solid opening, generous examples, effective closing—you may want to experiment with metaphor and figurative language. This writing is a private one to be shared with friends and family. This is a safe time to try your hand at enriching the language of your writing. Look at Workbench 1 again. Can you develop a fresh metaphor or two in your writing? Can you plant a few surprises in the piece?

Recopy your final version of your writing. Share the finished piece with friends or your parents. Watch them smile and nod as you reveal the many selves of you.

**Getting
It
Right**

Chapter 4

Coming of Age

Adolescence is the bridge young people in our society must cross on their journey to adulthood. While adolescence links childhood and adulthood, it also blurs the dividing line between the two. In our culture a young person does not go to sleep a child and awaken an adult. The transition between childhood and adulthood is gradual. At some point during their passage into maturity, young people gain the rights of adulthood . . . but when?

Some believe adulthood is linked to age, yet the exact age is unclear. At what age are young people considered adult? Is it at 16 when they can be licensed to drive a car, at 17 when they may view "R" rated movies, at 18 when they inherit the right to vote, or 21, the age traditionally associated with adulthood?

The controversial age question is complicated by circumstance. Maturity sometimes defies age. Should the 18-year-old serving in the armed forces be denied adult status? And what about the 19-year-old providing for a family? Should the legal age be lowered in certain instances?

The Adult Dilemma

Adolescence is an age of uncertainty for adults as well as for teen-agers. As adults, parents are responsible for protecting and guiding their young. Most parents take their responsibility seriously. But what is to be done with the almost-adult offspring?

Even state legislatures disagree about many facets of adolescence. Legal age for certain activities varies from state to state. The legal drinking age, for example, is controversial. Whether the age at which alcoholic beverages may be purchased should be raised or lowered is frequently disputed. In some states the legal drinking age is as low as 18. In other states it is as high as 21.

~~~~~~

The Age of Maturity

**Getting
It
Started**

The age of maturity question is a complex issue. In a free writing, voice your opinion on the matter. What are your feelings? Where do you stand on the age of maturity controversy? You may choose to explore the full range of age-related questions or to focus your writing on one topic, such as the legal drinking age. In your Writer's Notebook write down your thoughts as fast as you can. Write for at least ten minutes. When you have finished writing, share your piece with a partner.

~~~~~~

While some stick by the age theory, others maintain that age alone is an unreliable barometer for gauging maturity. Advocates of the responsibility hypothesis argue that adult status must be earned. This camp contends that young people should be viewed as adults only when they prove their competence in the adult world. They feel that young people must act as adults in order to be treated as adults.

But what does "act as an adult" mean? To some, mature behavior may include considering consequences before making decisions and earning your own way in the world. To others acting as an adult may mean accepting responsibility in relationships or considering the feelings of others before your own. The fact is that many young people take on adult responsibilities such as caring for younger brothers and sisters and holding down a job. They exhibit behaviors adults value, such as honoring school and social commitments. Nonetheless, grownups are reluctant to use responsibility as the sole criterion for adulthood.

The Adolescent Quandary
(or The Double Standard Crunch)

Young people frequently complain that they're asked to be an adult one minute, then treated as children the next. Forgetting to hang up your clothes may be met with "Act responsibly! You're not a child anymore," while a request to own your own motorcycle may provoke, "You're too young for that kind of responsibility." While many young people understand that parental restrictions grow out of love, there is still some frustration with the demand for a dual child-adult role.

A double standard exists in society at large. When it comes to purchasing tickets to movies or amusement parks, adolescents are considered adults. They pay adult admission prices. On the other hand, adolescents are turned away from other places of business with, "Sorry. No minors allowed."

The hazy distinction between childhood and adulthood may leave you uncertain as to where you fit in. You may wonder if there isn't a simpler, more straightforward approach to attaining adult status. Looking at how other cultures determine adulthood may provide some unexpected insights.

In Chapter 3 you explored the pressures and joys of growing up and wrote a "Notes to Myself" piece in which you took a closer look at yourself. In a "Many Selves of Me" writing you discovered the various selves that make you unique.

SPOTLIGHT

In Chapter 4 you will continue to investigate the complex process of growing up. So far you have examined the social practices surrounding passage into adulthood in our society. Now you will turn your attention to initiation customs in other cultures.

Through several free writings you will explore the complexities of coming-of-age. Workbenches will give you an opportunity to sharpen your skills as a writer. Relying on writings completed in Chapters 3 and 4, you will create a piece entitled "On Growing Up" for an adult audience. To give you maximum freedom as a writer, several options will be provided.

Rites of Passage

In our society growing up is a complicated process. Gaining acceptance as an adult often depends on subtle factors. In primitive societies life is much simpler. The passage from childhood to adulthood is clearly marked. Transition from one stage to the next is signaled by formal ceremonies called rituals. These formal, sometimes elaborate, rituals are called rites of passage. The following description of initiation for the Manus boy of New Guinea illustrates the drama surrounding the ritual.

The Adolescent Boy
. . . At some time between twelve and sixteen, when his family finances suggest the advisability, his ears are pierced. The feasts of ear piercing pay back the great display which his father made at his silver wedding. Much property must be collected, many plans laid.

The boy's size or age are relatively unimportant. But some day a boy comes home from playing with his companions, to be told that his ears will be pierced in a month. If he is the first among his age mates to undergo the tiresome ceremony, he rebels. Occasionally a father will follow his pattern of indulgence, more often he insists. The wives of the boy's mother's brothers come in a body to stay in the house with him. His father's family prepares a feast of cooked food. He himself is dressed in his very best—his small neck bristles with dogs' teeth, a gorgeous new laplap proclaims his special state. He sits beside his father, very stiff and straight, divided between embarrassment and pride. None of his friends come to the ceremony, only grown people and little children. His father's sisters take him by the hands and lead him down the ladder to the platform. Here his mother's brother pierces his ears with a sharpened bit of hard wood. Bits of soft wood are inserted in the newly made hole, and small protectors of sago bark are placed over each ear. Now the boy is under strict tabu. He cannot cut with a knife; he cannot kindle a fire; he cannot bathe for five days. He must eat only of the food which his mother's brothers' wives cook for him. When he leaves the house, he sits very erect and gaudy upon the canoe platform while the other boys punt him. His companions are very impressed with his strange state. They gladly act as oarsmen. They take him all the tobacco they can beg. At the end of the five days, he may wash, and he is free to move quietly about the village. The other prohibitions hold until his mother's relatives make a big feast for his father's relatives. Until then his ears are in danger should he be unobservant of the tabus. . . .

Margaret Mead

Ear-piercing feasts proclaim the Manus boy's initiation. Hereafter, younger boys will look up to the newly initiated youth. What is your reaction to this ceremony and its effect on the Manus boy's status?

Think of ceremonies in our society such as religious rites or high school graduation. How do these ceremonies affect the status of young people in our culture?

Secrecy surrounds most coming-of-age ceremonies. In certain villages tribal secrets and mythology are withheld from children. Only when adulthood is attained are the tribal mysteries revealed to the novice. Novices are young people newly initiated into adulthood. They are considered beginners in the adult world. Until initiation, novices live in the protected world of childhood innocence. To the novices of many cultures, initiation means the unfolding of profound religious secrets.

Some societies reserve tribal secrets for male novices. Anthropologists, who study human cultures, their behaviors, and customs, report that girls do not participate in rites of passage in all cultures. The highly symbolic initiation rituals of the Apache, however, include girls.

. . . a young Apache maiden had her time in the sun before the routine of married life began. At the age of 12 to 14 she starred in a four-day drama that would launch her properly into womanhood. The whole tribe gathered to share in the festivities.

Today as in aboriginal times, cattail fronds, symbol of renewal, carpet the entrance to the tipi; inside the girl kneels, clad in golden buckskin, the color of pollen. Attending shamans wail their high-pitched songs:

. . . the rainbow moves forward, dawn maidens . . .

Beautifully over us it is dawning.

A "godmother" paints the young maiden with pollen from cheek to cheek, then pushes her toward a tray laden with ritual objects, which she circles four times. Every night the girl dances until midnight, while outside, her people dance and feast. On the last day a shaman blesses her, a sun symbol in his palm:

The sun . . . has come down to the earth,

It has come to her . . .

Long life! Its power is good.

Meekly the girl submits to the demanding rite, for if she behaves well on this day, the Apache believe, she will always be a good woman.

Jules B. Billard, ed.

Cattail fronds

Symbolic articles such as cattail fronds—leaves from a flowery marsh plant—are highly significant in many rites of passage. Think of articles in our culture, such as the American flag, that are symbolic. What do these objects symbolize? How important are they in our society? Can you think of articles associated with the American teen-ager that are, in some ways, symbolic? If so, what do these articles signify?

Patterns

The initiation rites of the Manus boy and the Apache girl illustrate the diversity of rites of passage. Each society signifies its youths' passage into adulthood in slightly different ways. Anthropological studies have uncovered a basic pattern in initiation rites. While anthropologists admit that not all the stages appear in all primitive rites, they feel confident enough to propose three stages: separation, transition, and reincorporation.

Separation marks stage one. By separation, observers mean that initiates, or novices, are literally set apart from their community and its members. Separation may last a short time or may span many days. To many societies the separation stage represents the symbolic death of childhood.

The second stage, transition, is often a period of testing. In this stage young people perform ritualistic feats or face strenuous ordeals. Instruction in tribal tradition is another aspect of the transition stage. All trials prepare youth for the third stage of initiation.

The final stage of the rites of passage is reincorporation. Entry into the adult world is finalized in this stage. New members of adult society are frequently celebrated by the entire community. Initiates are symbolically reborn as adults. There is cause for much joy and feasting.

Coming-Of-Age

Getting It Down

It is said that there are no formal initiation rites in American culture. Perhaps that's only fair since there is no "adolescence" in primitive cultures. Young people in tribal societies don't skip the teen years, of course. They simply miss out on the teen age—the age of uncertainty, of turmoil, confusion; the age for dreaming, for reflecting, and for finding themselves.

Think of this free writing as an exploratory piece. Sit back for a minute. Contemplate coming-of-age in a primitive society.

Reflect on your own passage into adulthood. Now weigh the pros and cons of attaining adulthood in these contrastive cultures.

Explore one of the following three options in a free writing. Read through all options before making a decision. Once you have selected an option, allow yourself to think on paper. Let your thoughts spill out for at least ten minutes.

Option 1: Draft a reaction piece. React to the initiation rites of a specific society. Reread the descriptions of the Manus and Apache initiation ceremonies. Put yourself there. Become the initiate. In what ways is your initiation a positive experience? In what ways is it a negative experience? What are your feelings as you cross the line between childhood and adulthood?

Option 2: Look for similarities in coming-of-age customs in America and in those of primitive societies. Find parallels between the informal American passage into adulthood and formal rites of passage. You may want to consider adolescence itself as a rite of passage. Explore the ordeals American youth must endure. Point to American ceremonies similar to those in primitive cultures. Discuss symbols in American cultures that are connected to coming-of-age. Consider how the journey toward adulthood is much the same for young people in America and in primitive societies.

Option 3: Focus on sharp contrasts. How do coming-of-age rituals in primitive cultures stand out in comparison to American coming-of-age customs? Stress features which distinguish rites in primitive cultures from the American passage into adulthood. Which features do you find appealing? Which traditions would you prefer to omit?

~~~~~~

After writing your piece, meet in small groups for sharing. Take time to explore divergent viewpoints. Talk through questions that puzzle or intrigue you. Then file your piece in your Writer's Notebook. You'll come back to it later.

**Checking
It
Out**

~~~~~~

Writer's Workbench 1

The Care and Feeding of Paragraphs

If you are a practiced writer, you may already be an expert paragrapher. In that case this Workbench will be merely a review. If, on the other hand, you are confused about when and where to begin and end paragraphs, the Workbench is right on time.

Paragraphing is difficult for inexperienced writers. They become involved in getting their words on paper, and forget that readers depend on paragraphs to direct their reading. Paragraphs are used by writers to organize and make their messages easier to read. Writers also use paragraphs to create dramatic effects, separate ideas, and pace readers.

Paragraphs are particularly important in transactional writing. When writers try to convey information or persuade their audience, they use paragraphs to organize their main points so that their audience will see their message clearly.

Paragraphing problems are best solved in two ways. First through *planning*—sometimes writers can decide where paragraphs should be by examining their jot lists and free writings. They mark their important ideas and decide on a rough order before they write a draft. They make a guess about how many paragraphs they will need and try their plan in a draft. If the plan doesn't work, they solve paragraphing problems by revising the draft, shifting the order of paragraphs, and combining too-short paragraphs. They may need some expert advice at the revision stage from a teacher or consultant.

Here's a review of common paragraphing problems.

Problem 1—The undernourished weakling

One- or two-sentence paragraphs are often a sign that the writer has not fully developed the ideas.

Look at this example:

My favorite sport is sailing. I sail every Saturday even in bad weather.

My brother is an excellent sailor. He has taught me everything I know.

I have my own Sunfish, but I hope to buy a daysailer after high school.

Racing a sailboat takes strength and courage. My brother won a race last week in a catamaran.   *Dan*

The writer's problem here is the collection of four undernourished paragraphs. Try rewriting this passage into two healthy paragraphs. Add more details if necessary to fatten up your paragraphs.

Problem 2—The overstuffed blimp

Sometimes writers stuff paragraphs so full of ideas that readers are overwhelmed. Take a look at this blimpy paragraph. How many well-developed paragraphs can you make from the blimp? Try a rewrite. Reorder the sentences any way you wish. Add or delete information as necessary.

Who took the vending machines out of this school? Teachers get to drink pop any time they want to. Some kids hate cafeteria food and eat that stuff in the vending machines. Maybe the principal thought there was too much trash in the halls. We're supposed to be mature enough to decide whether or not to eat the junk food in vending machines. Taking those machines away is treating us like babies. Taking those machines away will not get more kids to eat in the cafeteria. More pizza and fewer fish fillets and soy burgers will get kids to eat lunch. Teachers have a private room for vending machines. Students are supposed to last 7 hours without eating junk food. It's not fair to ask more of students than teachers.

Sharon

Problem 3—The formless blob

Nothing drives readers up the wall as much as the "Look Ma, no paragraphs!" piece. Readers depend on paragraphs to focus their reading and help them get the writer's message. Paragraphs say to the reader, "Look at this point; now think about this; next consider these facts." A writing without paragraphs is a writing without an obvious structure. Many readers will simply lose the message if you omit paragraphs.

Final Word

When you revise your writing, use this paragraphing checklist:

1. Take a hard look at any one- or two-sentence paragraphs in your draft. Do they need to be fattened up? If they contain the kernel of a good idea, develop them more fully. Cite an example that illustrates the point. Elaborate, tell the full story, use facts and figures, descriptions, quotations, anecdotes to put some meat on your bare-bones paragraph.
2. Look carefully at any long paragraphs. Are there any overstuffed blimps? Do you need to rewrite any paragraphs to slim them down? Remember a good paragraph develops *one* idea thoroughly.
3. Check to see that each important idea has a paragraph of its own.

SPOTLIGHT

Have you ever looked at your younger brothers and sisters and thought, "Gee, you have it made"? Unencumbered by adult pressures, children indulge in hours of carefree play. A child's life seems so simple, so full of surprise.

The Book of Merlyn concludes the fantasy *The Once and Future King*. The tales revolve around the life of King Arthur under the tutelage of Merlyn the Magician. At Merlyn's insistence, King Arthur returns to his boyhood in this final tale.

> But it made him remember his first childhood vividly, the happy times swimming in moats or flying with Archimedes, and he realised that he had lost something since those days. It was something which he thought of now as the faculty of wonder. Then, his delights had been indiscriminate. His attention, or his sense of beauty, or whatever it was to be called, had attached itself fortuitously to oddments. Perhaps, while Archimedes had been lecturing him about the flight of birds, he himself would have been lost in admiration at the way in

which the fur went on the mouse in the owl's claws. Or the great Mr. M. might have been making him a speech about Dictatorship, while he, all the time, would have seen only the bony teeth, poring on them in an ecstasy of experience.

This, his faculty of wonder, was gone from inside him, however much Merlyn might have furbished up his brain. It was exchanged—for the faculty of discrimination, he supposed. Now would never have seen the grey fur or the yellow teeth. He did not feel proud of the change.

T. H. White

Merlyn feels that children have special qualities which make them more open to learning. Do you believe that qualities such as innocence and a sense of wonder aid the learning process? Why or why not?

In this excerpt Arthur grieves over the loss of his sense of wonder. Why is he so sad? What does the speaker mean when he says, "His attention . . . attached itself fortuitously to oddments"? What examples illustrate this point? What has the King gained to replace his sense of wonder? Do you think Arthur would be happy as an adult without this latter quality?

Losses and Gains

Adulthood is just out of reach. You seem so close, yet so far from your goal. In your quest for adulthood, take time to glance over your shoulder. As a class, brainstorm the *losses* of childhood. On the board, have someone record the qualities you've left behind.

Now look ahead. Adulthood holds a mysterious fascination. Why? What do you hope to achieve in winning adult status? With classmates, brainstorm the *gains* of adulthood. Record the gains on the board beside the losses column.

Your childhood lies behind you; your adulthood looms ahead, but you're in neither place. Write a piece from your vantage point. Use the brainstorm lists to look at what you've left behind and at what you hope to gain. Write for at least 15 minutes. When you complete your draft, file it in your Writer's Notebook. You will use this draft as a resource for your major writing assignment on growing up.

Writer's Workbench 2

Sentence Control

Before you begin the next major writing assignment, take time out to do this sentence-combining Workbench. It will help you get your sentences under control, and could make the sentences in your next paper stronger.
● See your Handbook if you need to check on grammar.

Section 1, adjectives.

Adjectives are descriptive words. They are like the underlined words in the following sentence-combining problem:

>   The dog ran after the children.
>   The dog was angry.
>   The dog was stray.
>   The children were frightened.

These sentences may be combined to produce the following sentence:
>   The *angry, stray* dog ran after the *frightened* children.

Since *angry* and *stray* refer to the dog, they appear near the word *dog* in the sentence. They are adjectives, and they modify or describe *dog*. *Frightened* refers to the *children*: thus it appears next to the word *children*. It is also an adjective, since it describes the word *children*, a noun. Adjectives modify nouns.

Do the following sentence-combining problems. The underlined words are all adjectives: they should be placed near the nouns they modify.

1.   Aspens surround the lake.
The aspens are tall.
The aspens are leafy.
The lake is calm.
2.   The fire started in the hills.
The fire was in the forest.
The hills were dry.
The hills were wooded.
3.   The building was littered with garbage.
The building was an apartment.
The building was vacant.
The garbage was old.
4.   The girl is selling flowers.
The girl is young.
The girl is pretty.
The flowers are plastic.
5.   The complex towered above the houses.
The complex was a building.
The complex was new.
The houses were decrepit.
6.   The crowd shouted insults at the umpire.
The crowd was boisterous.
The insults were vulgar.
The umpire was umpiring baseball.
7.   The neighbors had a party.
The neighbors were noisy.
The party was all-night.
The party was for a victory.
8.   The cows headed for the barn.
The cows were hungry.
The cows were cold.
The barn was comforting.

9. The hikers sat around the fire.
   The hikers were weary.
   The hikers were lonely.
   The fire was warm.
10. The swimmers plunged their faces into the water.
    The swimmers were enthusiastic.
    Their faces were smiling.
    The water was cool.

Section 2, participles.

Participles are also descriptive words. They are verbs that end in "ing,"
"ed," or "d" and function as adjectives. The underlined words in the
following sentence-combining problems are participles.

> In a locked area behind the family's house lay the food.
> The family was starving.
> The food was rotting.

These sentences may be combined to produce the following sentence:

> In a locked area behind the *starving* family's house lay the *rotting*
> food.

The participle *starving* refers to the word *family* and the participle *rotting*
refers to the word *food*. Participles modify nouns just as adjectives do.

Do the following sentence-combining problems. The underlined
words are all participles, and should be placed near the *nouns* they
modify.

1. The coach was trying to quiet the crowd.
   The coach was embarrassed.
   The crowd was jeering.
2. The goose chased the boys.
   The goose was hissing.
   The boys were running.
3. The passengers evacuated the ship.
   The passengers were screaming.
   The ship was sinking.
4. The pilot brought the plane to safety.
   The pilot was well-trained.
   The plane was disabled.
5. We found a photograph in the attic.
   The photograph was faded.
   The attic was crumbling.

6. The scouts were gathered around the fire.
    The scouts were <u>singing.</u>
    The fire was <u>blazing.</u>
7. The man held onto the vine.
    The man was <u>frightened.</u>
    The vine was <u>breaking.</u>
8. The policeman stopped the motorcycle.
    The policeman was <u>pursuing.</u>
    The motorcycle was <u>speeding.</u>
9. The teacher read the story.
    The teacher was <u>excited.</u>
    The story was <u>thrilling.</u>
10. The child cut herself on a bottle.
    The child was <u>abandoned.</u>
    The bottle was <u>broken.</u>

<u>Section 3, phrases.</u>

Both participles and adjectives can be used as phrases. An adjective
phrase is a group of words that modifies a noun. The underlined words in
the following sentence-combining problems are phrases.

> The chemicals kill the bacteria.
> The chemicals are <u>in the pool.</u>
> The bacteria are <u>swimming in the water.</u>

These sentences may be combined to produce the following sentence:

The chemicals *in the pool* kill the bacteria *swimming in the water*.

The adjective phrase *in the pool* refers to the noun *chemicals*. The participial phrase *swimming in the water* refers to the noun *bacteria*. Both phrases act as adjectives because they modify nouns.

Do the following sentence-combining problems. The underlined words are all phrases used as adjectives. Be sure to place the participial phrases close to the nouns they modify.

1. Sheila shut the door.
   Sheila was disturbed by the noise.
   The door was to her bedroom.

Did you write "Disturbed by the noise, Sheila shut the door to her bedroom" or "Sheila, disturbed by the noise, shut the door to her bedroom"? Either is correct. Choose the order which best fits the situation in which you use the sentence.

2. The dog tried to bite the mailman.
   The dog was guarding the porch.
   The mailman was delivering a package.
3. The speaker answered many questions.
   The speaker was from Washington, D.C.
   The questions were about energy problems.
4. Put the luggage on the rack.
   The luggage is for your trip.
   The rack is above your seat.
5. Ann called her boyfriend.
   Ann was delighted with the news.
   Her boyfriend lived in Iowa.
6. Sue drew a picture.
   She was using her artistic ability.
   The picture was of a winter scene.
7. The guests will be given a tour.
   The guests are waiting in the lobby.
   The tour will be of the museum.
8. Marty found a coin.
   Marty was looking for his watch.
   The coin was in the mud.

9. The man spent endless days.
   The man is <u>recovering from burns</u>.
   The days are <u>in the hospital</u>.
10. Bob left his suitcase.
    Bob was <u>hurrying to the airport</u>.
    His suitcase was <u>in the taxi</u>.

<u>Section 4, clauses.</u>

An adjective clause is a group of words which modifies a noun. A clause differs from a phrase because it has a subject and a verb. Note the following sentences.

> Ted brought the dog to the veterinarian.
> The dog was not feeling well.   (which)
> The veterinarian gave it a shot.   (who)

These sentences may be combined to produce the following sentence:

> Ted brought the dog *which was not feeling well* to the veterinarian
> *who gave it a shot.*

The adjective clause *which was not feeling well* refers to the noun *dog*. The adjective clause *who gave it a shot* refers to the noun *veterinarian*. Both clauses act as adjectives since they modify nouns.

Do the following sentence-combining problems. The word in parentheses signals an adjective clause.

1. Each student received a pen.
   The student wrote a composition.   (who)
   The pen was donated by the Chamber of Commerce.   (which)
2. The book describes the life of the Secretary of State.
   The book is a biography.   (which)
   The Secretary of State helped bring peace to the Middle East.
      (who)
3. The antique sits on a table.
   The antique was bought at the auction.   (which)
   The table is in the living room.   (which)
4. The old lady stared out a window.
   The lady was bored.   (who)
   The window opened onto the street.   (which)
5. The motorists drive onto a freeway.
   The motorists are going to work.   (who)
   The freeway is full of cars.   (which)
6. The woman yelled for the boy.
   The woman had supper waiting.   (who)
   The boy wanted to shoot marbles rather than eat.   (who)
7. The pharmacist did not have the medicine.
   The pharmacist was very busy.   (who)
   I needed the medicine.   (which)
8. The desk is cluttered with debris.
   The desk is used for studying.   (which)
   The debris was left by my younger brother.   (which)
9. Sally looked at herself in the mirror.
   Sally is a perfectionist.   (who)
   The mirror was in the hallway.   (which)
10. The ticking came from the clock.
    The ticking kept me up all night.   (which)
    The clock was repaired yesterday.   (which)

On Growing Up

Getting It Started

This writing assignment culminates two chapters of explorations on adolescence. You have explored personal feelings about your own adolescence. You've read and reacted to growing-up rituals in our own culture and in more primitive cultures. You've contemplated the losses and gains associated with your passage from childhood into teen years. In short, you've been doing groundwork for this assignment. The activity is a major writing assignment which will ask you to pull together your best thinking and transactional writing abilities. Your final product will be evaluated carefully by your teacher using the Checkpoint at the end of this chapter.

The words "major writing assignment" should not strike terror in your heart. You do have to face a blank sheet of paper, but you have been developing ideas and strategies for this assignment for several days. If you follow a step-by-step approach to the writing assignment, you should be pleased with the results.

Step One—Considering topic options

The theme for this writing assignment is "On Growing Up." Here are some possible approaches to the topic.

Option A.   "On Growing Up: Advice to Parents"

This piece speaks directly to parents of teen-agers. You should avoid preachy writing which talks down to parents. Your purpose is to inform and even encourage parents to support and understand their adolescents. Your advice should be concrete, helpful, and positive.

Option B.   "On Growing Up: The Passage from Childhood to Adulthood"

Here you might discuss some of the subtle and obvious changes young people undergo as they grow up. Comment on what you consider to be normal adolescent attitudes and feelings which might threaten adults. Your purpose might be to anticipate adult frustrations with adolescent behavior. You might remind adults of their own adolescence and reassure them that growing up is a chaotic process. Your audience in this piece is a more general adult audience than the audience in Option A.

Option C: "On Growing Up: A Metaphor"

For this assignment you might think about some natural process, such as metamorphosis, change of seasons or weather, or growth of plants and other animals which might serve as a metaphor for your discussion on growing up. This is a creative assignment giving you maximum freedom to develop a unique metaphor. The biggest challenge of this option may be to avoid trite or overused language. Your audience for this piece is adults and your purpose is to help them understand adolescence better than they now do.

Option D: "On Growing Up: The In-Between Years"

In this topic you might compare and contrast childhood and adulthood, pointing out advantages and disadvantages of each. Then talk about being caught in the transition between the two, and the difficulties of being treated alternately as child and adult. The purpose of this piece is to describe as vividly as possible the frustrations of adolescence. Your purpose is to help an adult audience better understand and appreciate young people. You might find humor, exaggeration, even satire helpful in developing this topic.

Option E.   "On Growing Up: ___ ___ ___ ___ ___ "

This is the "make-it-up-yourself" option. If options A through D don't inspire you or if you have a better idea, develop your own topic. Fix clearly in mind a purpose for your piece and an adult audience who will read your writing. Experiment, create, develop a unique approach to the topic.

Step Two—Rereading Your Writings

**Checking
It
Out**

Ease into this assignment by rereading all of your writings from Chapters 3 and 4. Mark any passages you like. Look for anything which might be worth using in this writing assignment.

Step Three—Exploring Options

**Getting
It
Down**

After you have read through your writings, explore several topic options. Try a preliminary jot list on several different ideas. If one of the jot lists takes off, you may want to use that topic. Use a consultant to help in the decision making if you wish. Discuss your thoughts with your teacher if you need to. Take some time exploring. Don't be in too much of a hurry to begin writing.

Step Four—Decision Time

Decide on a topic. Develop a complete jot list on that topic. Look back through earlier writings again for anything you might use in this writing. Talk through your jot list with a consultant. Think about a good way to begin your writing. Keep working on that jot list until you feel the topic growing.

Getting
It
Down

Step Five—Thinking About Audience

Take a few minutes to reflect on potential readers of this writing. They will be adults. Try a short free writing about adults and their attitudes toward teen-agers. What are some possible things to avoid in your writing? What are some ways you might hook them into your writing?

Getting
It
Down

Step Six—Discovery Draft

There's been enough delaying. It's time to write a first draft. You may wish to organize your jot list before you write the draft, or you may wish to put away your jot list and not look at it during drafting. Use your own personal approach to the draft, but try to write the whole piece from start to finish. If you get stuck or bogged down, leave that part and keep writing. Write the ending first, start in the middle, or begin at the beginning. The most important thing is to get words on the page. Take your time. Let your draft grow as you write it.

Getting
It
Down

Step Seven—Sharing the Draft

Read your draft aloud to a consultant. Try out your writing. Have someone react. Get some feedback. Listen to the sound of your writing as you read it aloud. Let it talk to you.

Checking
It
Out

Step Eight—Revision

Use the following checklist to rework that draft.

1. Paragraphs—Do I have fully developed paragraphs? Do I have any underdeveloped or overstuffed paragraphs?

2. Transitions—Does the piece move smoothly from beginning to end? Do I help the reader sense the movement by using transitions? Where are the rough spots?

3. Development—Do I have plenty of meat in this paper? Should I add more facts, examples, opinions, or anecdotes to fill up the paper? What about the order of my paragraphs?

4. Opening/Conclusion—Does the writing invite a reader into the piece? Check that opening paragraph. Does it need to be reworked? What about the concluding paragraph. Does it flow logically from the piece? Does it give the writer a feeling of closure?

Spend time in careful, thoughtful revision. Seek opinions and advice from consultants if you need to.

Step Nine—Final Draft

Work your writing into a final draft. Proofread this draft for spelling errors, punctuation problems, and any questionable usage. ● Take care at this stage to use a dictionary, your Handbook, or a consultant.

Step Ten—Finish

Turn in a clean, final copy. Proofread this final draft several times. Don't let careless errors detract from the effectiveness of your piece. Enjoy your finished product.

Writer's Workbench 3

Transitions

A good piece of transactional writing is not a series of isolated paragraphs. Good writing hooks the reader in the first paragraph and then moves him or her along smoothly from paragraph to paragraph. The movement may have some twists and turns in it and may have a few surprises hidden there, but the reader senses the movement. When readers comment, "Your writing flows together" or "This is a tight piece of writing," you know you have succeeded in creating a feeling of movement.

One of the most obvious ways to create a sense of movement in your writing is through the use of transitions. Transitions are words and phrases which help the reader move from paragraph to paragraph. Sometimes transitions reach back to connect with earlier ideas. Sometimes transitions reach ahead helping the reader to anticipate the direction of the writing.

Reaching Back

Such phrases as . . .

As I pointed out earlier . . .
In summary let me say . . .
More importantly than that . . .
While my earlier examples illustrated . . .
After you have followed steps one and two carefully . . .
Writing, on the other hand, is a very different process . . .
Remember the purpose of these activities is . . .
Another good way to . . .

all serve to tie a new paragraph to earlier paragraphs. They smooth the movement from one paragraph to another. They let readers know the writer is trying to help them understand the message.

Words such as *after, when, while, however, beyond,* and words such as *during, in the meantime, nevertheless, throughout* are word cues for the reader. They signal movement and direction in the writings. They help readers get the point.

Reaching Ahead

Some transitions direct the reader to the next paragraph or series of paragraphs.

1. As I will demonstrate in this paper . . .
2. But there was more to the story than that . . .
3. The list of injustices is long, but I will only comment on a few . . .
4. But would the police officer buy his story?
5. That's exactly when the problems begin.

These phrases alert the reader to what lies ahead in the writing. Sometimes they are obvious, preparing the reader for specific facts or opinions (Examples 1 and 3). Sometimes they create suspense and get the reader's imagination working (Examples 2 and 4). Transitions which reach ahead cue the reader and enable writers to set up important paragraphs in the writing.

Experimenting with Transitions

Because you may feel awkward the first time you begin experimenting with transitions, the best time to try them out may be after you have written a discovery draft. If you worry about working in transitions while you are writing the draft, you may frustrate your own process.

Experienced writers have an intuitive sense for transitions. These writers have a feel for appropriate transitions and create movement with relative ease. Don't be discouraged if your use of transitions is more obvious at first. Like most other parts of the writing process, the use of transitions improves with practice.

Checking
It
Out

Reread your draft. Can you improve the movement from paragraph to paragraph through the use of transitions?

Getting
It
Right

Recopy your paper if necessary. You will be rated according to the following Checkpoint.

CHECKPOINT 1

1	2	3	4	5

Paragraphing   ×3=

Your paper is without any solid paragraphs. See me for help.

You still have a few undernourished or over-stuffed paragraphs. Spend more time in revision.

All paragraphs are well-developed.

Movement (transitions)   ×3=

Many of your paragraphs stand alone. The piece does not feel connected. (See Workbench 1)

You are trying out some transitions. Keep practicing.

Your writing moves smoothly from opening paragraph to conclusion.

Development (by example, anecdote, or fact)   ×5=

Your paper is short on specific information. Spend more time on jot lists and free writing.

One or more of your main points is underdeveloped. Rewriting weakly developed paragraphs will help.

There is meat in this paper. You reward the reader with substance.

Punctuation/Mechanics   ×2=

Frequent and varied errors. Proofread carefully. Check the Handbook.

No serious errors. Avoid careless omissions through proofreading.

Error-free. Excellent!

Spelling   ×1=

Four or more errors. Use a consultant at proofing stage. Use the Handbook.

Two errors. Double check any questionable spelling during proofreading.

No Errors. Good eyes!

Overall Effectiveness   ×6=

The piece does not work. You have not given your reader much to go on. Follow the steps more carefully.

The piece almost works. More care both during revision and proofreading will help.

This is a strong, well-conceived piece. I enjoyed reading it.

Chapter 5

Reflections of Childhood

Visit to Grandpa's

In the middle of the night I woke from a dream full of whips and lariats as long as serpents, and runaway coaches on mountain passes, and wide, windy gallops over cactus fields, and I heard the old man in the next room crying, "Gee-up!" and "Whoa!" and trotting his tongue on the roof of his mouth.

It was the first time I had stayed in grandpa's house. The floorboards had squeaked like mice as I climbed into bed, and the mice between the walls had creaked like wood as though another visitor was walking on them. It was a mild summer night, but curtains had flapped and branches beaten against the window. I had pulled the sheets over my head, and soon was roaring and riding in a book.

"Whoa there, my beauties!" cried grandpa. His voice sounded very young and loud, and his tongue had powerful hooves, and he made his bedroom into a great meadow. I thought I would see if he was ill, or had set his bedclothes on fire, for my mother said that he lit his pipe under the blankets, and had warned me to run to his help if I smelled smoke in the night. I went on tiptoe through the darkness to his bedroom door, brushing against the furniture and upsetting a candlestick with a thump. When I saw there was a light in the room I felt frightened, and as I opened the door I heard grandpa shout, "Gee-up!" as loudly as a bull with a megaphone.

He was sitting straight up in bed and rocking from side to side as though the bed were on a rough road; the knotted edges of the counterpane were his reins; his invisible horses stood in a shadow beyond the bedside candle. Over a white flannel nightshirt he was wearing a red waistcoat with walnut-sized brass buttons. The over-filled bowl of his pipe smouldered among his whiskers like a little, burning hayrick on a stick. At the sight of me, his hands dropped from the reins and lay blue and quiet, the bed stopped still on a level road, he muffled his tongue into silence, and the horses drew softly up.

"Is there anything the matter, grandpa?" I asked, though the clothes were not on fire. His face in the candlelight looked like a ragged quilt pinned upright on the black air and patched all over with goat beards.

He stared at me mildly. Then he blew down his pipe, scattering the sparks and making a high, wet dog-whistle of the stem, and shouted: "Ask no questions."

After a pause, he said slyly: "Do you ever have nightmares, boy?"

I said: "No."

"Oh, yes, you do," he said.

I said I was awakened by a voice that was shouting to horses.

"What did I tell you?" he said. "You eat too much. Who ever heard of horses in a bedroom?"

He fumbled under his pillow, brought out a small, tinkling bag, and carefully untied its strings. He put a sovereign in my hand, and said "Buy a cake." I thanked him and wished him good night.

As I closed my bedroom door, I heard his voice crying loudly and gaily, "Gee-up!" and the rocking of the traveling bed.

Dylan Thomas

Dylan Thomas recounts a strange evening at his grandpa's house. He tells the story with an amazing memory recalling sounds, smells, exact words, and important details. Good writers use memory as an important source for writing ideas. In this chapter you will rely on your memory to recount strong childhood memories. Your memories will be written as personal narratives—stories from your childhood which can be shared with your classmates. You are the curator of a private stock of stories from your childhood. Sharing these unique experiences can be pleasant for you and your audience.

Looking back is a most human trait. Whether it's daydreams about a pleasant weekend or remembrances of a light-hearted summer or an elaborate memory of a dramatic childhood experience such as the one Dylan Thomas wrote about, all of us spend a portion of each day replaying past experiences in our heads. Strangely enough we have the ability to forget bad experiences quickly and retain pleasant memories.

Sometimes we recall the past sentimentally, remembering events and people wistfully and a little sadly. This tendency to indulge ourselves in memories is called nostalgia. Nostalgia is a popular national hobby.

Fifties dances complete with bobby sox, fifties movies, television shows, and fifties music have all enjoyed a revival in recent years.

Remembering has always been a favorite activity of older people. Grandparents spin yarns about overcoming poverty and the Depression; old cheerleaders get out the high school yearbook once in awhile and thumb the pages, occasionally stopping to read a note from a forgotten classmate. Parents get out the baby pictures to remember when their children were cuter and more dependent on them. Former athletes read their clippings. Former teachers, secretly hoping they are not forgotten, keep track of their successful students. Remembering is a pleasant and healthy activity which puts us in touch with long-forgotten feelings.

At your age most of your thought time is now-directed. What do I want to do? How can I survive high school? Is college worth it? How can I afford a car? You probably do not spend much time sitting around contemplating your lost childhood. You have not been overcome with a nostalgic wish to return to the third grade or go through violin lessons again. But somewhere among the kaleidoscopic childish years are a number of good potential writing topics. Most writers cite their own personal memories and past experience as the most consistently helpful source of ideas for writing. Even though your past is recent, the writing activities of this chapter will ask you to search among childhood memories.

~~~~~~

Getting
It
Started

Let your mind wander back to the good old days when you were really young. What memories pop up? Have a pen and your Writer's Notebook handy. List four memories with potential for writing. Was there a time when you learned an important lesson the hard way? Was there a time when something totally unexpected happened? Was there a time when you snatched defeat from the jaws of victory? Was there an event that still brings proud or happy feelings to mind? Was there a happening that changed your life? Maybe you don't remember anything as earth shaking as all this. Sometimes relatively routine events make for good writings. Maybe you remember a particularly memorable birthday or holiday. Maybe this memory is of your first bike or your first dress-up dance or the first time you were really on your own. Maybe it's something you can laugh about now but which was no laughing matter at the time. Let your mind wander. Replay the videotape of past experience. Jot down the most vividly remembered scenes in your Notebook.

If you draw a blank, find some time at home or a quiet place somewhere where you can think. Talk to your parents or a relative about your childhood. Talk to a brother or sister or a school friend from elementary days. Spend some reflective time and compile a list of four or five memories.

SPOTLIGHT

Dan's List

1. The time we hit the bridge in the green, '48 sports car.
2. Giving my two-year-old sister an impromptu haircut.
3. The first time I went fishing alone on the Mad River.
4. My short career as a peach picker in the San Joaquin sun.
5. My first real date. Italian Restaurant, Arcata, California.

Sketching a Memory

Checking It Out

Look at your list of memories. Which one is most vivid or most poignant? Which one will work well with your audience? Check your list with a consultant. Briefly tell your consultant about each memory. Get some help making choices, then choose a memory to work with.

Jot List

Getting It Down

Replay that memory in your head. Jot down as many details as you can. See the memory; hear the memory. Collect a list of 15 or 20 specific details. Don't stop too soon. Get inside the memory and walk around. Notice the weather; notice other people; notice your own feelings; see and hear as much as you can. Keep jotting.

Read over your jot list several times. Add little details you think of as you're reading the list. Mark the details you like. Evaluate your jot list. Are the details *specific*? Are the details *complete*? What was the weather like that day? What song was playing on the radio? Who else was with you? What were the

physical surroundings like? What were you feeling at the time?
Try to recall fine details. Try to recall large details. Zoom in.
Zoom out. See the memory as if it were a movie. Keep jotting.
Here is Dan's jot list.

SPOTLIGHT

Dan's Jot List

Impromptu haircut

Linda's curly blond hair
Recently styled
Getting ready to visit my grandparents
Hot Sunday afternoon
Slight breeze in the tops of the sycamore trees

I was a very confident five year old.
The big brother—the guy in charge
Linda is three in pinafore and white sandals.
She follows me around waiting for me to think up games to play.
My parents are taking a Sunday afternoon nap.
It is quiet in the old house on Vine Street.
"Let's play barber shop. I'll cut your hair."
"OK, Bubba"
Out on the screen porch on a kitchen stool
Dish towel draped around her neck
At first I pretend to cut, making "snip snip" noises as I work the
    scissors.
Then I can't resist. I cut off a beautiful curl.
"Snip snip." More frizzy blond hair falls to the floor.
My mother/sleepy stands in the door/look of horror.
"What on earth . . .? Danny you give me those scissors . . . I
    can't believe it . . . Barrett come straighten this child
    out . . . Danny how could you do it . . .?"
Linda's crying, "Bubba cut my hair off."
The spanking
Somebody takes a picture of my "haircut."
My handiwork is a matter of family record in the picture
    album.
Explaining to grandparents how Linda used to have long hair
    before Danny took up barbering

Dan chose a memory he had not thought about in a long time. The jot list moves basically from beginning to end of the incident. Yours may not. Dan remembers what he did, and he remembers voices. He particularly remembers his mother's shocked reactions, and he remembers getting one of the few spankings of his entire childhood. The jot list takes off and Dan finds he has a potential piece of writing.

If your jot list does not grow rapidly, you may have selected the wrong memory. Choose a different memory from your list and try doing another jot list.

Free Writing

Once you are satisfied with your jot list, it is time to begin writing. Try a free writing at first. Start with anything on your jot list and just begin telling the story, or, put your jot list away and write the experience from memory, without notes. You can check your jot list later to see what you might add. If you need more structure, organize some of the details on your jot list. Think about when you want to begin and end.

Whatever strategy you select for writing, get started putting words on paper. Keep writing until you have told the whole story. If you run into problems, write around them. If you can't think of a word, leave a space and go on. Begin anywhere and keep writing. Don't take time to check spelling or to look in a thesaurus. The important point right now is to get the story on the page.

SPOTLIGHT

Kurt has been working on a piece about a time when he broke his collar bone while playing with his brother. Read his draft.

A plastic streak of colors rolls over me and I run and laugh beneath it. Karl yells, "Bring it back up and I'll let it go again!" I jump through ivy off a short stone wall that splits the back-yard into two levels. Standing on my toes in a summer layer of pine needles and leaves, I reach up and grab the cable car bouncing against the tree trunk. My chubby fingers remove the pully wheel from the string taken from the kitchen drawer, and I clutch the cable car to my chest. "Hurry up, Kurt!" Karl yells again and I race up the stone steps and dash around to the porch stairs. Eagerly I hand <u>his</u> creation of plastic bricks up and he takes it without a word. I watch him disappear over the top of the porch stairs; then I run back around and wait patiently at the spot under the porch where one end of the string is tied to the railing. "Hurry up!" I whine in an attempt to imitate his command; and he takes all the time in the world to make sure <u>his</u> cable car is attached securely. Suddenly, he lets it go and, taken by surprise, I sprint to get under it, to fly with it. I fly over the ivy. I fly along a thin white string suspended between porch and tree. I fly off the wall. The layer of pine needles and leaves flies up to catch me and I crash-land into ivy, tree, and ground. The harmless colorful plastic laughs down at me and dares me to fly again. Dazed and confused, I slowly stand up and <u>walk</u> over the pine needles, up the stone steps, down the sidewalk, up the porch stairs, down the porch, past now-silent Karl, through the kitchen door, over the tile floor, down the hallway, into the T.V. room, lie down on the couch, and blink. The tears don't start till Mom and Dad run into the room. Outside, Karl unties the string from the railing and watches <u>our</u> cable car drop to the foot of the tree and shatter. Harmless colorful bricks of plastic fly one last time over the pine needles and leaves.

Kurt

Kurt retells the story as though it is happening right now. How does he achieve that effect? How does he put the reader there? What subtle point is Kurt trying to make with the underlined words <u>his,</u> <u>his,</u> <u>our?</u>

Notice Kurt's use of repetition: "I sprint . . . I fly over. . . . I fly along . . . I crash . . ." Notice Kurt's short prepositional phrases as he walks into the house: "over the pine needles, up the porch stairs, down the porch," etc. What effect does he create by using these phrases? What about Kurt's ending? Do you like it?

Free Writing

Checking It Out

Getting that first draft is always the hardest part of any writing assignment. The process from remembering to listing potential topics to jot listing is usually fun and painless enough. Sometimes the leap from jot list to first draft is difficult. You have good ideas on that jot list, but they refuse to organize themselves into a coherent piece of writing.

Most student writers are their own harshest critics. They hand their papers tentatively to other readers with a "This isn't very good, is it?" look in their eyes. Share your writing with a sympathetic consultant who will mark successful sections of your draft. Ask the consultant to point to surprising words, strong verbs, light touches, good transitions—anything that works. If you serve as a consultant, look hard for *good* things in the piece you are reading. Encourage the writer.

The consultant should suggest one *next step* for the writer. What is the most immediate project for the writer? What suggestions, options, or experiments should the author consider? The consultant should be specific, concrete, and helpful.

SPOTLIGHT

Selecting Revision Strategies

When you begin to revise and fine tune a piece of writing you like, there are at least two pitfalls:

Pitfall No. 1

Changing words and phrases may make your piece worse instead of better. One of the reasons this book stresses free writing so heavily is to encourage you to learn to use the words in your own head. When you are writing quickly and spontaneously, you are relying on your intuitions as a writer. When you go back to that free writing and begin to pick at individual words, you may weaken your piece by substituting less precise, less concrete language.

Look at Kurt's piece again (page 99). One of its strengths is his consistent use of strong verbs: "I reach up and grab the cable car," "I clutch the cable car to my chest." Suppose Kurt starts tinkering with single words in his writing and decides that "grab" and "clutch" are too informal or too dramatic. Suppose he substitutes "take" for "grab" and "hold" for "clutch." The piece would then read, "I reach up and take the cable car . . . I hold the cable car to my chest." By substituting safer, less precise words, Kurt would have sapped some of the strength from his writing. When you rework words and phrases in your piece, try not to give in to the temptation to "play it safe." Check with a consultant for support. Substitute strong verbs for weak verbs. Substitute concrete, specific details for vague, general details. Keep your nerve when you revise. Don't play it safe. Trust your intuitions.

Pitfall No. 2

The old "recopy it and turn it in" strategy is another pitfall. Few pieces of writing are ever complete and polished in the first draft stage. It is sometimes painful to reread your drafts, and yes, too often you won't have any idea where to begin to fix it up. But if the piece has promise, if your consultant, you, or your writing teacher likes it, it is worth reworking. Resist the temptation to do only cosmetic revision. If the piece has power and audience appeal; if you like it; take some time for careful revision.

When you revise, don't try to "fix" everything all at once; a better strategy for revision is to choose two or three things to work on and stay with them throughout the whole piece.

Things to Consider for Revision

1. <u>Personal Voice</u>.   The one essential ingredient of an effective personal narrative is that it has the sound of the author's voice. Start there. Reread your piece *aloud* several times. Can you hear the narrator's voice? Does it sound like a live human being talking? Listen for the rhythms of a human voice. Free write any sections which sound more like a computer than a human being.

<u>Voice-Killers</u>
Some language choices work against finding your own voice. The "woulds," the passive voice, and the third person impersonal all smother voice in writing. Learn to spot these voice-killers in your drafts and experiment with more direct language.

<u>A serious case of the "woulds."</u>

Original: Every Christmas I would get up before anyone else. I would stumble out of my bed at first light, and I would hurry into the living room.

Revision: Every Christmas I'm the first one up. I stumble out of my bed at first light and hurry into the living room.

Original: Sometimes I would be afraid to go to school. I would complain of a million illnesses: stomach aches, headaches, and even pneumonia. I would cry and plead with my parents to let me stay home in bed.

Revision: Sometimes I was afraid to go to school. I complained of a million illnesses: stomach aches, headaches, and even pneumonia. I cried and pleaded with my parents not to send me to school.

Curing the "woulds" is usually a simple surgical procedure. Cut them out, and the piece picks up the voice of the author immediately.

<u>Passive Voice</u>

Original: The bridge was hit by the car.
Revision: The car smacked the bridge.
Original: The gold chain was given to me by my father.
Revision: My father gave me that gold chain.

For some mysterious reason a few writers get trapped into passive verb constructions. To keep the sound of a human voice in your writing, use active verbs.

Third-Person Impersonal

Original: If one is confused about the most direct route, one should recheck the map.

Revision: If you get lost, check your map.

Original: One is never fully satisfied with a first draft. One must continually rework one's writing to write something of which one can be proud.

Revision: I am never fully satisfied with my first drafts. I rework them continually until I am satisfied.

There remains some controversy among teachers about whether the second person familiar "you" is ever appropriate for formal written discourse. However, in personal narrative the familiar pronouns "I" and "you" are always preferred. Do not hide behind impersonal pronouns in personal writing.

———

2. Dialogue.   Let your characters tell the story. Some students are hesitant to use dialogue because they know that punctuating it is troublesome. See page 108 for some guidelines for punctuating dialogue.

• See the Handbook as well, page H-20.

3. Photographic Details.   Carefully chosen details are critical to any effective personal narrative. Professional writers seem to use them with such ease. There they are all laid out in picture-perfect fashion. However, even accomplished writers do not find just the right details haphazardly. They rework their pieces carefully, adding and subtracting details to create the picture they want.

Reread your piece, deliberately examining details. Have you given the readers enough for them to *see* your narrative? Can you add more concrete descriptive terms?

Read this passage written by a professional writer.

I was raised in Westchester, Illinois, one of the towns that rose from the prairies around Chicago as a result of post-war affluence, VA mortgage loans, and the migratory urge and housing shortage that sent millions of people out of the cities in the years following World War II. It had everything a suburb is supposed to have: sleek, new schools smelling of fresh plaster and floor wax; supermarkets full of Wonder Bread and Bird's Eye frozen peas; rows of centrally heated split-levels that lined dirtless streets on which nothing ever happened.

It was pleasant enough at first, but by the time I entered my late teens I could not stand the place, the dullness of it, the summer barbecues eaten to the lulling drone of power mowers. During the years I grew up there, Westchester stood on or near the edge of the built-up area. Beyond stretched the Illinois farm and pasture lands, where I used to hunt on weekends. I remember the fields as they were in the late fall: the corn stubble brown against the snow, dead husks rasping dryly in the wind; abandoned farm houses waiting for the bulldozers that would tear them down to clear space for a new subdivision; and off on the horizon, a few stripped sycamores silhouetted against a bleak November sky. I can still see myself roaming around out there, scaring rabbits from the brambles, the tract houses a few miles behind me, the vast, vacant prairies in front, a restless boy caught between suburban boredom and rural desolation.

The only thing I really liked about my boyhood surroundings were the Cook and DuPage County forest preserves, a belt of virgin woodland through which flowed a muddy stream called Salt Creek. It was not too polluted then, and its sluggish waters yielded bullhead, catfish, carp, and a rare bass. There was small game in the woods, sometimes a deer or two, but most of all a hint of the wild past, when moccasined feet trod the forest paths and fur trappers cruised the rivers in bark canoes. Once in a while, I found flint arrowheads in the muddy creek bank. Looking at them, I would dream of that savage, heroic time and wish I had lived then, before America became a land of salesmen and shopping centers.

Phillip Caputo

In your Notebook, list some of the most specific and precise details the author includes. Notice that he uses sensory details: sounds, smells, and sights. Point to some of the most effective of these.

As you consider reworking your narrative for more precise details, examine Caputo's choices. Work to create a photograph. Help your reader see, hear, and feel your piece.

4. <u>Beginnings and endings.</u>   There are two important moments in every well-written, short piece of writing: the opening paragraph and the final paragraph. The opening paragraph is critical because in those few lines you must *hook* your reader. See that beginning paragraph as your invitation to the reader. If your invitation is clever or surprising or honest or imaginative, your reader will accept your offer and continue reading. Rework your opening considering these options.

Sometimes short sentences work well:

I was alone. It was dark. I was scared.

Sometimes you can talk directly to your reader:

Have you ever thought you might like to try backpacking alone? I thought I was ready for a solo adventure. So much for the over-confidence of youth.

Sometimes scene-setting is a good way to bring your reader into the piece:

The wind was warm and beads of sweat trickled down the back of my neck. I stopped to catch my breath and grab a handful of trail mix from the zippered pouch in my backpack. I leaned the pack against a young hickory tree and squatted in the shade. I tingled with my aloneness. I listened to the wind.

Sometimes a little foreshadowing or mystery works:

I should have known better. Me who slept with the closet light on until I was twelve. Me who used to see shadows on my window shades and chill at the sound of tree limbs scraping the roof of our house in night winds. I should have known the Jack River Trail would make me a boy again.

Sometimes you just launch into your narrative:

I was sixteen and restless and I was driving my folks crazy. I remember bugging my dad for over a week to let me pack into the Cohutta wilderness by myself. I had just read Thoreau's *Walden*, and I was itching to get into the woods and return to the simple life.

Experiment with several beginnings for your narrative. Try them out on a consultant. Get some advice on the more effective opening. Now, write your personal narrative.

Getting It Down

Writer's Workbench

Proofreading: The Final Touch

You've written a personal narrative. You've even spent time reworking the troublesome spots. Don't neglect the final step—proofreading. Before you submit a clean copy for your teacher's scrutiny, take some time for a deliberate and careful proofing of your paper. This is the time to play hawk-eyed error-finder. Be picky. Check and recheck. Let a consultant help. Sometimes it's difficult to find your own errors. Use this checklist.

1. <u>Spelling.</u>   You know your own strengths and weaknesses with spelling. If you are prone to spelling errors and have difficulty recognizing them, enlist the aid of a consultant. If you are a natural speller with few problems, share your gifts, and work as a spelling consultant for others.
● Use the list of freqently misspelled words in your Handbook (p. H-40) or a dictionary for help.

2. <u>Punctuation.</u>   ● The Handbook section of this text provides brief, clear guidelines for punctuation decisions. Reference that Handbook for specific problems. Few inexperienced writers know *all* the complex punctuation rules. Even professional writers rely on proofreaders to clarify punctuation tangles. If in doubt, check it out.

Some words on the comma . . .

The comma is the most consistently misused punctuation mark. A myth is abroad about the comma: "Use it whenever you need to take a breath." The "inhale/exhale comma theory" inevitably leads writers to overuse the comma, sometimes even separating verbs and their subjects just to catch a breath.

Breathing oxygenates the blood; commas clarify complicated syntax and separate parts of the sentence. Breathing is a natural function regulated by the brain, but the use of commas is rule-governed. Commas should be placed in your writings only when you have a clear reason to do so.

Refresh your memory by examining these two particularly troublesome comma conventions.

When you join two complete sentences with a conjunction, you also need a comma.

<u>Model 1</u>

Sentence A:	I am sixteen today.
Sentence B:	I get my driver's license tomorrow.
Combined Sentence:	I am sixteen today, and I get my driver's license tomorrow.

Sentence A:	I was supposed to jog today.
Sentence B:	It poured down rain.
Combined Sentence:	I was supposed to jog today, but it poured down rain.

A sophisticated alternative to the comma and the coordinating conjunction is the semi-colon.

I am sixteen today; I get my driver's license tomorrow.

Check all coordinating conjunctions in your paper. If you are joining two *complete* sentences, be sure a comma precedes the conjunction.

Watch for the dreaded comma-splice. Inexperienced writers sometimes substitute commas for periods, semicolons, or comma and coordinating conjunction.

Model 2

	Correct:	I wasn't ready for the movie to end. I was just beginning to understand it.
	Correct:	I wasn't ready for the movie to end; I was just beginning to understand it.
	Correct:	I wasn't ready for the movie to end, because I was just beginning to understand it.
Dreaded comma-splice:		I wasn't ready for the movie to end, I was just beginning to understand it.

A comma-splice occurs when you join two independent clauses with *only a comma*.

Proofread your paper carefully looking particularly at those points where complete sentences end.

~~~~~~

Getting It Right

Go over your paper again, polishing where necessary, and paying particular attention to the categories in the Checkpoint on page 111. Your teacher will evaluate your paper using this Checkpoint.

~~~~~~

CHECKPOINT 2

	1		2		3		4		5	

Personal Voice: ×3=

Speak directly. Use your own voice. Did you free write first?

I hear your voice some of the time. Review voice-killers. Read your draft aloud.

Yes. I hear you. Your piece has a distinct voice.

Beginning: ×3=

Did you rework that opening? The piece moves slowly at first.

Experiment more. Try several openings. Use your consultant.

Good invitation. I was drawn into your piece immediately.

Detail: ×3=

Use more concrete, more photographic detail. What kind of tree? What brand of car?

Look at your jot list. Did you forget to use some of those details? Use all five senses.

You put me there! Choice of detail is excellent.

Dialogue: ×3=

Let your characters tell the story. Use their exact words.

Read your dialogue aloud to capture the sound of real people talking.

Yes. Effective and accurate.

Proofreading: ×3=

Spend more time. Check spelling. Use your Handbook.

Only a few errors. Did you use your consultant?

No errors. Good eyes.

Overall Impression: ×5=

Spend more time in the process. Work deliberately. Use a jot list.

Not a bad effort. More revision and proofreading time will improve your effectiveness.

A moving piece. Very effective narrative.

Reaching Out

Chapter 6

Sensing an Audience

It's easy to keep audience in mind when speaking. Talking to other people seems natural. They respond as you speak. If your message is garbled, listeners let you know. At times they stop you in midstream to ask questions. Often, however, their reactions are subtle. Eyebrows knit into frowns or faces wrinkle into quizzical expressions. Whatever their feedback, your audience is present to tell you it needs help. If your intended message is not getting across, you automatically adjust to assist listeners.

When you are writing, the task isn't so simple. There is no audience present, no exchange to depend on. Writers have to envision an invisible audience; they guess what readers will need. For this reason writing often feels unnatural. Writing, a solitary act, is often lonely. Inexperienced writers sometimes get trapped by the seclusion. They begin talking only to themselves in writing, forgetting about their audience altogether.

Chapter 6 reminds you that your readers are out there, even if they seem distant. The audience-directed activities in this chapter will help you bring readers into focus. By writing what appeals, you will discover that good writers, like good speakers, have a developed sense of audience. Writers, too, make adjustments to accommodate audience. Through role playing, you will experiment with audience maneuvers and recognize levels of language. Throughout the chapter, you will rehearse audience strategies in preparation for a reasoned piece for your paper that you will write in Chapter 7.

Think of Chapter 6 as a laboratory for audience experiments. Practice; explore the ways to reach audiences. Take risks; experiment with audience ploys. Try out a new voice: persuade, banter playfully, speak forcefully or implore appealingly. Convince readers to see things your way.

Use the activities in Chapter 6 to keep in touch with audience. Discover how to alter your voice purposefully and to adjust language strategically. Select tactics that reach audiences; slough off those that fail to connect.

~~~~~~

Adapting to Audience

You have a finely tuned sense of audience in speaking situations. One expert terms your savvy *audience sensitivity*. That means you know what to say (and what not to say) when speaking.

When talking to parents, you know what is required. You shift easily into another voice to accommodate friends. Subtly, you adjust your voice for teachers and school officials.

You probably wouldn't dream of addressing school principals by their first names—unless you wanted to be purposely defiant. Calling your friends by their last names would be ridiculous—unless you were trying to be funny. You know what shifts to make when. These sophisticated audience skills can inform your intuitions as a writer.

For this activity you will role-play one or more scenes. Ask volunteers to act out the scenes for the entire class or form small groups. It's helpful to have the same student play the "you" within each scene. Use different group members for the various audience roles.

Scene One: You have a guest over for dinner. Your mother has gone to great lengths to see that everything is just right. In the middle of dinner, your sister, the clutz, spills a glass of milk in your lap. Role-play what you say when

> the "guest" is your best friend,
> the "guest" is your sister's boyfriend,
> the "guest" is your mother's new boss.

Scene Two: You leave school early for a dental appointment. Unfortunately, you have a wreck in the parking lot. You're okay, but the car sustains about $300 worth of damage. Role-play what you say to

> the oaf who backed into you,
> the friend from whom you borrowed the car,
> the school official who heard the crash,
> the parent who assumed you were taking the city bus to the dentist's office.

As a class, discuss audience strategies employed by the "you" in each scene:

What voice changes did you note as audience changed?

Did the speaker alter language choices? Explain.

Did you note any changes in the speaker's story? Talk about that.

If applicable, give examples of the speaker being blatantly dishonest as opposed to being sensitive to audience.

Adjusting Voice

In previous chapters, you've been using your own voice in writing. You've practiced listening for your own voice and using it with confidence. Now you are ready to begin exploring the full range of your voice. With this chapter you will begin altering your voice for different audiences.

At times you have altered your voice purposefully. If your baby sister ambles toward traffic, you speak forcefully, compelling her attention. In response to a friend's hurt, your voice is gentle to reassure her. When your boss's hiring decision hangs on your recommendation, you speak frankly, weighing each word for its accuracy. When arbitrating a dispute, your voice is even, comanding reason in place of emotionalism. Purpose often dictates tone of voice.

Audience also affects voice. Think of the reprimand you aim at a twelve year old. Now consider the one you target at a three year old. Imagine yourself angry at your best friend—at your grandmother—at your teacher—at a police officer. Think of what you might say to each audience.

When you speak you alter the tone of your voice to accommodate your audience. Effective writers realize the importance of adjusting their voices in writing, too. A finely tuned sense of audience marks the mature writer.

Appealing to a Teacher

Sometimes you're sure you've done well on an assignment. There's a surge of triumph deep down as you hand in your paper. When the teacher returns the assignment, you reach for yours

Getting
It
Down

with confidence. But have you ever opened that paper, startled to find a grade lower than you expected?

You possibly swallowed the pang of disappointment. The paper wasn't that good after all, you tell yourself. Perhaps you rationalized the grade, wallowed in self-pity, or simply smouldered in silence.

If you're like many students, you've suffered through this scenario. Days later you kick yourself realizing what you should have done or could have said. Here's your chance to recover.

Think of a recent graded assignment. Make it one on which you'd like a higher evaluation. In your Writer's Notebook, appeal to your teacher to change your grade.

Explore a range of appeals. Deliberately alter your voice in three different pieces. In your first appeal, deny any responsibility for the grade. Place the blame squarely on the teacher.

In a second piece grovel for a higher grade; be humble and ingratiating. Beg if you must, but get that grade changed.

In a third piece, reason with your teacher. Lay out the facts in no-nonsense fashion. Be courteous but unyielding. Convince your teacher to change your grade in a coldly logical piece.

**Checking
It
Out**

After free writing your appeals, form small groups for discussion. Examine your three pieces for similarities and differences. Ask each group member to reveal the most comfortable voice.

Speculate about the voices. Would the first voice work on any teacher you know? Would the second or third voice work?

Zero in on the audience to whom each appeal is directed. Would a fourth voice or perhaps a combination of voices be more convincing? What kind of appeals will the person listen to? What kind of appeal will put this teacher off? Can you alter the language to elicit a more favorable response? Where? How?

**Getting
It
Right**

After receiving feedback from the group, remold a fourth appeal. Think carefully about your audience, then shape the appeal. Use any you think will help. Fine tune the appeal; remold; reshape. File the piece for emergency use with this teacher.

Writer's Workbench

Manipulating Language

This Workbench will help you develop your ability to use language more effectively. If you're insecure about your language skills, we understand. As yet, you are an immature writer. You are stubborn when it comes to putting down words. To your ear, your words sound clumsy. You lack the guts to trust your own words. In many ways you're a nincompoop. Nonetheless, as a writer, you have peculiar potential. That's why we have nightmares about your future.

Reread the preceding paragraph. How do those words make you feel? What words trigger your reaction? At what point do you realize you're being manipulated?

Now read this next version.

This Workbench will help you develop your ability to use language more effectively. If you're insecure about your language skills, we understand. As yet, you are an <u>inexperienced</u> writer. You are <u>reluctant</u> when it comes to putting down words. To your ear, your words sound <u>awkward</u>. You lack the <u>courage</u> to trust your own words. In many ways you're a <u>novice</u>. Nonetheless, as a writer, you have <u>unique</u> potential. That's why we have <u>dreams</u> for your future.

How does the substitution of the underlined words change the effect? In the first version, words such as <u>immature,</u> taunt you; derogatory terms such as <u>nincompoop,</u> insult your intelligence. The voice takes on a surly, superior tone. The second passage is soothing. A gentle voice reassures you; it encourages your efforts as a writer.

Denotation—Connotation

Good writers understand the power of words and select words purposefully. Your choice of words can profoundly affect your appeal. Look at a few of the substitutions made in the two previous passages.

First Version	Second Version
immature	inexperienced
stubborn	hesitant
clumsy	awkward
peculiar	unique

At first glance the words look deceptively similar. For example, a dictionary may list *clumsy* and *awkward* as synonyms. That is, the dictionary suggests that the two words may be used interchangeably. But look at the difference the two words make in the two passages.

You can easily see the problem with borrowing words freely from a dictionary or thesaurus. That's why you're encouraged to use your own words first. It's a good idea to expand your vocabulary, but you should also use your intuitions as a speaker of the English language. These informed intuitions keep you from making haphazard word choices.

Denotation—Connotation: Letting Your Experience Guide You

Words that share the same *denotation* frequently have different *connotations*. *Denotation* refers to the meaning of words found in a dictionary. *Connotation* refers to the subtle meaning distinctions experience teaches you.

Examine the following situations. Put yourself there. Select the word that accurately captures the scene as you see it. There are no right or wrong answers. Be ready to defend your choices. Be prepared to explain how the word's connotation fits the scene.

1. laid back, apathetic, calm
    a. Your English class faces a mid-term exam. You describe the class attitude as. . . .
    b. The principal complains that there is no school spirit. He describes your class as. . . .
2. fun-loving, spirited, wild
    a. You want to go out with a group of friends to the game. Your mother wants to know what kind of people they are. You say that they're. . . .
    b. The manager of a pizza parlor later describes your group to your mother as. . . .
3. shy, stuck up, aloof
    a. You're trying to get your cousin a date. You describe her to a likely date as. . . .
    b. You're trying to discourage your friend's interest in a boy you like. To your friend you described this person as. . . .
4. aroma, stench, smell
    a. Your mother is cooking a new dish. You don't want to hurt her feelings. You tell her the entrée has a strong. . . .
    b. You open your locker to discover your p.e. uniform, left there over the week-end. You describe the greeting you receive as a strong . . .

5. skinny, bony, slim
   a. You're describing your new boyfriend to a hypercritical friend. You refer to your new friend's physique as. . . .
   b. You reach for the last piece of chicken on the platter. You complain that it's. . . .
6. determined, stubborn, persistent
   a. You refuse to attend your father's cherished alma mater. He describes your decision as. . . .
   b. In anticipation of cheerleading tryouts, you've practiced every day for four weeks. Your father congratulates you for being so. . . .

7. lazy, relaxed, listless
   a. Your pet hasn't felt well all week. You tell the vet that your pet has been. . . .
   b. You haven't cleaned your room in three weeks. Your dad insists that you've been. . . .
8. discussion, argument, shouting match
   a. You're explaining to your parents a disagreement you had with your teacher. You tell them you and your teacher had a . . .
   b. You're batting in a game. The ump makes a bad call. The ump's error costs your team the city championship. The ensuing exchange between you and the ump is best described as a . . .

Free Advice

In making your appeal, avoid name-calling. Inflammatory terms, such as *nincompoop*, make audiences hostile. Use loaded words carefully. They may backfire.

Keeping the Audience in View

When writers put pen to paper, they usually create a piece to be read by someone else. If you won't be home for dinner, you probably write a note before leaving the house. You write your message for someone, perhaps explaining where you'll be, possibly letting that person know when you will return, or maybe persuading the person that your absence is mandatory. Whatever your purpose, you direct your message to an audience. Writing is usually audience-directed. Executives write letters to clients; mothers or fathers make lists for babysitters; working people leave instructions for carpet cleaners; and teachers write directions for students. A famous cartoon character even pens love notes to a cute, little red-headed girl. In our daily transactions, most writing is written to be read by others.

In transactional writing the writer's primary goal is to connect with an audience. The writer's ability to tune in to an audience determines the success of the piece. Audience consideration necessarily absorbs a large part of the writer's time. Good writers know their audiences; they are sensitive to readers' needs and expectations. Good transactional writing reflects a keen awareness of audience. The best transactional writing gets things done by reaching an audience.

Appealing to a Parent

If you're ever tried to persuade your parents to let you stay out late on a school night, buy a new sound system, or drive the family car, you've had experience in making appeals. You have no doubt learned to anticipate audience response. Anticipating response means figuring out in advance how your parents will react. You've probably discovered that making informed guesses about their responses can give you valuable information about how to approach them. This is particularly important when parents are hesitant about your request.

How successful are you in anticipating your parents' responses? Can you predict their objections? Do you know their attitudes? Are you aware of their concerns? Can you guess what questions they will ask?

In the following activity you will shape a piece with an audience, your parents, clearly in mind. Although you will begin by talking to yourself, you will gradually shape the piece for delivery. At the end of the process you will evaluate your sensitivity to your audience, your parents.

~~~~~~

Discovering—Free Write a Wish

Think of something you really want. Make it a situation that requires a parent's approval. Perhaps you've earned part of the money to buy a portable tape deck but need help with the balance. Maybe you want to take a job after school or need transportation to do volunteer work at a local hospital. The Spanish Club may be planning a trip to Madrid or you may have an invitation to go on vacation with your best friend's family.

If you can't think of anything you want, concentrate on something you *don't* want. Maybe you don't want to share a bedroom with your sibling. Perhaps you'd like to stop being the family "go-for," dishwasher, or sanitation engineer. You may want to get out of a family responsibility that stands in the way of opportunity. You may have a part in the school play, but the cast practices every Wednesday night—your night to babysit baby brother. Maybe you're tired of shopping for school clothes with your mother, and want to be on your own. Whatever the situation you choose, be sure it is real.

In your Writer's Notebook free write about your wish. You won't have to share this writing, so just talk to yourself about anything you wish you could have. Think about why this yearning is important to you. Talk about how it can benefit you. Focus on how the attainment of this dream will affect your life. Jot down what sacrifices you are willing to make to convince your parents to grant their permission.

Caution: Avoid selecting an appeal you have your hopes and dreams pinned on. Remember that your first appeal is practice. Learn from this experimental round.

Getting
It
Down

~~~~~~

SPOTLIGHT

Take a look at Brett's free writing. Brett couldn't think of anything he needed from his parents, but he knew he desperately wanted to leave English class early Friday, so his appeal is directed at his English teacher.

As the writer, you have the option to direct your appeal to a different audience. The key is in choosing a real issue important to you. Here's Brett's free writing.

A little tyke armed in pads and helmet trudged onto the playing field. "He's too small," someone whispered. "My kid'll kill him," another jeered. Minutes later he limped off the field. "You did okay, kid," the coach's voice echoed. "You'll be a great manager some-day."

Manager?! Who wants to be a manager. I want to be a football star. At least that's what I thought then.

Being a manager's okay, as long as you're the best manager the team's ever had. And I am.

Friday's the big day. Six foot four giants will trudge onto the field, helmets in hand and hope in their hearts. I need to be there to greet them, calm their nerves, have their equipment ready. That's my job.

Okay, so I want a few brownie points from the coach. I'm human. But I also want to be there when that five foot eleven inch tyke limps off the field.

Old man Hardliner, that's not his real name, of course, is all right. He hates sports, but he understands us. Deep down inside he knows I'll learn more about communication on that field Friday than in any class in school. I'll even write a report on it.

Brett

Developing—Make a Jot List

Getting It Down

As a son or daughter you've cultivated reliable intuitions about your parents; use them. Once you've decided on an issue, use informed guesses to anticipate your parents' responses. Think about possible objections, questions, attitudes and concerns your audience may have, and make a jot list.

SPOTLIGHT

Brett's Jot List

What I want—to get out of class early Friday so I can be ready for
varsity try-outs. Audience—Teacher.

Audience Questions

    Is this a school-approved activity?

    Why should I excuse you from English Class to do extra-
        curricular work?

    Why can't you do this after school?

    Are you trying to put one over on me?

    What about your responsibility to your group?

Audience Attitudes

    Academics—more important than sports

    Students belong in class

    Believes in being fair

    Likes students

    Values honesty

    Is impressed by responsible students

    Believes in independent learning

    Responds to students who show initiative

Audience Concerns

    That this request not become a habit

    That learning take place

    That I'm not goofing off or just trying to get out of class

    That I live up to my responsibility to my group

    That he not be seen as a "pushover"

    That other group members feel I'm doing my share in the group

Drafting—Draft an Experimental Piece

Now draft an appeal to your parent. Your jot list will help you
anticipate audience response. Include anticipated responses
(AR's) as you draft your appeal. In parentheses actually jot down
how you think your audience will respond. Let these responses
shape your appeal.

Getting
It
Down

SPOTLIGHT

Here's Brett's first draft. Remember that his is addressed to his teacher.

Dear Dr. Murphy,

Try-outs for the varsity football team are Friday. (AR: *Uh, oh. Here it comes. He wants to know if he can get out of class so he can fool around.*")

I'd like to be excused from class Friday about twenty minutes early. I know this is not your usual policy, but try-outs occur only once a year. (AR: *"That's the same story I hear about cheerleading, band, chorus, track, and basketball tryouts. Why can't you do this after school?"*)

Since try-outs begin *immediately* after school, it is impossible to be ready unless I get on the field at least thirty minutes prior to everyone else. As team manager, it's my responsibility to coordinate the preliminary activities. These preliminaries take time. Jerseys must be sorted, first aid materials checked, and equipment carried to the field. (AR: *"I'm glad to see you taking responsibility, but what about your commitment to your group and to this class?"*)

My first responsibility, of course, is to this class and to my group. Group projects are due Friday, so I've taken the initiative to discuss my predicament with the group. The group insists on presenting first. Tracy, Frank, and Alice are willing to help me out; in return I've agreed to be the spokesperson for our group. Everyone feels this is fair. (AR: *"But you'll miss the other group presentations. What does football have to do with English?"*)

Dr. Murphy, I know how interested you are in communication. To be perfectly honest, I know what it's like to be told you didn't make the team. I think I'll get a great deal of practice in communication out there on the field Friday. I'm even willing to do some independent research on the silent communication of body language. There's plenty of data on that field.

If you approve, I can share my independent research with the class on Monday. (AR: *"Okay, okay. You may leave early, but I expect that report on Monday!"*)

Brett

Look back at Brett's jot list. Point to places in which Brett uses informed guesses in drafting his appeal. How do anticipated responses shape what Brett says next?

Read Brett's appeal aloud, omitting anticipated responses. Listen to the voice and language of this piece. How do Brett's perceptions of Dr. Murphy influence his language choices and voice? Point to words or phrases targeted to an adult audience. Do you think Brett has a "feel" for his audience? Explain.

Consulting

Find a partner with whom you feel comfortable. Share your appeal, explaining the informed guesses you made about audience. You may want to show your consultant your jot list. Talk through your strategy with your consultant.

Checking
It
Out

A Word to Consultants

Remember that the activities in this chapter are for practice. Be as supportive as possible without lying. Show the writer specific phrases you think will "hook" the audience. If you think the writer says something that will "turn off" the audience, you have an obligation to point that out *gently*. Search for the *good* parts. Encourage the writer.

Focus your comments. It's more helpful to give two concrete suggestions than to make ten general comments. Here are some points to check.

First, look at the writer's jot list. Has the writer addressed the audience's major concerns? Has the writer played off the audience's interests and attitudes? Show the writer a place where he or she might develop the piece further.

Second, look at the anticipated responses the writer included. Does the writer use those responses to shape the next point? Has the writer left out a reaction the audience is bound to have? Give him or her some pointers.

Third, look at the language of the piece. Is there a more flattering term the writer can use? Is there a loaded word that should be replaced? Can you think of a more appealing phrase? Make one suggestion.

Getting It Right

Shaping

Based on feedback from your consultant, reshape the piece. This time don't write anticipated responses. In remolding the piece, work deliberately to hook the audience. Ask the crucial question. What voice will this audience listen to? Think about your audience's concerns; address those concerns. Keep audience attitudes in mind; work those attitudes to your advantage. Remember question marks in the audience's mind; erase doubts. Finally, look at language with a critical eye. Manipulate language to make your appeal strong.

Delivering

Find a time when your parent is relaxed. Avoid short circuiting your appeal by selecting an inopportune moment to make your pitch. Keep your main points in mind but don't try to quote your appeal verbatim. Show your parent you've thought this through. Remember to mention that you're willing to do your part.

Evaluating

In your Writer's Notebook, free write an evaluation. Were your guesses about audience valid? How helpful were your hunches? How well did you read your audience? Did you accurately anticipate responses? Were you successful in persuading your parent? If not, what happened? Were there extenuating circum-stances you could not control (family budget, an unexpected illness, a family priority)? What did you learn about this audience that will strengthen your next appeal?

Chapter 7

Connecting with an Audience

One of the unrealized joys of being an American is being able to voice our opinions. We sometimes take for granted the extent to which we are able to offer our views without fear. People can voice their convictions around breakfast tables, in elevators, on street corners, from pulpits, and in subways. We are free to applaud the good and complain about the ill. Americans can freely criticize the government, bemoan the economy, and protest injustices wherever they appear.

Americans take advantage of their right to voice discontent. Expressing displeasure often takes the form of griping. Grumbling and muttering hardly raise eyebrows. Grouching is not only acceptable, it's quite common. Even hard-core optimists occasionally give in to it. Humans seem to need griping as an outlet for daily pressures.

Getting It off Your Chest

Give it a try; sound off about an irritating incident that happened in your school career. Think of a time when circumstances beyond your control trapped you in a compromising position. Perhaps you innocently passed on a piece of paper that contained a request for a date, and the teacher intercepted it at your desk. You were possibly in the right place at the wrong time—such as the time you stepped into the wash room and found yourself

Getting
It
Down

serving as a prop in a senior's demonstration of how to stuff a sophomore into a trash can. How about your only tardy? You remember; it occurred on the day your teacher inaugurated his "get tough" policy. There's a chance you were misunderstood—how about the time when your comment about the principal's new toupée resulted in ten days of detention.

On some days you have probably regretted leaving the security of your snug bed to venture into the killer world of academe. If so, here's your chance to sound off. Use pseudonyms to protect the identities of those you thrash in your "getting it off your chest" paper. Recall the specific incident that miffed you; get mad again. Use your Writer's Notebook to release that pent-up fury. Free write for at least 15 minutes.

**Checking
It
Out**

Now share your complaint with one other person. When you've finished sharing, file the piece in your Notebook. You may want to rework it into a more reasoned piece later.

Taking a stand is a national pastime. While most people simply blow off steam without accomplishing much, many organizations and people effectively air their grievances. Groups of all descriptions champion causes: major corporations, garden clubs, labor unions, service organizations, and other special interest groups state their cases persuasively. Consumer advocate groups square off with producers; citizen action groups lobby for legislation; junior service leagues sponsor drives; and health organizations speak out against practices harmful to people's physical well-being.

Anyone can sound off. There are always many issues around the old school to get heated up over. Why do we have to eat lunch in the cafeteria? Who says teachers should get to park near the building while we have to park in the adjoining county? Why don't we get a break during the school day the way teachers do? Ah, the list of injustices goes on and on . . . and the griping goes on and on, too. While you no doubt know people who complain constantly, seldom getting anything changed, you also know those who make their stands count. Those individuals state their cases persuasively.

SPOTLIGHT

While some of you may be comfortable in the role of "angry young adult out to right wrongs," others of you may feel less comfortable. Although effective positions call for carefully thought out strategies and a large dose of audience awareness, such papers don't automatically signal an unimaginative writing experience. As the following piece about a frustrating school experience illustrates, there's more than one way to make a point persuasively.

I was remembering some of the library rules at my high school:

—Thou shalt not touch a book unless your hands have been scrubbed clean and thoroughly inspected by the head librarian. ("A smudge on a book is an insult to literature.")

—Thou shalt not wear wristwatches or bracelets into the library because a wristwatch or a bracelet could make a scratch on one of the library tables. . . .

(I am convinced anybody caught scratching a library table at my high school would have been dragged out behind the auditorium and shot, not to mention having his or her library privileges taken away.)

—Thou shalt not talk while in the library, nor giggle nor grunt nor pull a chair from under a table so as to make the noise a chair being pulled from under a table will inevitably make.

(Once a fat girl, who was stronger than I, punched me in the belly in the library because I wouldn't give her the sports section of the newspaper. I grunted from the punch and attempted to flee for fear of further blows.

(In my haste, I pulled my chair from under the table and it made a noise. I had to stay after school every day for a week and my stomach hurt for a month. The fat girl's nickname was "Mean Mama," incidentally.)

Irregardless—which isn't a word but was used a hundred times a day by one of the coaches—I still look back on my high school years with favor.

Lewis Grizzard

What is your reaction to Lewis Grizzard's piece? Notice the devices of humor he uses. He repeats the phrase "Thou shalt not" three times. What effect do you think he wants to create by using repetition? Is he successful? Point to places in which Grizzard uses exaggeration as a technique. Do you think the strategy works in the piece? Grizzard avoids venomous sarcasm, opting instead for a light touch. In this piece, how effective is humor as an audience strategy? Do you think Grizzard actually experienced the situation he describes? What makes you think so?

Who would enjoy such writing?—bracelet wearers?—high school librarians?—coaches? Maybe all of these people would enjoy it. Lewis Grizzard, newspaper columnist for *The Atlanta Constitution*, has a large readership, and for good reason. His writing connects with readers: the powerful—politicians, corporate executives, bureaucrats, financiers; the beautiful—models, fashion designers, actors and dancers; the hoi polloi—sanitation engineers, cooks, sales clerks, commuters, and pipe welders. Jim Minter, Manager Editor of *The Atlanta Journal*, describes Grizzard as "the hottest thing in Southern newsprint." Grizzard knows his audience. He uses strategies calculated to drive home his point without driving away his audience.

As any writer will tell you, effective opinion pieces convincingly stated seldom come off the pen that way. Instead, writers first envision their audiences; then they work on the paper until they have created a piece that has impact. They work and rework their pieces, keeping intended audience in mind, considering which voice the audience will listen to, experimenting with lines of support, and assuring technical accuracy. In the final analysis the best writers speak with authority—they communicate to their audiences a sense of knowledge about and confidence in their positions.

That voice of authority is not reserved for professional writers alone. Jim, a student, realized that too much of his school career had been spent in a purple haze. Rather than dropping out of school in disgust, refusing ever again to fill out a dittoed sheet, or taking any of a dozen other irrational actions, Jim decided to take a positive stand by bringing the matter to the attention of the school at large. He did this through an opinion piece written for and published in the school paper.

Busywork: A Sea of Purple Sheets

"That concludes our lesson today, students. There are a few minutes left before the bell rings, so. . . ."

THUD.

Stacks of dittoed sheets, also called "purple sheets" and "purple passions" drop like heavy hearts on each desk. In robot fashion I pick up my pencil and begin:

Which verb best fits the following sentence?
Scott ____ the log.
  a.   Caressed
  b.   Betrayed
  c.   Fumigated

John has 234 apples. If he bought them for five cents apiece, and sold 93 to Mary at a 23 per cent profit, and sold 18 to Joe for twice as much money as what he sold Jane one fourth of his remaining apples for, and rented 6 to his brother at 26 cents an hour, and sent 5 to his granny in Chicago at a cost to himself of 17 cents, and then pulled out a magic wand and made apples numbering five times more than the amount of hours that his brother kept his apples, how many apples does the Japanese ambassador to Sweden have in his orchard?

Use 12 references that are listed to find out whether or not Marie Antoinette had cake crumbs on her dress when she was executed.

To be fair, everything found on purple sheets is not busywork. Sometimes you'll find an assignment that really calls for some creative thinking. Too often, however, the exercises and activities on purple passions are simply time fillers.

Why do we have busywork?

I believe there are two main reasons. First, busywork has a close cousin known as "learning by repetition." It is most often found in math and vocational classrooms where you are dealing with ideas that need to be repeated to be grasped, i.e., doing five geometry problems using the same formula. Learning by repetition is an integral part of our educational system, but calling busywork "learning by repetition" is like putting a wolf in sheep's clothing.

Second, some students simply do not react reasonably when given freedom. Teachers become disheartened and resort to giving busywork. Proponents of busywork see it as their only hope until someone discovers a less brutal substitute for keeping people quiet. The fallacy of this logic is that busywork punishes the responsible as well as the irresponsible.

What is the defense for busywork?

"Idle hands are the devil's workshop."

"This is the only way to keep you quiet."

These are the two most frequently used defenses of busywork. One is a realistic comment, and the other is a tired old cliché. I would like to make a few observations.

First of all, the idea that students should constantly be doing something productive is fortunately unfeasible. It can't be done, and yet, busywork is often used to keep students occupied. Just because you're pushing a pencil doesn't mean you're doing something productive.

What would you be doing if you weren't pushing a pencil? Probably reading, talking, or thinking. If you just sit there and think, it is my opinion that you are doing something productive. One of the things school should teach you to do is to think through a problem or decision, and a little practice never hurt anybody. As for talking, it can get out of hand. However, we sometimes make the mistake of thinking that the only way that you can learn by word of mouth is if the mouth possesses a college degree. Reading is great, if you are free to get what you want out of it. Often, though, you have to get what a purple sheet with 20 questions wants you to get out of it, but still. . . .

. . . . ."Idle hands are the devil's workshop, and this is the only way to keep you quiet. Besides, these repetitive exercises will help you learn." Learn. LEARN?! It hits me like an atomic bomb! NOBODY LEARNS FROM BUSYWORK!!!

Right now, I'm typing. If my fingers weren't busy I'd be shaking my fists at the heavens and asking "How many more times? How many more times will this scene take place?"

Jim Veal

Both the Grizzard excerpt and this student-written piece address problems in schools. While their subjects are similar, the intended audiences differ. What clues tell you that the professional piece is written for a large and varied readership, while the student piece is strictly intended for a school population? If the student writer decided to rewrite this piece for a major newspaper such as *The Los Angeles Times, The Chicago Tribune,* or *The New York Times,* what suggestions for revision would you give him? What parts would you urge him to leave unchanged? Do you agree or disagree with the student author's opinion of busy work? Explain in your Writer's Notebook.

Like the Grizzard piece, this student writing connects with its intended audience. The writer pulls in his readers with two opening questions: "What is busywork?" and "Why do we have busywork?" While "Busywork" is not a five-paragraph theme, it is well-organized. The question technique sets up an organizational structure within which the writer coherently, yet imaginatively, expresses his opinions. The writer convincingly states his points, supporting them with humorous examples. Even though the examples are amusing, they mirror the reality of busywork. Readers sense that the writer knows his subject; he speaks with authority. A finely tuned sense of audience, a light touch, and strong supporting examples contribute to effective opinion writing.

In this chapter you will share your point of view in a carefully written opinion paper. Your audience will be the readers of your school newspaper—other students, teachers, administrators, and in all likelihood, some parents. Plan to shape your paper for that audience; then submit your final version for possible publication. If your school does not have a paper, plan to publish a class paper. It need not be expensive. You may be able to get an extra ream of paper from the school, and you may also be able to use the school's copying machine. Target your audience; know who they are. As a writer, your job will be to cultivate that audience. Later in the chapter you'll profile your audience so you can make informed decisions about which strategies to try.

You'll want to consider purpose as well as audience for this piece. The intent of the piece is not to grumble, grouch, or whimper. The intent is to point out inequities and inefficiencies through convincing prose. Your topic will be a school issue of your choice. Since the key to writing a paper that has the voice of authority lies in finding the right topic, select one that genuinely riles or disturbs or touches you. Let the topic find you. Using brainstorming and the jot list as discovery tools, explore several issues until one reaches out and grabs you.

Discovering a Topic

Getting
It
Started

You are vaguely aware of some school problems and are intimately acquainted with others. If the mere thought of an injustice puts you in orbit, that issue is probably not for you—unless you can step away from it long enough to evaluate fairly all sides of the problem. If you can only mumble a few unintelligible pieces of hearsay about a topic, that one's not for you either. Out there amidst the maze of complex issues lies one waiting for you.

Brainstorming

Begin by brainstorming a list of school issues that deserve attention. The topics on your list may range from personal injuries to school-wide concerns. Accept all contributions. The most unlikely contribution may spark a spin-off issue that reaches out to you.

Brainstorming List

Personal injustices—involving other students, teachers, administrators

Replacement of junk food vending machines with those dispensing nutritional goodies

Inordinate amount of attention given to certain student groups—cheerleaders, the band, athletes

Senior Skip Day

Student government—a viable entity?

Policing the school—student responsibility for monitoring halls, rule making, serving on judicial committees

The value (or lack of value) of schooling

Contributions of the class clown

The exploitation of substitutes

Conformity and peer pressure

Grading vs. Non-grading

It may be helpful to make a class list of the issues in question form. The topic "Policing the school . . ." can be rewritten as "Can and should students be responsible for the general policing of school?" The issue "The value of schooling" may now become "What is the value of schooling? Do schools really educate or do they merely indoctrinate?"

On your own, select two or three questions about which you have a definite opinion. Avoid topics you feel wishy-washy about. You don't want fence-straddling issues.

~~~~~~~~~~~~~~~~~~~~~~~~~~~~~~~~~~~~~

Exploratory Jotting

Pinpoint three topics about which you have a definite view—pro or con. Don't overlook the issue you used for Getting It Down on page 131; that, too, may have possibilities.

Using the jot list, find out how much you know about the

**Getting
It
Down**

topics. Take a few minutes to explore the issues. In your jottings, list experiences, snatches of conversations, strong sentiments, or factual evidence supporting your view.

～～～～～～～～～～～～～～～～～～～～～

Developing the Jot List

Getting It Down

Look over your three exploratory jot lists. Which jot list has the most information? Which topic interests you most? Which jot list has potential audience appeal? Which topic feels most comfortable? Discuss your options with a consultant or your teacher. Let the topic choose you.

Rework your jot list. Develop it by including anything which might relate to your topic: descriptive words and phrases, conversations you have overheard, your own personal feelings, hard facts, other sides to the issue, tentative solutions, examples, analogies, and key words. Don't censor your thinking at this time. Jot down anything that comes to mind.

～～～～～～～～～～～～～～～～～～～～～

Profiling an Audience

Getting It Started

As a student, you more than likely read the school newspaper, so you know how it goes. You pick up the paper, thumb through it to see if anything catches your eye, then turn to your favorite section, or possibly flip to an article written by a friend. If you have time during the last few minutes of study hall, you may glance over the paper once more.

Let's face it. Your peers are a tough audience. Your teachers and administrators are kind people, but they don't have time to waste. Make sure that your piece gets the audience it deserves by shaping it to captivate audience interest. To accomplish that, you must first figure out the connection between your topic and your audience. Complete the Audience Profile for help.

Audience Profile

1. Who is my audience?
2. What common experiences do I share with my audience?
3. What kind of voice will they listen to?
4. How do they feel about this issue?
5. Will they agree with my point of view? If so, how can I capitalize on that support?

6. If they disagree, what arguments will they counter with?
7. How can my point of view make a difference? How can my stand improve their life here at school?

As a final audience check, skim some back issues of the school paper. Jar your memory. Which articles were widely read and discussed? Which pieces got things done? Jot down your impressions about why certain articles were popular with the school audience.

~~~~~~

Free Writing a Position

Look back at your jot list. Mark your strongest points. Try a free writing around those lines. See what you can make of them.

Getting
It
Down

~~~~~~

Writer's Workbench 1

Appositives

An appositive is a word or group of words which identifies a noun or noun phrase in a sentence. An appositive is also set off from the rest of the sentence by commas and placed as close as possible to the noun it identifies. Look at the following example, and then do the sentence-combining activities that use appositives.

Example: Tony is the quarterback on the football team.
Tony is *my best friend.*   (, ,)

Tony, my best friend, is the quarterback on the football team.

1. Mr. Brockman was born in West Berlin.
   My Brockman is *my German teacher.*   (, ,)
2. The doctor rushed to the hospital.
   The doctor is *a specialist in internal medicine.*   (, ,)
3. The dog sat by the table but did not beg for food.
   The dog is *a graduate of obedience school.*   (, ,)

4. Gwenn's father will visit China.
   Gwenn's father is *the president of an oil company.*   (, ,)
5. Mrs. Allen is tutoring students during the summer.
   Mrs. Allen is *a former English teacher.*   (, ,)
6. The man witnessed the accident.
   The man is *the operator of the diner.*   (, ,)
7. Because food prices are high, Mr. Welsh decided to grow a garden.
   Mr. Welsh is *our next door neighbor.*   (, ,)
8. Atkinson was injured last night in the three-alarm blaze.
   Atkinson is *the fire marshal.*   (, ,)
9. The daily special was the best choice on the menu.
   The daily special was *liver and onions.*   (, ,)
10. The storm destroyed my flower garden.
    The storm was *a mixture of rain and hail.*   (, ,)

Experiment with several different openings for your paper. Try at least two short free writings from your list of possible openings. Ask your teacher or a consultant for advice in creating the most powerful opening for your paper.

Getting
It
Started

Drafting the Piece

You now have a developed jot list, several possible openings, and a free writing on the heart of your paper. In short, you have done the groundwork for a complete draft of this paper. Now try drafting your paper from start to finish. Write the draft in one sitting. Leave out the hard parts. Try to get a whole piece even if it is weak in some places. Listen to your intuitions. Speak directly to your audience. Read your draft aloud to a consultant when you have completed it.

Getting
It
Down

SPOTLIGHT

Revision Strategies

Organization

Hazy organization lessens the effectiveness of any piece of writing. When a writer's purpose is to call an inefficiency or injustice to someone's attention, organization is critical. Your paper must provide the reader with a readable, understandable structure. In Grizzard's piece, page 133, the author uses something as obvious as repetition: "Thou shalt not. . . ." In Jim Veal's piece on busy work, page 135, the author uses questions to direct the reader: "What is busy work?" "Why do we have busy work?"

Many traditional writing texts ask writers to make outlines. The theory is that writers who can't develop an outline for writings have no clear idea of what they want to say. An outline may work for you. Try one if you wish.

Many successful writers avoid outlines. They rely on their own intuitions and their own sense of order to structure their writings. They discover organizational structures as they write and revise. Such an approach may work for you.

The bottom line for your paper is an organized intelligible presentation of your ideas. Check your organizational strategies by *talking through* your paper with a consultant.

Support and Substance

To be entirely effective, your paper needs some "meat" in it. Remember that while the ravings of fanatics mildly amuse some, unfounded babbling seldom holds audiences. Readers grow impatient with pieces which have logic so flawed that it can be recognized by the average fifth grader. If, however, major points are clearly stated and well supported, audiences often hear out even those notions with which they disagree. That gives writers a chance to change the minds of readers. Unlike emotionally charged rantings and opinionated conjectures, carefully articulated stances command attention.

Check to be sure that you have supported each of your main ideas with examples, facts, evidence, the opinions of others, or personal observation.

Tone of Voice

The human voice is a miraculously versatile communication instrument. By the time you reach adolescence you have mastered the more subtle use of tone to express exact feelings. Mastering tone of voice in written communication is more difficult. Punctuation can help; word choice is important, but a consistent tone is essential. An inconsistent tone may confuse readers.

Even more importantly, when stating your opinions in writing, be careful not to antagonize readers with inappropriate tone. Opinion papers speak directly to an audience. You want that audience to listen to you—to hear you out. An audience will do just that if you give them something to think about and if you don't turn them off with an inappropriate tone in your voice. Ranting and raving seldom produce effective writing. Whining and moaning seldom evoke a sympathetic ear.

Check the tone of voice in your writing. Watch for these audience turn-offs.

Turn-off 1: "Anyone who doesn't agree with me is stupid . . ."

You might not ever say this directly in your writing, but your tone can imply such an inflammatory stance. Such words as "obviously," "without a doubt," "as anyone can plainly see," imply that your readers are nitwits if they don't see your point of view.

Inflammatory: It should be perfectly obvious to anyone that student parking is simply inadequate.

Reasoned: The students I have talked to are unanimous in their opinion: parking facilities are inadequate.

Turn-off 2: "Because I said so . . ."

We have suggested that you use the voice of authority in your paper. State your opinions with firmness and conviction. Be careful, however, that your firmness is not mistaken for inflexibility. Any complex issue will have many sides. When you make strong statements, support them with facts and avoid an arbitrary tone.

Inflexible: There *is* no other solution. Students must be allowed to leave campus for lunch. We have been stalled long enough. The administration must act at once. We are fed up!

Reasonable: The open-lunch issue continues to ferment. Many students have expressed their preference for an open lunch. The administration is apparently convinced that open-lunch would create new problems. The impasse needs to be resolved soon to avoid hard feelings.

Turn-off 3: Why? Why? "Whyney" Questions

Questioning your readers is an effective technique—if your questions cause readers to consider your position. The overuse of questions, particularly "whyney" ones, weakens your paper.

"Whyney" Questions: Why can't we leave campus at noon? Why do we have to stay around the cafeteria just because a few kids might get in trouble? How come they have an open lunch over at Miller High School and we don't? Why is our administration so stubborn? Why do they always assume that kids will get in trouble?

Effective Questions: What then is a satisfactory solution to the open lunch controversy? Should open lunch be a privilege to be earned? Should such freedom be reserved for juniors and seniors? Could we develop a student commons area on campus as an alternative to open lunch? Students and administrators working cooperatively can find a positive solution.

You practiced using effective rhetorical questions in Chapter 2, and you may want to experiment with rhetorical questions in your opinion piece. They often advance your point of view, and suggest possible solutions. They always speak directly to audiences.

**Checking
It
Out**

Read your paper critically. Watch for audience turn-offs; check for solid support and a comprehensible organizational pattern. Check with your teacher or a consultant for assistance.

**Getting
It
Right**

Now, write the revised version of your paper. Checkpoint 3 on page 147 will be used by your teacher for evaluation.

CHECKPOINT 3

1	2	3	4	5

Effective Opening   ×3=

You fail to hook your reader. Did you try some experimental openings?

Try a less conventional opening. Spend more time experimenting with your opening.

Powerful! Engages the reader immediately.

Voice   ×3=

Too many audience turn-offs. Be sensitive to your readers.

Speak with more authority. Avoid put-downs. Work for consistency. Feel your audience out there.

Convincing. Confident. Matches your intent. Speaks directly to your audience.

Organization   ×3=

I'm confused. I can't follow your thinking. Plan carefully.

I lost your logic in a few places. Did you use a consultant?

Tightly structured. Logical. Orderly. Takes the reader somewhere.

Support   ×3=

The paper is thin. Ideas are inadequately supported. Work harder on your jot list.

One or two of your main points need more facts or examples. Strengthen your jot list.

Meaty. Well-developed. You have something to say.

Technical Accuracy   ×3=

Many careless errors. See me for help.

A few errors. Be a careful proofreader. Check your Handbook.

No serious errors. Good proofreading.

Overall Effectiveness   ×3=

This writing did not connect with your audience. Spend more time on the writing process.

This paper has potential. Spend more time in thoughtful revision.

Strong piece. You know your topic, and you connect with your audience.

Chapter 8

Clarifying a Community Issue

SPOTLIGHT

Bulldozers 20—Magnolias 0

A bulldozer—the logo of progress—idles roughly; its driver, a picture of boredom, spits into the red dirt clinging to its massive treads.

The old house sits quietly among years-old magnolia trees, its white columns peeling into bone-bleached grey.

With a snort of black smoke the bulldozer lurches forward, tracks squeaking, dust rising. With herky-jerky clumsiness a blade smashes into a bleached column amidst the haunting sound of bones breaking. The roof of the veranda sags then settles to the ground in a sigh of resignation.

A wiry old man leans on his cane watching from the safety of the sidewalk. "It's sad. That O'Malley place has been there over a hundred years. I remember when those magnolias were planted. Now they just break them up like so much firewood. People don't respect the past. One more convenience store-gas station, one less reminder of our heritage." The old man watched the last column crash to the ground. "So that's progress." He turned his back and shuffled down the sidewalk musing to himself.

The O'Malley house is just one of 20 hundred-year-old homes which have been razed in the Prince Avenue area in the past two years. "That's a boom area," says City Manager Allen Bradley. "The center of population is shifting to the north side of town and builders and merchants are capitalizing on it. If you have people, you have to have services."

There in a nutshell is a community issue which has polarized opinion in our city. As a beautiful old southern town, we have prided ourselves on our stately homes set back on tree-lined streets. The ambience, the grace of those old homes has set the tone for our town—a friendly, refined town with respect for tradition.

Enter the villain progress in the guise of new industry, new jobs, new opportunity. The delicate balance of growth and tradition is upset. First an apartment complex claims a block of row houses, then a shopette vanquishes the Morton house. One by one the fast food chains knife into the tree-lined boulevard. A burger stand is juxtaposed to a three-story Victorian—a donut shop, an historic bungalow, a parking lot, a church with a new neon sign. In a roar of bulldozers, Prince Avenue—old, historic Prince Avenue—has become just another urban, neon four lane. Tacos and fish sticks and French fries and plastic shrubbery have supplanted column and wrought-iron gate and magnolia and dogwood. How did a proud, old southern town let this happen? Did no one try to stop progress?

"We tried to get the townfolk excited five years ago about this" says Lloyd Waters, president of historic Milledgeville, "the very first time someone requested a zoning variance on Prince Avenue. The developers of that apartment complex wanted permission to tear down those row houses and build a 'tastefully traditional' group of townhouses. We got 40 or 50 people out to that zoning hearing, but the developers were smart. They had beautiful drawings with trees and landscaping showing how their apartments would only 'enhance' the neighborhood. We tried to tell people that apartments bring a lot more than people to a neighborhood, but no one listened. The local newspaper called us 'anti-progress' and 'alarmists.' Well, I hate to say 'I told you so,' but look at that mess on Prince Avenue; tradition's gone forever."

Is Prince Avenue's metamorphosis a simple case of progress vs. past or are there larger issues at stake here? How do progress and tradition co-exist?

Sheila Forsyth

All communities have issues which divide them: zoning, better services, more recreational areas, law enforcement, property taxes, a new fire station, store hours, traffic flow. The list goes on.

The piece you have just read is an introduction to a position paper on a community issue of historic preservation in a southern city. What position do you think the writer will take? How do you think she will support her position?

"Bulldozers 20—Magnolias 0" is transactional writing; the author is trying to inform, explain, and perhaps persuade her readers. Discuss some of the techniques she uses in this excerpt to contact her audience.

This opening by Sheila has the *sound* of a well-informed writer. Sheila sounds knowledgeable because she is knowledgeable. She has done her homework. She has read articles on the issue, talked to the people involved, and formulated her own synthesis of the various sides of the issue. Behind such a paper is a careful research process which is invisible to her readers. Chapters 8 and 9 work together to step you through the preparation for writing a paper similar to Sheila's. You will begin by exploring topic options to discover one that appeals to you. You will gather information for your paper by reading relevant information and interviewing people, taking notes from your sources as you explore them. You will then work to clarify the points of view around your issue and draft a synthesis of all you have learned. Finally you will draft a position paper weaving in specific information you have discovered. The final result will be an informative and clearly stated position paper which frames the issue you have selected.

Your Writer's Notebook will be an important tool throughout this experience. Keep it handy for all of your research work. It will become the record of every piece of writing that you do.

Community Issues: Something Worth Writing About . . .
Wherever you live, people around you are concerned about the quality of life in their community. Folks in small-town Iowa may be debating the merits of a new high school. People in Eugene, Oregon are discussing bike paths. Residents of Atlanta are concerned about more people-space for recreation. Citizens of a growing city in Ohio are working for a by-pass highway to alleviate traffic in residential areas. Homeowners in a Chicago suburb want stricter enforcement of leash laws to curb roaming animals.

These issues and hundreds more like them fill local newspapers and local radio station talk shows. What are the community issues that people in your town are excited about? What issues fill your local paper? Spend some time exploring issues in your community which might become workable topics for your paper. Your teacher may plan a class brainstorming session, you may work with a partner, or you may need to spend some time looking through the newspaper. Use your Writer's Notebook to list a few

Getting It Started

possible topics. Select something that interests you. You do not have to be an expert on this issue. You can find information and formulate a position as you work through your topic. In fact, topics which you do not already have strong feelings about may work best. The purpose of this assignment is to help you think through an issue, develop a position, and state that opinion in even-handed, firm language.

SPOTLIGHT

Study this list of issues which a high school class brainstormed. See if any of them are relevant to your community:

> *Space Issues*
> Parks and recreation areas
> Green space
> Sidewalks for kids and elderly
> Bike trails for safety
> New Community center . . . When?

Historic Preservation
Save the old buildings
Historic sites around town should be marked.

Community Services
More funding for mental-health center
Alcoholics' rehabilitation center needed.
Half-way house for paroled offenders needed.
Health services for aged are inadequate.
City land-fill site is a disgrace and a hazard.

Beautification
Tree plantings needed.
Maintenance of city-owned land is inadequate.
Replacement of diseased trees needed.
Sign ordinance needed.

Community Spirit Projects
Spring or summer festival would boost community.
New signs of welcome at city entrance

Nuisance Issues
Leash laws
Improper dumping of trash
Traffic-flow problems
Noise pollution
Zoning and land use
Law enforcement
Store hours

All of these issues were being debated and discussed recently in a mid-west community. Are any of these issues current topics of discussion in your community? Use your Writer's Notebook to explore issues which interest you. Talk to friends, parents, and other adults.

**Getting
It
Started**

Getting Your Bearings

Getting
It
Down

Any writing task looks formidable before you begin it. This writing assignment which asks you to develop a position paper on a community issue using a variety of resources from print to personal interviews, will stretch you a bit. A little churning in the stomach and some fleeting moments of panic are natural at this point even for experienced writers.

The best medicine for such pre-writing trauma is an enforced period of reflection on the topic and deliberate planning for the job ahead. Fight temptations to fly off in a hundred directions or to succumb to hopelessness. Do some constructive list making. Using your Writer's Notebook develop three lists: List one—print sources, List two—people sources, List three—a plan. Read the following material for strategies on how to do this assignment.

List One—Print Sources   Where can you find articles and other written information on your topic? If your topic is a localized issue particular to your community alone, your local newspaper will be an important source. Chances are there have been a number of news stories, editorials, interviews, even editorial cartoons printed on your topic in the past few months or years. Try an exploratory phone call to the newspaper. Ask for the newsroom. Explain your topic and your purpose for writing your paper. Ask if they have a file of stories on your topic.

If you cannot speak directly to newspaper people, begin your search for print sources by talking with your school media specialist or public librarian. Libraries and media centers may index back issues of newspapers. Additionally, libraries have vertical files containing clippings on current issues. Librarians are trained resource people. They can be helpful not only in providing specific resources, but also in suggesting strategies for learning more about your topic. Librarians are at their best when they are serving as resource people. Cultivate their expertise.

If your topic is an issue of more general concern to many communities, you may want to read articles in news magazines to get a better background about the problem. *The Readers' Guide to Periodical Literature* in the library is an excellent index to such sources. Block out some research time in the library. Don't try to get much out of *The Readers' Guide* in ten minutes. You need time to find out the various ways in which your topic is indexed. List titles of articles which sound promising. Work on your list before you start trying to round up magazines. ● The Handbook contains directions for using the Readers' Guide (page H-52).

List Two—People Sources.   An important step in the process of writing this piece is interviewing. People's opinions and knowledge about your topic are essential. Brainstorm a list of people or types of people who might offer different perspectives on your topic. Don't be reluctant to put down names of city officials and names which appear in the newspaper frequently. These people may be willing to talk to you. Check with your teacher and parents. Maybe they know people whom you can interview. Parents of friends, members of your church or synagogue, members of your parent's social clubs, people who work with your parents, people who own businesses in your neighborhood, even "the person on the street" may be good resources. Brainstorm your list without worrying about how you will interview the people who are most directly affected by your issue. If your issue concerns young people, interview your peers. If your issue concerns property owners, interview people in your neighborhood. If your issue concerns the entire community, a random sample of citizens may be appropriate. Plan to get as much first-hand information as possible. Your paper will be more accurate, more immediate, and more convincing if you have the actual words of the actors in the drama.

List Three—A Plan.   Begin to develop a plan for your investigation by making a list of things you need to do. Don't rely on your memory to direct your work. Write things down. What needs to be done first? —second? What can wait until later? Keep the list handy in your Writer's Notebook. Add to it when you have a flash of brilliance. Cross off things when you complete them. Let this list be an on-going record of your activity with this project.

~~~~~~

Charting Your Course

With the Writer's Notebook containing your three lists close at hand and your topic clearly in mind, you're ready to begin your research. Conducting a logically organized search will prevent

Getting
It
Down

the GTTH Syndrome (the Gnashing of Teeth and Tearing of Hair Syndrome) which commonly afflicts disorganized research-ers. Victims of the GTTH Syndrome find themselves waist deep in newspapers and magazines hours before deadline. While the clock ticks relentlessly on, GTTH victims run around in circles bewildered by the knowledge that they've spent countless hours in the library—seemingly to no avail. Avoid last-minute jitters by following List Three—your clearly-thought-out plan of action.

If you're making your debut as a researcher or even if you're a research whiz, you'll want to try some of the strategies good researchers use for conducting the search for print sources. Remember that not all of the strategies will apply. If your topic concerns a localized issue, checking major magazines and newspapers will be an exercise in futility. If, however, your topic focuses on an issue affecting many communities, you won't want to overlook a wider range of resources. Select from the following the strategies that will help you work more intelligently.

Research Strategy 1: Checking for Indexes.   Organized researchers check first to see whether indexes exist. No matter what your topic is, you'll want to look first for an index to your source. If you're searching for magazine articles, check out *The Readers' Guide to Periodical Literature*; if a larger issue leads you to major newspapers, look for indexes such as *The New York Times Index*; if yours is a hometown concern, ask your local paper whether they index their back issues.

Indexes are generally organized alphabetically by subject. If an index to your source is available, brainstorm ideas of how your topic may be listed. Articles related to a city park may be listed under geographical headings such as the city's name, under "Amusement Parks," "Playground and Other Recreational Areas," or even under "Proposed Recreational Sites." Don't give up too easily. Keep your sense of humor; index-makers sometimes use imaginative headings. Indexes are easy to use if you take time to read the directions located near the front of the volume. Ask the librarian or person in charge for assistance if you get bogged down.

Research Strategy 2: Rummaging Through the Vertical File. Because of their expense, indexes are not always available. Your next move may be to look for the vertical file. The vertical file is too often the library's best kept secret. Ask about it if you don't see it around. The vertical file is the librarian's personal file of pamphlets, governmental agency reports, news clippings, pictures, and bulletins on current topics. You may or may not find your issue among the topics listed in the vertical file. The vertical file may be a collection of manila folders rubber-banded together and stashed under the library counter. Topics are usually arranged alphabetically by subject.

Research Strategy 3: Searching Through News Files.   Local papers will naturally cover issues of interest to the community and may comment on issues of concern to communities-at-large. If your local paper doesn't have an index, it may well have a file on your issue stuffed full of all articles, editorials, news clippings, and political cartoons written by the paper's staff. The possibility is worth a telephone call to the news office of your local paper. Explain what you're doing and why: try to speak directly to the file clerk in charge or to the reporter who has covered your issue.

Make an appointment to go in and peruse the files. Some newspapers may be more helpful than others. Be persistent without being pushy. Volunteer to search the files yourself.

When you visit the news office, remember to take a pocket full of change if you intend to photocopy any of the paper's articles. The advantage of photocopying is that you can look back at the original source if questions later develop. It helps you avoid having to go back to the news office or library to clarify points or verify information at a later time. You may want to compromise, copying two or three of the articles or political cartoons and taking notes on the remaining clippings. If an index or news files are not available, ask to see the bound copies of newspaper back issues. Request bound copies for the last six months or for whatever time span you're interested in seeing. Bound copies are frequently kept in regional libraries, too, so if there's a mad rush on the news office, check the library.

Research Strategy 4: Flipping Through the Card Catalogue.   A library's card catalogue generally lists most of its books. While the chances of your finding a book addressing your current issue are slim, you may find city maps, charts, or even pictures related to your topic. It's worth a quick check. Look for subject cards on topics connected to your area of interest. Jot down the call number and title of materials you want to check. See your librarian, media specialist, or teacher if you need help using the card catalogue. ● The Handbook includes helpful information on using the card catalogue (page H-52).

Research Strategy 5: Plowing Through the Pages.   If all else fails, you may have to go directly to back issues of newspapers or magazines. Be certain that you have not overlooked indexes before you start digging through mounds of back issues. In searching through old newspapers, resist the temptation to dawdle over the sports page, the cartoon section, or letters from the lovelorn. Scanning the front page, news or business sections, and editorial pages will be your best bet. When researching magazines, also check the table of contents to see whether other sections look promising. You may find back issues in bound books, on microfilm, or on microfiche. In all cases, librarians and media specialists will be ready to assist. Set goals for yourself. After you've found three articles—or whatever your personal goal—treat yourself to fifteen minutes or so of free reading.

Conducting Your Search

Equipped with List One, Print Sources, and Research Strategies 1 through 5, you're now ready to launch your search. Settle for no fewer than five or six print resources. If you can get materials from different sources, all the better. A variety of print sources insures a broader view of the issue and lessens the likelihood of reading articles expressing only one point of view. As you make discoveries, free write your reactions in your Writer's Notebook. Record your frustrations and successes as you explore resource possibilities. See the following for help.

Indexes.   Are indexes available? If so, which is most helpful? Are indexes readily accessible to students? How easy or difficult are they to use? If indexes do exist but aren't carried in one library, are they available at a nearby facility? If not, are purchases planned?

Vertical File.   Does your school media specialist maintain a vertical file? How complete is it? Is there a file on a subject related to your topic? What kinds of materials do you find there? If no file related to your topic exists, bring this to the attention of your media specialist. Does the media specialist have other suggestions? Does the regional library also have a vertical file?

News Files.   Does your local newspaper index its back issues, maintain news files, or provide bound copies for public use? Are newspaper personnel helpful? Note with whom you speak. Talk about the kind of reception you receive. If you're able to visit the news room, comment on the finds you uncover there.

The Card Catalogue.   A card catalogue search may lead you to other print sources—speeches, city charters, by-laws, maps. If you turn up intriguing materials as a result of your card catalogue search, comment briefly on your success. If you have a suggestion for how the library might assist students—placing the card catalogue in the center of the library instead of next to the wall, posting sample cards from the catalogue with directions in bold print, or using student aides to assist bewildered card catalogue users—talk through your proposal in your Writer's Notebook.

Getting
It
Down

<u>Back Issues of Newspapers and Magazines.</u>   If other strategies are dead-ends, your manual search through back issues may uncover materials nothing less than spectacular. If you know how to use microfilm or microfiche readers, talk about that experience. If you have a flash on how the school can raise the necessary funds to purchase indexes, explore that idea on paper. Jot down the high and low points of your dig.

Writer's Workbench 1

Taking Notes on Print Materials

Now that you've found your topic, explored print resources, conducted your search, and located your print materials, you're ready to take notes. Your notes will form the basis of your interview questions, so take some time on this part of the research process. Good notes carry only the essence of an article's content and are more concise than the original source. Remember that notes *take the place of* print materials, so you'll want your notes to be legible and to reflect accurately the information you want to capture. Meaningful notes are a researcher's best friend. They help researchers piece together loose ends, sort out jumbled details, and often give them a "feel" for the topic.

If your note-taking skills are a bit rusty or if you simply want a quick review, here are some pointers.

1. *Jot down a brief source entry.*
The source entry simply tells you the source of your information. Writing a source entry is a quick and painless step that can save you from an interview scene such as the following:

Interviewer

(You):   I read somewhere that you said 'City Hall should be abolished.'

Interviewee

(The Mayor):   Where? Did I say that?

Interviewer: Umm. I think so. It says so right here in my notes. I don't remember where I read that. I've been reading so much. Hmmm, I just don't know . . .

Interviewee: I don't remember *ever* saying that.

Fade to interviewer (you) crawling under carpet . . .

With source entry noted, you can confidently conduct an intelligent, honest interview.

Interviewer: According to *Today*, you are quoted as saying, 'City Hall should be abolished.' I'd be interested in hearing more about your views.

Interviewee: Where? Did I say that?

Interviewer: The January 3, 1985 issue of *Today* contained an article entitled "Mayor Uses Strong Language" in which you're quoted as using those exact words.

Interviewee: I was quoted out of context there. Let me explain what I really said . . .

In your Writer's Notebook jot down a brief source entry before taking notes on any source. The entry is for you, so use a form you can

understand. Your teacher may have a particular form he or she favors. If not, we've included some examples. ● Check also with the Handbook, page H-62.

A Newspaper Article

> Sanders, Bill, "Mayor Uses Strong Language," <u>Today,</u> Jan. 3, 1985, p. 1, cols. 1–3.

Jot down the writer's name, the title of the article, the name of the newspaper, the date, page, and columns in which you find information. Follow the punctuation and indentation used in the preceding example.

A Magazine Article

> Conyers, Sarah, "Mayors Talk Back," <u>Our Magazine,</u> Jan. 20, 1985, pp. 20–23.

If no author is given, simply begin your entry with the name of the article.

A Magazine Interview

> "An Interview with Outspoken Mayors," Interview with Mayors Sloan, Tate, and Cunningham, <u>Life in Big Cities,</u> Jan. 25, 1985, pp. 60–62.

No matter which form you adopt, be certain to write down the information that can quickly direct you to the original source.

2. *Use your own short-hand system.*

Develop short-hand symbols that make your note-taking job quicker. Make sure you understand what the symbols mean. Being consistent helps. Here are some examples.

& = and	cc = city council
w = with	cit = citizen
w/o = without	

Create symbols meaningful to you.

3. *Take notes only on key information.*

If you copy down everything, you defeat the purpose of taking notes. Make note only of facts that enlighten you. Remember that you want to explore *all* sides of the issue. Look for key information that expands your knowledge—original concepts, opinions, facts, figures, explanations, and statistics.

4. *Use your own words.*

Notes are seen only by you. It makes sense to use the words you know best—your own. In your own words jot down notes that capture the writer's meaning. There are two exceptions to the "use your own words" philosophy.

Exception 1: Direct Quotes

When you want to record a direct quote—a person's exact words—copy the quote just as it appears. Quotation marks tell you that a person's exact words are being quoted. When you see words enclosed in quotation marks, copy them exactly. Accuracy is important. ● For help with direct quotations see Writer's Handbook, page H-20.

Exception 2: Buzz Words

If you see key words or phrases popping up again and again in an article or group of articles, chances are that you've discovered buzz words. Buzz words are frequently-used jargon. Every field has its jargon. If you're a rock-music enthusiast, you're familiar with these buzz words: "jam session," "going gold," "roadies," and "groupies." For practice, look at the following buzz words. With what field are they associated? What do the buzz words mean?

Group 1	Group 2	Group 3	Group 4
block buster	gridiron	the warm down	rush
superstar	pigskin	runner's knee	preppy
flicks	clothesline	jogging gurus	freaks
	huddle up		

While taking notes, be on the lookout for buzz words. If buzz words connected with your issue baffle you, check with your teacher or parents. If their answers are a bit hazy, you've discovered your first interview question.

5. *Record your impressions.*

Reflect on the material you read. Spend a few moments evaluating the source. An editorial is an opinion piece. You don't expect objectivity. By definition an editorial is one person's opinion. A good news story, on the other hand, tries to present an objective report. In evaluating a news story, consider these questions: Is the situation described reported in an even-handed manner? Do you detect the writer's biases? Is the report slanted? For all materials you read, ask: Does the content of the piece match the form in which it is presented? You might make a brief note commenting on the value of the source for your purposes. Note the following example.

> Editorial—good source for the *pro* side of my issue. Would like to interview this person.

Writer's Workbench 2

Notes Toward a Position Paper

Since you've been taking notes in classes for some time, you may already have a reliable note-taking system you feel comfortable using. If not, see Writer's Workbench 1, page 160. Before you jot down a word, reflect on your purposes for taking notes on your print sources. You're still exploring your issue, still probing to discover all you can about all sides of the topic, and still trying to get a grasp on the issue. Think of the note-taking process as a way to accomplish that goal. Use this process to gather a base of facts, figures, opinions, and points of view. When your notes are complete, you should have a good idea of where the gaps are, what questions still plague you, and to whom you want to speak to fill in those blank spots and to answer your questions.

Step One: Skim print materials.

Quickly glance over your materials. Read through them rapidly to get a "feel" for your topic. Make sure this is the issue you want to investigate for the next several days. Are you still interested in this topic? Are there at least two sides to the issue? Is genuine interest or concern by the community reflected in your materials?

If you answered "No!" to any of these questions, see your teacher. It's not too late to select another topic from your brainstorm list. The best research topic will both intrigue you and be of interest to the community.

Step Two: Reread materials closely; take careful notes.

Begin by writing a source entry. (See Writer's Workbench 1 on page 160.) Then jot down key information from each print resource. If you can sum up that information in one sentence, do so. More often, however, you will want to note specific details. Think of your issue as a skeleton. Note information that helps you flesh it out. Look for specific points of view, proposed solutions, unique suggestions, and diverse opinions. If you note direct quotes, copy them down *exactly* as they appear; enclose them in quotation marks. Be alert for names which keep cropping up. Write down the names and titles of community members who are outspoken; note which side of the issue they speak for. Write down facts, figures, and statistics used in support of the viewpoints expressed. You may get a good bit of information from some clippings and almost none from others.

From a two-column newspaper article a student took these notes:

Osley, M. Diane, "Impact Of Proposed Regional Mall—Good or Evil?" Today, Feb. 8, 1985, p. 1. col. 3–4.

News Article—Two Sides Presented

Downtown Merchants' Side.   Fears: 1. downtown may become ghost town, 2. high cost of move to mall, 3. # of vacant bldgs. may invite more crime (vandalism) in downtown area, 4. overhead in mall prohibitive to small business person.

Mall Developers' Side.   Claim: mall will "enhance" downtown by cutting down # of shoppers' trips to large cities & by keeping local $ at home.

Possible Interviewees.   Retail Merchants' Side—Bill Bradley, Director of Central Business Authority. Mall Developers' Side—Mark Hawk, spokesperson for Taylor Shopping Centers, Inc.

Quotes.   Bradley, "The majority of downtown merchants can't possibly pay the overhead in a regional shopping mall." Hawk, "Experience tells us that this (proposed mall) will enhance the central business district."

Miscellaneous.   Merchants now agree—"Stop the mall" efforts useless.

Evaluation.   Mostly shows plight of small downtown business people. 2/3rds of article discusses merchants' side. Two good interview possibilities.

Cathy

Cathy has adapted the note-taking format suggested in Writer's Workbench 1, page 160, to suit her own needs. Feel free to do the same. Notice the abbreviations Cathy uses. Can you suggest others she might use? Take a few minutes to talk about Cathy's note-taking style. What are the strengths? Do you have questions about taking notes? If so, discuss those questions as a class.

Step Three: Synthesize Your Notes.

An important part of the note-taking process is pulling together the loose ends. Once you've taken notes on each clipping, synthesize your notes in this fashion:

1. *State the issue you're exploring.*
Keep this to one sentence. When Cathy explored topic options in her Writer's Notebook, she envisioned the issue to be:

Should we or should we not have a regional shopping mall?

Now that she's done some reading on the issue, Cathy sees that the real issue looks more like this:

Can our community have *both* a regional shopping mall and an economically viable central business district?

2. *Determine how many sides to the issue exist. Identify those sides.* Re-state the concerns of each side in list form. While many issues have only two sides, more complex issues may have more sides. Look carefully for all sides of the issue.

Cathy jotted down the concerns of those who feel her community can have the best of both worlds (YES) and those who feel that downtown will suffer as the result of a new mall (NO).

YES

Stores can increase their floor space and can offer a wider variety of merchandise.

Mall will keep hometown $ at home and will attract buyers from surrounding counties.

Mall will generate local option taxes and property tax $$$ for the city.

New jobs will be created.

More convenient parking will be at the mall.

Mall will "force" downtown to be competitive. Business will have to cater more to customers' needs. Perhaps downtown will respond by converting to a unique specialty shop center.

Consumers will come to view our community as an attractive entertainment center.

NO

Growth cycle of downtown will be effectively halted.

A large portion of small local business people will be driven out of business.

Small business can't afford the move to the mall.

Even if small business makes it out there, they can't afford the overhead to stay there.

Downtown will not be active for awhile. (Who knows for how long?)

Empty bldgs. may invite more crime downtown.

Majority of business people in the mall will be out-of-town folks.

Trade will shift from downtown to mall area. With the shift will come shifts in residential patterns, increases in demands —police protection, fire protection, utilities, etc. that we can't handle now.

3. *Determine how the community is divided on the issue.*
Cathy looked through her notes and made this list:

YES

Mark Hawk, spokesperson for Taylor Shopping Centers, Inc.

Tina Newton, manager of *Sensational Cities* and all the other big businesses moving to the mall.

Kathy Kelser, owner of *Systems Unlimited* and other small businesses moving to the mall.

Some shoppers.

NO

Bill Bradley, Director of Central Business Authority.

Brenda Cheekster, owner of Balloons Bountiful and other merchants who can't make the move.

Some shoppers.

4. *Decide how you're doing.*

Look over your synthesis. Do you need more print sources? Are you ready to interview? Do you have an idea of who you want to speak to? Do you need to consult with your teacher? Are you ready for a little break? Assess your progress. Talk to yourself in a free writing.

This is what Cathy wrote.

I'm excited about this. This is really a tough problem. As a shopper, I'd love to have a few more dress shops and a few *good* places to eat. I'm sick of *Taco's Tonight* and *Hotdog Heaven*. On the other hand, if my mom or dad owned a small business, I'd really be worried. I'd like to talk to some business people and find out how they feel. I want to know the odds of downtown folding. Maybe if I just let all this settle in my mind

Writer's Notebook Check

To help you avoid putting all this off until the last moment, your teacher may want to check your progress in your Writer's Notebook, where by now you should have the following:

**Checking
It
Out**

1. Topic explorations
2. Selected topic
3. List One—Print Sources
4. List Two—People Sources
5. List Three—A Plan for Your Research
6. Notes on 5 or 6 print sources; synthesis of notes

Chapter 9

Voicing Your Convictions

SPOTLIGHT

An interview with Brenda Cheekster, Downtown Merchant—Owner of Balloons Bountiful. Interview by Cathy Andersen. February 4, 198-, 4:30 p.m.

> **Interviewer:** When did you and other merchants first hear about the proposed regional mall?
>
> **Interviewee:** Rumors about mall construction have floated around this city for as long as I can remember, and I've been here fifteen years. Signs saying "Future Site of Axel Mall" or "Coming Soon—Ashley Square" stayed on that land until the weeds stood taller than the signposts . . . Up until three years ago, talk by the latest out-of-town developer about a new mall barely raised an eyebrow. The community remained unimpressed— maybe slightly bemused by the developer's "dream." Folks around here thought of the "dream" as a "hallucination."
>
> **Interviewer:** Do you think the community's feeling changed?
>
> **Interviewee:** Yes. That's exactly what happened.
>
> **Interviewer:** What do you think caused the community to change its attitudes?
>
> **Interviewee:** Well, the community itself changed. We still have the old families—the ones who founded this community—but we have new families, too. We're no longer a sleepy, little college town nestled in the back woods. We're now the "bedroom community" of the capital. A large proportion of our people live here but work fifty miles away.

Interviewer: You seem to be saying that there's a connection between our being a "bedroom community" and the change in community interest about the proposed mall. Tell me more about that. What's your theory?

Interviewee: People have gotten a taste of big city life. In the capital there are places to go, things to do. People are scratching their heads and wondering why they're having to travel fifty miles just to eat in a fancy restaurant, see a good play, or shop in a convenient mall. After all, with the influx of industry, we've grown by leaps and bounds over the past few years. People are finally realizing that our community doesn't have to remain a nostalgic town of yesteryear. They see that our community can join the twentieth century any time we want.

Interviewer: Many people think that becoming just another booming metropolis is not really progress. They say that more is not necessarily better. You're one of the few downtown merchants *not* moving to the mall who seems philosophic about the dramatic effect of the mall. As a downtown merchant who stands to lose a great deal, what are your feelings on the issue?

Interviewee: To be honest, I was initially angry and frightened when I realized that the community was behind this mall. I thought it spelled the beginning of the end for downtown merchants. Now I feel differently. The challenge of the proposed mall has united the business people in the central business district. It's brought out the best in us. There's a great deal of innovative thinking going on. The merchandising expertise of the downtown merchants is coming to light. To survive we've got to be competitive. I have great hopes for the future of downtown.

Interviewer: How do you envision the central business district ten years from now?

Interviewee: I see unique boutiques and specialty shops. Our merchants can offer the personal service . . .

Reread Cathy's opening question. Why do you think she chooses a low-key question to begin? How do Cathy's questions show that she is interested in and listening to her interviewee? Most of Cathy's questions encourage her interviewee to share her thoughts. Notice how they are worded. Cathy's second question produced a limited response. What went wrong in that question? How could she have re-phrased it? How would you evaluate Cathy's interview?

Writer's Workbench 1

The Interviewer's Guide to Good Questions

Question-asking looks deceptively simple. Television news reporters and talk-show hosts ask a few natural-sounding questions and the interviewee launches into a lengthy discussion. The reporter or host then asks a few clarifying questions and the guest gives animated responses. The interviewee talks; the interviewer listens. That seems simple enough. What viewers may be unaware of is the careful preparation interviewers go through before such successful discussions. Interviewers do their homework. They learn as much as they can about the person they are interviewing by reading statements their interviewee has made and by familiarizing themselves with the interviewee's work experience and personal background.

The most important homework interviewers do, however, is the careful planning of the questions they will ask. As a beginning interviewer, you will need a set of written questions. They will help you relax and listen to your interviewee, and they will keep the interview on track. The key to successful interviewing is asking good questions.

Here are some tips on asking good questions:

Opening Questions

Plan to ask a question or two which will put both you and your interviewee at ease. These do not have to be throw-away questions like, "What is your job here at the newspaper?" (The sign on the desk says "editor.") They should be questions which give interviewees a chance to talk a little bit about themselves. Here are some examples.

"How did you first become interested in the mall issue?"

"How long have you been concerned about the need for bike paths in our community?"

"Would you be comfortable answering some questions about . . .?"

Steer away from questions which might put the interviewee on the defensive, such as the following:

"How come you think your solution to airport congestion is best?"

"What makes you think you're an expert?"

Brainstorm some opening questions for your interviewee; jot them in your Writer's Notebook.

Open-Ended Questions

The best questions draw out the interviewee. Simple yes/no questions provide little information. Try to word your questions so that they invite the speaker to give extended answers.

Reword the following questions into more open-ended ones:

"Do you favor extending the by-pass beyond Hall Street?"

"Is a sign ordinance really necessary in this town?"

"Do kids need a new recreation center?"

Probing Questions

If the interview is going well and you are feeling confident, you may want to probe the interviewee with some tough questions:

"Isn't progress inevitable? Aren't attempts to save old buildings just wishful thinking?"

"Aren't the fears of those residents near the proposed halfway house reasonable? Isn't the placement of a home for the mentally retarded in a residential neighborhood just another good theory? Can it really work if neighbors don't want it?"

The intent of probing questions is not to make your interviewee angry, but to take the discussion beyond superficial talk. By accurately stating the concerns of those opposed to your interviewee's position, you are intensifying the responses and sharpening the discussion.

What are some probing questions you might like to ask your interviewee? Experiment with wording some of these tough questions in your Writer's Notebook. Be sure they are fair.

Two Sides to the Issue

Your questions can help your interviewee focus his or her response by presenting the other side of an issue in your question, and by inviting your interviewee to rebut it. Here are some examples.

"How do you respond to those critics of a new regional mall who suggest that it will be the end of downtown business?"

"Are there other alternatives to pet control than strict leash laws with fines and loss of animals?"

Try formulating a question which presents the other side of the issue.

Formulating Interview Questions

Plan to interview at least one person representing each side of your issue. If there are two sides to your issue, count on conducting at least two interviews. Decide on the people you want to interview; assume they will agree to talk with you. For each interviewee develop a set of from five to eight interview questions. Experiment with the types of questions described in Writer's Workbench 1. Try writing several openers and a probing question or two. Develop at least one question designed to get your interviewee to respond to the opposing side of the issue. Reread all of your formulated questions, making sure they are open-ended invitations.

**Getting
It
Down**

〜〜〜〜〜〜〜〜〜〜〜〜〜〜〜〜〜〜

**Checking
It
Out**

In pairs, conduct practice interviews. Brief your partner on the issue. Tell your partner the role he or she will play in explaining the side of the issue he or she will represent. Role-play the interviews as you expect to conduct them. After role playing, analyze the interview. Swap places and repeat the process so that both of you have practiced conducting an interview with your list of questions.

〜〜〜〜〜〜〜〜〜〜〜〜〜〜〜〜〜〜

Interviewing the Experts

**Getting
It
Down**

Speaking to those most directly affected by your issue is your single best source of information. If you've worked through Chapters 8 and 9 to this point, you're all set. Relax and enjoy conducting a skillful interview.

Tips For Interviewers

1. Make an appointment.   Be sure your interviewee knows that you're coming and has some time for the interview.

2. Be ready.   Have your pencils sharpened before you get to the interview. Check to be sure you have your Writer's Notebook for taking notes.

3. Use a tape recorder.   If your interviewee agrees, you may want to tape the interview as well as take notes. Check your equipment and its use in advance. If your interviewee shows any signs of discomfort, shut off the tape recorder and rely on your notes.

4. Jot down key words and phrases.   You can't possibly write your interviewee's words verbatim, but you can note key phrases. Use your best note-taking skills.

5. Stay calm.   Take your time. You're talking to another human being, someone just like you. Think before you speak. Rely on the questions you've brought with you.

6. Tune in.   Even though you have your questions before you, you may want to stray from them a bit. *Listen* to what your interviewee has to say. Follow good leads that your interviewee gives you. If you're unsure about a comment, ask the interviewee to repeat or restate it.

7. <u>Thank your interviewee.</u>   Before you leave, express your appreciation for the time your interviewee has given you. Consider writing a thank-you note when you return to school.

8. <u>Transcribe notes immediately.</u>   While the interview is still fresh, transcribe your jottings. Re-play your tape. Get quotes down exactly as you hear them. See Writer's Workbench 1, pages 173–175 for help.

~~~~~~

Pulling It All Together

If you've done a thorough job of reading and interviewing, you should be ready for your most challenging assignment— summarizing your findings. This is the time to try to pull together all the information necessary for making some sense of it in your mind, and to formulate your personal position on the issue.

Since writing clarifies thinking, it may be helpful to try a free writing which summarizes the issue as you see it. You might give the issue a chronological treatment, that is, begin your free writing at the point when the issue first surfaced in the community, then follow it to its conclusion.

Getting It Down

~~~~~~

SPOTLIGHT

When you have completed your free writing, read Cathy's free-writing summary using a chronological approach.

Initially, retail merchants and shopping mall developers were portrayed as "the good guys" vs. "the bad guys." The media showed "the little guys"—local business people—fighting for survival against the mighty and moneyed—the powerful regional shopping center developers. Pros and cons of mall construction sparked heated debate. When the air cleared, the community supported the pro side. The gains for the community-at-large seem to have outweighed possible losses to individual business people.

Gradually, lines dividing downtown merchants and mall developers softened. Developers convinced merchants that they were not intent upon destroying downtown. Merchants realized that they could compete by turning the downtown area into a unique specialty shops center which could offer the personal service the mall couldn't match.

Now "the good guys" and "the bad guys" speak with one voice. To the community and the surrounding area, both groups promote the city as a future retail trade center. They envision a city where there is something for everyone.

Cathy

Getting It Down

Another approach to the summary is a pro/con treatment. In Chapter 8 you identified the various sides of the issue and the principal speakers for each side. Try a free writing which presents each side and your own concluding position.

A third approach to your summary is to begin with a statement of your own position. Develop your reasons for coming to this conclusion, citing the information which influenced your decision. Conclude your summary with your reasons for rejecting the other sides of the controversy.

Checking It Out

Try at least two of these three free-writing approaches. Select the free writing you like best to share with a consultant. Together, look for places that need further facts, figures, or quotes. Look over your quotes and select the ones that most vividly bring your position statement to life.

Writer's Workbench 2

The Writer's Guide to Using Quotations

With a voice as calm as his serene blue eyes, Mr. Brody noted, "City and county officials work harder on resisting the proposed merger of governments than they work solving the problems of this community."

Types of Quotations—Direct and Indirect

Direct Quotations

Direct quotations indicate that an interviewee's *exact* words are being used. In transcribing the notes from your interviews, use a direct quotation only when you are repeating exactly what your interviewee said. When you use exact words, enclose your interviewee's remarks in quotation marks. The preceding quote is an example of a *direct quotation*. What are Mr. Brody's *exact* words? How can you tell?

Indirect Quotations

Indirect quotations tell readers that you are *not* using your interviewee's exact words. In most cases an indirect quotation indicates *paraphrasing*. In your own words you're summing up what your interviewee said as succinctly and as honestly as memory allows. No quotation marks appear in indirect quotations.

Reread the opening quote in this Workbench. Try paraphrasing or summing up Mr. Brody's comment as objectively as possible.

Your efforts may look something like this:

Paraphrase (Indirect Quotation)
Mr. Brody feels that the officials of both governments devote more energy to blocking the merger than they do in unraveling area problems.

Writers have problems when they twist an interviewee's words to support their own viewpoints. Some interviewee's comments may be so involved and jargon-laden that you feel compelled to translate or interpret them so that your readers can understand them. Exercise judgment; interpret with caution. Don't allow your personal feelings to color your translation.

The "Putting Your Words in Their Mouths" Translation
Mr. Brody thinks the officials of city and county government are wrong because they spend all of their time bucking this merger. He thinks our community's problems would be solved if only those people would do what they get paid for doing.

The Cautious Translation
Mr. Brody voiced his concern over the issue by implying that city and county officials spend an inordinate amount of time trying to block the proposed merger.

Direct Quotation Reminders

Stems

The *quotation stem* tells readers the person whose exact words are being used.

Stem   *Direct Quotation*
Julie said, "I'm in favor of a half-way house for first offenders."

A string of he *saids*, she *saids*, they *saids* will drive your readers to distraction. Explore more precise alternatives. Put some life into quotation stems; begin by getting rid of *said* stems.

Strong Verb Stems

Use strong verbs that *show* readers *how* interviewees speak their words:

Julie snorted,   Julie volunteered,
Julie ventured,   Julie cried,
Julie interrupted,   Julie whispered,
Julie suggested,   Julie insisted,

Reread Julie's quote using these stems. Can you *hear* the intensity in Julie's words? Use quotation stems to help readers "hear" *how* interviewees express themselves.

Scene-Setters

Effective writers use quotation stems to set the scene. Good stems put the reader there.

Scene-Setter
It seemed that no one would speak for the first offenders; then Julie's clear voice broke the silence, "I'm in favor of a half-way house for first offenders."

Look at the quote from Mr. Brody at the beginning of the Workbench. Point out the *quotation stem*. Comment on its effectiveness as a scene-setter.

Punctuating Quotations

When to capitalize what and whether to use a comma or a period often depends upon the placement of the quotation stem. Look at the patterns of punctuation in these examples.

Pattern 1: Quotation Stem at the Beginning of Direct Quotation

> /Stem—
>
> Mr. Brody observed, "Official insensitivity to the hardship this deadlock imposes on taxpayers frustrates them."

Pattern 2: Quotation Stem in the Middle of Direct Quotation

> "Official insensitivity to the hardship this deadlock imposes on taxpayers," Mr. Brody observed, "frustrates them."
>
> ＼Stem—

Pattern 3: Quotation Stem at the End of Direct Quotation

> "Official insensitivity to the hardship this deadlock imposes on taxpayers frustrates them," Mr. Brody observed.
>
> ＼Stem—

Admittedly, not all punctuation patterns are this simple. Questions may arise: What do I do if the quote I'm using is a question, but the sentence in which it appears is a statement? *or* What if the quote is a statement, but the sentence is a question? Relax. ● The essential rules for punctuating quotations in the situations you're likely to encounter as a writer are contained in the Writer's Handbook, pages H-20, 29–31. Refer to your Handbook as questions arise. The more you use quotations in your writing, the more comfortable you will feel with handling their punctuation.

Special Problems

The Sandwich Quote

As interviewees share their views, they, too, may quote other people. Here's how to handle the quote within a quote or the "sandwich quote."

> The comments of Mayor Hall irritated Mr. Brody. "When she (Mayor Hall) told the media, 'We'll never see these governments merge in our lifetime,' I telephoned the Mayor to express my displeasure."

Notice that single quotation marks encase the quote within; double quotation marks are used to indicate the words of Mr. Brody.

The Extensive Quote

You may find that an interviewee articulates a point with such clarity and insight that you want to use every word. A controversial stand or an original concept too good to miss may present itself. In such cases you may find yourself quoting several lines. When using an extensive quotation, indent five extra spaces from the left and the right margins. If you are typing your final draft, single-space extensive quotations. Omit quotation marks when using extensive quotations; the extra indentation takes the place of quotation marks.

> I pressed Mr. Brody to explain why the Mayor's remark distressed him.
>
> People look up to Mayor Hall. She's an intelligent, well-spoken individual with a wealth of experience. When she speaks, people listen. I do not believe she enhanced our chances for merger by making that remark. Frankly, I think she blundered; that single error in judgment could cost us this merger. I believe the Mayor regrets having made the statement. I think the public can expect a retraction or, at the least, a *clarification* of that comment.

Extensive quotations should be used sparingly. Limit yourself to one or two extensive quotations in your position piece.

SPOTLIGHT

Good Transactional Writing

A good position paper has something to say and says it well. Dull, dry, lifeless prose will not connect with an audience regardless of how carefully the writer has collected the information. Read this transactional writing, a position paper about tallgrass prairies, by Dennis Farney. Notice how the writer gives life to a potentially mundane issue.

The Tallgrass Prairie:
Can It Be Saved?

> There is hardly any prairie left in Illinois, the Prairie State. And when I finally found the prairie there, it was caged in like a prisoner.
> A prairie is not, as you may think, any old piece of flatland in the Midwest. No, a prairie is wine-colored grass, dancing in the

wind. A prairie is a sun-splashed hillside, bright with wild flowers. A prairie is a fleeting cloud shadow, the song of a meadowlark. It is wild land that has never felt the slash of the plow.

I drove out one October afternoon, through the spreading suburbs west of Chicago, searching for these things. I found tollbooths. Bulldozers, gouging out basements. Billboards. And everywhere, the subdivisions the billboards advertised.

Then I saw it, a remnant of the landscape that once covered much of Illinois.

The prairie was there, in a pioneer cemetery surrounded by a chain link fence.

And outside the fence was the most encouraging sight I'd seen all day. A young man was walking, head down, collecting wildflower seeds in an old bakery sack.

"You look like a prairie restorationist," I hailed him. Ken Klick looked up, then grinned his confirmation. "My 'prairie's' only fifteen feet by five—my backyard," he said. "But these wild flowers are so rare I want to do whatever I can to save them. I'm taking these few seeds home to plant." . . .

The autumn wind moaned in the chain link fence and rustled dryly in a clump of coarse leaves at our feet. "That's the compass plant," Ken said, pointing out that the vertical leaves face east and west to best catch the sun.

"There's the rattlesnake master," he continued. It was reputedly used as folk medicine to cure snakebite. "Over there is the shooting star." Come May, its pale pink, swept-back petals suggesting falling stars would blanket the slope.

Ken stopped to pick up a beer can and paused among the headstones. A milkweed seed drifted by on its puffy parachute. A wedge of geese honked across the sky, heading south.

"This prairie makes me sad," Ken said softly. I felt it too. That tiny caged-in prairie symbolized a loss so vast as to be almost incomprehensible to modern Americans. It symbolized a lost landscape—the landscape of the tallgrass prairie.

Once that landscape stretched from Ohio to eastern Kansas and the Dakotas, and from Texas into Canada, a great triangle beneath an empty sky . . .

It's almost gone now, that shining, swirling landscape. Other prairie survives, characterized by shorter grasses, on the dry, thinly populated Great Plains to the west. But the tallgrass prairie, the king of prairies, became the corn belt. Became Chicago, became Des Moines, became home for 25 million people. As the homesteaders' steel plows sliced through its matted roots, it all but vanished in a ringing, tearing sound.

That didn't happen in the Flint Hills of eastern Kansas, a fifty-mile-wide swath that runs north-south across the state. There the plow ran into a thin and stony soil, and so today the Flint Hills remain cloaked in prairie and in a kind of turn-of-the-century peacefulness as well. . . . It remains a country of cattle, boots, and branding irons, and of stone barns and houses that seem as rooted to the land as the grass itself.

Almost all these flat-topped hills are wrapped around limestone, deposited by an ancient sea more than 200 million years ago. Embedded in the limestone are nodules of flint, which give the region its name. Here environmentalists are pressing for a Tallgrass Prairie National Park. A proposal to be presented to the U.S. House of

Representatives seeks a park of 320,000 acres, split into three parcels. It would fill a gap in the National Park System, which contains no significant reserve of tallgrass prairie.

Vehemently opposed to the park are the Flint Hills ranchers. KEEP THE GRASSLANDS FREE read bumper stickers on their cattle trucks. The ranchers fear government condemnation of their land and the changes an influx of tourists might bring to their thinly populated region. They argue that they're already preserving the prairie—in the form of ranches . . . .

"You know, by golly, what would happen then?" demanded Orville Burtis, an 87-year-old rancher. "Then they'll have to run blacktop roads through it. Have to have rest stations. Have to have a

place to buy pop and beer. And pretty soon the realistic part of it—the back-to-nature-just-exactly-like-God-Almighty-made-it part—*is gone.* Why can't they let it *alone?*"

"To be right honest with you," Jim Hess told me, "ranchers aren't much interested in having the government interfere with them. Ranchers are an independent bunch. What bothers us most is the use of eminent domain. We feel it's wrong for one group of people to take land from another." . . .

The 1970s have brought a great surge of prairie preservation and prairie restoration activity, a phenomenon seemingly bound up with some larger national search for continuity and permanence. I examined that phenomenon recently, returning to the wide and open country of my youth.

My journey took me to Ordway Memorial Prairie in South Dakota, a jumble of hills and wetlands deposited by glaciers. As I lay belly down in the grass at dusk, dark shapes suddenly loomed against the sky, rocking and pounding. Bison! Heads lowered, powerful shoulders working, they thundered by me into the darkening landscape.

I talked with John Humke, midwestern vice president of the Nature Conservancy, which preserved that prairie as a refuge for both plants and wildlife. Saving ecologically valuable land is the conservancy's sole function; it preserves plants, animals, and samples of ecosystems that might otherwise be obliterated—1.5 million acres nationally to date. In that total are 39,000 acres of prairie—74 projects in 11 states.

"I used to dream of a million dollars for buying prairie," Humke told me. "In the past decade we've spent ten million."

And I met the prairie restorationists—hundreds of them now, rescuing wild flowers and attempting the almost impossible: reconstructing the prairie on ground that was once plowed.

You can grow a prairie facsimile in five or ten years. But some scientists think it could take 200 years to reconstruct the intricate prairie ecosystem. Others think 500. Still others, never. No matter. The prairie-restoration movement continues to grow, part of the impulse that moves some people to restore old homes and trace genealogies.

"It's roots," restorationist Robert Betz told me. "That's why you've got this whole movement of trying to recapture the past. The prairie represents the past. It represents something you can grab onto, something that endures." . . .

Dennis Farney

Dennis Farney's piece on the tallgrass prairie is a particularly effective position paper. It is not a stuffy text-bookish, impersonal treatment of the topic. Neither is it a shrill, ranting piece of personal opinions and accusations.

What surprises you about this piece? How does Farney connect with his audience? Point to interesting or effective words and phrases.

How fairly does Farney present the issue? Does he accurately report both sides of the issue? Point to the subtle ways by which the author lets you know his position.

Notice the writer's use of direct and indirect quotations. How does he let you know he has done his homework? Is there anything the writer did not do in this piece that might have made it more effective?

Writing for a Larger Audience

In earlier chapters of this book you've spoken out on personal and school issues. You have expressed your views to friends, classmates, parents, and readers of the school newspaper. These writing challenges have gradually moved your topic and your audience further and further from you. In these two chapters you have been working through the process for writing a position paper on a community issue for a general audience. Experienced writers know that the more distant and generalized the audience, the more challenging the writing task.

When you write from your own experience, for yourself or your friends, you are more relaxed about word choices and form. You write in a chatty, almost conversational voice. When you write for a more general audience on a less personal topic, you must use more deliberate and careful language. This does not mean that your writing must become false or pretentious. It certainly does not mean that you should forget all you have learned about what good writing is. Ms. Forsyth (page 149) used some of the elements of the narrative—for example, sensory description and the voices of characters—to set the stage for her position paper. Writing for unknown audiences places a special burden on writers to research topics thoroughly and to discuss them in clear, precise language so that all readers may "listen" and understand the message.

Drafting the Paper
Your preparation for this draft has been frenzied. You've hustled around finding print sources, jotting notes, finding someone to interview, summarizing and making some sense of your notes.

Getting
It
Down

Don't worry. You've done your homework. The draft will come. Find a quiet place. Reflect a little on your topic. What are some things that come through loud and clear from all of your research? Where might you begin to unravel the conflicting sides of your issue?

Reread the openings to the Forsyth and Farney pieces (pages 149 and 182). Notice that both authors begin with some descriptive material as though they were writing a narrative. Maybe a good way for you to begin your draft is to start telling the story or describing something.

Reread your quotations. Maybe a good quotation from an interview or a newspaper article will get your piece started. Maybe several questions addressed directly to your readers will help you get started.

Rely on your hunches and intuitions about what your readers will want to know. Keep writing until you have completed your draft. Include information from at least three print sources; use at least two quotes from your interview.

Checking It Out

When you have a complete draft, read your paper aloud to a consultant. Ask the consultant to listen to your voice. Is it clear, consistent, fair? Ask the consultant whether all sides of the issue are stated clearly and whether your own position is apparent: Do I need more information anywhere? Is my paper easy to follow? Do I confuse you on any point? How can I make this better?

Revision Strategies

Getting It Right

1. *Voice.*   Listen carefully to the voice in your piece. Is it reasoned, even-handed, fair? Does it speak directly to readers? Is it the voice of an authority? Do you sound as if you know what you're talking about? Rework any sections that sound like a textbook or emotional babbling. Work for a firm, knowledgeable tone of voice. Compare these examples of voice:

Textbook voice.   It has become increasingly apparent that the citizenry are impatient with City Council reluctance to address this problem.

Emotional babbling.   The people in this town have had it! The bumblers on the City Council are scared to death of this issue. They're just too wishy-washy to make a decision.

Even-handed.   The City Council has been slow to make a decision on the issue. Most of the people I talked to are weary of the official foot-dragging.

2. *Show and Tell.*   Mere facts and figures about an issue can be pretty dry stuff. Telling readers *about* an issue may be less effective than showing the effects of an issue. Even something as mundane as a definition need not be drab dictionary-sounding prose:

A dictionary *tells*:

"A prairie is defined as a large grassy level or slightly rolling area of land."

Random House

A writer *shows*:

"A prairie is wine-colored grass dancing in the wind. A prairie is a sun-splashed hillside, bright with wild flowers. A prairie is a fleeting cloud shadow, the song of a meadowlark. It is wild land that has never felt the slash of a plow."

Dennis Farney

Rework parts of your writing to *show* rather than *tell*. Use the sensory detail of a good narrative.

3. *Quotations.*   Writers use quotations to do more than just repeat the exact words of a speaker. Effective writers surround quotations with words which reveal the speaker's tone of voice, level of volume, frame of mind, or personal appearance. These descriptive words help the writer re-create the moment when the words were spoken. Effective descriptive words around a quotation put the reader there. Here are some examples.

Ken Klick looked up, then grinned his confirmation. "My 'prairie's' only fifteen feet by five—my backyard," he said.

"I'll be out of business a month after that mall opens." Mr. Scott raised his hands in frustration.

"So that's progress!" He turned his back and shuffled down the sidewalk musing to himself.

Look over your quotations to see whether the addition of any descriptive words around them will add to the reader's understanding.

Strong verb stems and scene-setters are also effective writing techniques. See Writer's Workbench 2, page 178, for examples.

4. *Support.*   Check to see that you have supported your position adequately with quotations from print sources, interviews, and personal observations. Base your conclusions on the evidence you have gathered. Connect that evidence directly to your conclusions for your readers. Watch out for "I feel" and "It seems."

An *"I feel"*   I feel strongly that we need better police protection in the inner city.

A *supported conclusion*   Inner city residents live in fear of their neighbors. Crimes against people have risen 15% in the past 12 months. The police commissioner admits he has inadequate manpower. These conditions are intolerable. We must not abandon the inner-city to criminals and their victims. The City Council must commit additional resources to the protection of inner-city residents.

An *"It seems"*   It seems that recreational facilities are inadequate for the children who live in the Cedar Creek area.

A *supported conclusion*   When one five-acre plot of grass and a red clay ballfield with a broken backstop are the sole recreational facilities for the more than 1000 children who live in the Cedar Creek area, something must be done.

Checking It Out   Reread your draft looking for any unsupported statements of opinion. Beef them up with facts and specifics or remove them. Purge "I feel" and "It seems" statements from your paper.

Proofreader's Checklist

1. **Spelling.** You may have used words with which you are not familiar. Your interviewees may have used words you only guessed at. Take the time to double check the spelling of all questionable words in your paper. Don't let sloppy spelling detract from the impact of your paper. Borrow a consultant's eyes if your own tend to miss spelling errors.

2. **Punctuation.** There are at least two potentially troublesome areas for punctuation in your paper. First, using quotations adds to the likelihood of errors. ● Check Workbench 2, page 178 and the Handbook (pages H-20, 29–31). Then look carefully at any direct quotations in your paper. ● Compare your punctuation with the models provided in the Workbench and the Handbook.

The second troublesome area occurs in long, complicated sentences. As sentences grow longer, and phrases and clauses begin to sprout everywhere, you may become confused about the punctuation. It is impossible to give you a rule which will work in all cases. Some sentences are so tricky that you may need an expert's advice. However, these examples may help:

Simple Sentences: John Calhoun is mayor of Maysville. He is concerned about the annexation issue.

Combined Sentence: John Calhoun is mayor of Maysville, and he is vitally concerned about the annexation issue.

Notice that when two independent clauses are joined with a conjunction, a comma precedes the conjunction.

Compound Sentence: John Calhoun, the Mayor of Maysville, is vitally concerned about the annexation issue; and he is committed to bringing the issue to a vote.

Notice in this sentence that a semicolon now precedes the conjunction *and*. The semicolon is needed because there are commas in the first clause. Any time you join two independent clauses which contain commas within them, use a semicolon before the connecting conjunction.

3. **Manuscript Form.** Taking the time to make sure your writing looks good on the page may seem like a trivial point. Obviously what you say is far more important than how it looks, but—some readers are offended by sloppy handwriting, inconsistent margins, and improper spacing. Use these general guidelines to insure an attractive looking paper:

   a. Plan to leave an inch-wide margin at the top, the bottom, and the right side of each page.

   b. The left margin may be slightly wider than an inch and should be strictly maintained.

c. If you are typing your paper, double space between lines and keep the right margin roughly even. Try to avoid ending lines with hyphens.

d. Indent each new paragraph five spaces.

e. Be sure your handwriting or typing is neat and legible.

Writer's Workbench 3

Posting Your Position Statement

Between trips to the media center and mad dashes to interview appointments, you may have lost sight of all the issues being researched by your classmates. While drafting a well-written statement of purpose, and offering your views to a larger audience may be undeniably satisfying, you probably want to hear from your classmates and share your discoveries with them.

An endless succession of students marching to the podium to drone out their reports is a sure-fire sleep inducer. If you've noticed that the bright, alert audience expressions for report one shift to tense smiles by the sixth report, strained looks by the fifteenth, and pleading glances by the twentieth, consider posting results in the form of a visual.

The late Marshall McLuhan, guru of mass media, reminded us that "The medium is the message." The form you select when you share your position can be as important as your findings. Advertisers, architects, and designers know this. That's why they go to great lengths to create forms that enhance their products. To gain the audience you deserve, select a form that will display your results effectively. This text will offer suggestions, but you have the option of creating a form of your own and having it approved by your teacher. Before you post your visual, be sure your clearly stated position and your name appear in, on, or alongside your product. Your position statement may be worded as a slogan, a jingle, a straightforward statement, or perhaps as a question—provided your visual clearly illustrates your stand. Your visual should be self-explanatory.

Option 1: Mock-Ups

If you like hands-on projects, consider this option. Perhaps you have a vision of how the city's new recreational area should look, or maybe you have an alternate dream for your community's new zoo. A mock-up or model can illustrate your plan in miniature. Plan carefully; construct compartments, nooks, and crannies to show the ins and outs of your vision. See your school's vocational education teacher, talk to a salesperson at your local lumber yard, or nose around your garage or backyard for old scraps of plywood and other materials.

Option 2: Graphic Representation

If one side of your issue clearly outweighs the other or if facts and figures convincingly support your position, consider presenting your data in a chart or graph. Print legibly and write large enough for information to be read from a reasonable distance. For eye appeal try thin-tipped pens available in an assortment of colors. A blueprint of the proposed mall, a map of the controversial land-fill area, sketches of courtroom proceedings, or a collage of carefully selected magazine pictures can be effective.

Option 3: Slide Show

Ask your teacher to allow you to rummage through that old box of slides in the back cabinet. See if your media specialist will give you permission to go through slide kits owned by the school. Guard borrowed slides with your life. If all else fails, take your own slides. Once you have an assortment before you, choose the ones that reflect the message you want to communicate. Check out a slide projector from the media center. Write your own narration or set your slides to music. Cassette tapes work well; coordination of slides and sound takes patience, so get in plenty of practice before you attempt the slide/tape show in front of an audience.

Option 4: Photographic Documentation

If your classmates don't know about the plight of the elderly on fixed incomes, are unaware of deplorable prison conditions, or are oblivious to the health hazard posed by unauthorized dumping of trash in residential areas, use photographic documentation to jolt them into action. Share your position with pictures. If you're not a photo buff, borrow (or check out from your media center) an inexpensive, easy-to-operate camera. Read the directions carefully. Take more pictures than you need, since all of your pictures may not develop as you had envisioned them. Plan carefully; use long shots, medium shots, and close-ups depending on the effect you want to create. Experiment. Once your pictures have been developed, arrange them to tell your story. Use captions, record a taped narration, or attach a copy of your paper for viewers to glance through.

Option 5: Videotape or Film Documentary

This option is for the serious. Unless you have access to equipment, expertise in videotaping/filmmaking, or are willing to devote yourself to careful study under the watchful guidance of a patient media specialist, this option is not your wisest choice. A documentary involves selecting details, planning a sequence of shots, filming, working with lighting, and editing your product. While it is a time-consuming endeavor, students who have worked through the process claim it to be one of the more creative and enjoyable efforts of their high-school experience. A student-produced film or videotape presentation is a definite audience grabber and dramatizes your issue.

Writer's Workbench 5

The Writer's Guide to Preparing the Bibliography

In Chapter 8 you wrote a source entry for each print resource you consulted. In preparing your bibliography it is necessary to list *only* those resources you actually use in drafting your final paper. Resources include any quotes you use from the people you interviewed. Use this sample bibliography as a guide, unless your teacher asks you to follow another form. ● See the Handbook, pages H-54–H-55 for complete coverage of bibliography.

Bibliography

Conyers, Sarah, "Mayors Talk Back," Our Magazine, Jan. 20, 1985, pp. 20–23.

"An Interview with Outspoken Mayors," Interview with Mayors Sloan, Tate, and Cunningham, Life in Big Cities, Jan. 25, 1985, pp. 60–62.

Sanders, Bill, "Mayor Uses Strong Language," Today, Jan. 3, 1985, p. 1.

Sloan, Kate, Personal Interview, Feb. 4, 1985.

Tate, Sid, Personal Interview, Feb. 5, 1985.

Wilson, Hugh, Personal Interview, Feb. 5, 1985.

Alphabetize your entries by last names of authors/interviewees. If no author is listed, use the first word of the title excluding the words "a," "an," and "the." Single-space individual entries; double-space between entries. Note the pattern for indentation in the model bibliography.

**Getting
It
Right**

You have written your position paper on a community issue, and you have shared this paper in some way with a general audience. Now, check your paper again for accuracy, do any necessary polishing, and pass it in to your teacher, who will evaluate it according to Checkpoint 4 on page 197.

CHECKPOINT 4

1	2	3	4	5

Voice   ×2=

Inconsistent. Your voice won't reach your audience.

Occasional slips into babbling or textbookery. Work for consistency.

Even-handed. Fair. Authoritative.

Support   ×4=

Overuse of "I think" and "I feel."

Some statements unsupported by your evidence.

Strong. Convincing. Well-documented.

Quotations   ×3=

There are none. Look for some good ones.

More or better use of quotes would strengthen this paper.

Imaginative. Effective. Punctuation is correct.

Punctuation   ×2=

Too many serious errors. Use your Handbook or see me.

Only a few slip-ups. Proofread more carefully.

No major errors!

Spelling   ×2=

Five or more errors.

Three errors.

No errors. Good eyes.

Manuscript Form   ×1=

The form weakens your message.

Watch margins and spacing.

Professional looking. Neat and sharp!

Overall Impression   ×6=

Superficial treatment. You were not involved in your topic. See me to review the process.

You've done some good work. More care at each step of the process would improve this piece.

A thorough and convincing piece. Forceful. Convincing.

Publishing
Your Writing

Chapter 10

The Magazine Stand

Where can you get the hottest "inside" story, the latest "how-to-do's", the quickest in-depth reporting, or the most current movie reviews? Which print medium offers escape at the doctor's office, in the school library, on an airplane flight, or beside the grocer's check-out stand? What form of entertainment can you tuck into your back pocket, stash under your arm, toss onto your nightstand, or display on top of your living-room table? Which medium can you collect, clip, compare, and reread whether you're a peanut farmer, a model, a railroad engineer, a sky diver, a teacher, or a business executive? What will amuse you, activate you, or affect you whether you're a senior citizen, a first-grader, a middle-ager, or a teen-ager? If you answered, "MAGAZINES, MAGAZINES, MAGA-ZINES," to these questions, you're among thousands of magazine fans.

The popularity of magazines is no surprise; magazines offer something for everyone. If you're concerned with how to deal with blemishes, you'll find numerous articles illustrating how to have glowing skin. If how to transform the confusion of sweaters, shirts, jeans, boots, blazers, and belts into a "casual layered look" befuddles you, fashion magazines give advice. Whether you're an experienced fisher in search of a "never fails" lure, or you're trying to figure out why your sports idol turned down a million-dollar pro contract, there's a magazine for you.

Spend a few dollars for *Mad*, *Cracked*, or *Crazy* and you'll read jokes about current TV programming, cheap shots aimed at the political scene, and satirical sketches of famous people. Pick up a copy of *Geo* or *National Geographic* and you can take a world tour, experience life in village and jungle, or view scenic splendor. Sacrifice your family's *Audubon* and *Smithsonian* to cut and paste for a class project and your "France—A Land of Contrasts" or your "Plants and Trees I've Known" paper comes to life.

In this chapter you'll explore the magazine market as it reaches out to inform, entertain, and persuade. You'll see how magazines reflect the diversity in American culture and how they attempt to influence the reading public. By participating in exploratory activities you'll discover how magazines persuade readers to buy, support, and accept an infinite number of products, opinions, and ideas.

What is the outlook for the magazine in the 80's? Has television cast a spell impossible to break? Does the magazine appeal to a large audience or to a select few? According to the Ayer Directory of Publications, there are over 9,000 periodicals being published currently—depending on how the experts classify them. A periodical is a magazine; unlike the daily paper, most magazines are published periodically. Of those 9,000 periodicals, 600 are general-interest magazines. How many general-interest magazines can you name? You probably know a large number of them.

The Challenge

Getting
It
Started

In groups of three or four, brainstorm as many magazine titles as you can. Don't limit yourself to general-interest magazines only; name any you can think of. This is brainstorming, so don't worry about accuracy at this point—just get the names down. Ask one group member to record your collective responses.

At the end of 15 minutes, take a look at the types of magazines you've listed. Are all of the magazines on your brainstorm list "general-interest" magazines? Do you see some "specialized" magazines that appeal to a certain type of reader? Obviously, not all magazines appeal to the same audience.

Try creating categories to classify the magazines you brainstormed. Create your own labels for your categories. Consider labels such as: family interest, women's interest, men's interest, kids, teen, news, literary, business, career, technical, gossip. Be as creative as you wish; simply make your labels accurately describe the magazine categories. Make a chart for this activity by placing labels for your categories across the top, and the names of magazines along the left margin. Use a grid to check the appropriate categories for each magazine.

Share your brainstorm list and chart with other groups in the class. How do the efforts of other groups compare? Did other groups list similar or strikingly different magazines? Did they categorize magazines as your group did? Which group generated the most creative labels? Which group brainstormed the largest list of magazine titles? Which list reflects the broadest range of categories?

Checking
It
Out

Reaching into the Magazine Rack

After all this talk about magazines, you may be ready to see some real ones. From the following list of projects, choose one that interests you. These options may be adapted for individual or group use. If none of these appeals to you, create your own and get your teacher's approval.

Getting
It
Started

Option One: Loitering in Waiting Areas

Magazines are everywhere. Waiting areas in places of business—doctor's offices, airports, bus terminals, hotel lobbies, and libraries—invite you to leisurely browsing. Magazines in places of business often reinforce aspects of the business itself or reflect the political perspectives, religious values, interests, or projected images of those running the business. Think of the magazines displayed in your dentist's office, in the waiting area of the local auto-repair shop, or in the lounge of your favorite stereo shop. What types of magazines are displayed there? Why do you think the owner selected those particular magazines? What do you think of the selection? If you were in charge, would you offer the same magazines or choose others? Explain. For this option visit at least five places of business—for example, a local car dealer, an orthodontist, your pet's veterinarian, the outer office of a business executive, an attorney's office. List the magazines you find, and analyze them using the preceding questions.

Option Two: Snooping Around the Stands

Explore the magazine phenomenon by investigating a local magazine stand. Browse around and see what you can learn about magazines from the ways in which they are displayed. Think about these questions:

The pleasure is back

So new.

HOW YOU CAN SAVE 10% OR MORE

1. Which magazines are just below eye level, in the front row? Which magazines get the most visual exposure? Which magazines are difficult to find?

2. Browse through another magazine display at a supermarket or drug store. Look for similarities and differences in the displays. Can you detect any pattern in the organization of the magazines? Can you draw any conclusions about potential buyers in those surrounding neighborhoods? For example, your neighborhood newsstand may display "do-it-yourself" gardening, cooking, and decorating magazines in the front row. The newsstand downtown may prominently display news magazines and selections such as the *Saturday Review*, *Gourmet*, the *New Yorker*, and the *New Republic*. The grocery store's rack where you do your shopping may feature *Woman's Day*, *Family Circle*, *True Confessions*, and *Good Housekeeping* near the checkout stands. See what you can discover from looking at differences in magazine displays around your town.

3. What happens to all the unsold issues? Do they ever have any two-for-one sales at the end of the month? Ask what happens to outdated magazines.

4. What are the best-selling magazines in your neighborhood? Are *People*, *Reader's Digest*, and *TV Guide* among the top sellers? How do the buying trends reflect the needs and reading tastes of the community?

Option Three: Bringin' in the Mags

Investigating, scrutinizing, and making judgments about magazines can best be accomplished by collecting a wide sample of commonly read ones. Join a group of fearless solicitors who want to take on the task of getting magazines for the class to study. Scrounge, buy, or borrow magazines from home, neighbors, and newsstands. Bring them to class and store and display them so all may use them. You can make attractive "file" boxes for them out of heavy-duty laundry soap boxes. Simply cut part of the box away to expose the spine of the magazine, cover the box with contact paper, and file ten to twelve magazines per box.

Option Four: Talkin' to the Readers

Maybe none of these options has stirred you from your desk. You can't get to a newsstand and you don't want to put magazines in soap boxes. You're a creative and resourceful person, but you like to work with people, not mags—good. Somebody needs to interview magazine readers to find out what they are reading and why. Develop an informative survey of five or so questions to ask of peers, family, and immediate neighbors. Questions you may want to include on your survey are: What are the favorite magazines of students in your class? What magazines do they buy regularly? What mags do they subscribe to? Which mags do they save? Are there any magazines they no longer subscribe to? Why did they stop taking that mag? As you try to make some sense of your results of the survey, look to see how male answers differ from female and how older people's responses differ from those of younger readers. Summarize your findings in a chart or graph to be displayed in your classroom.

Reader Profiles

**Getting
It
Down**

Magazine publishers analyze their readers very carefully. They select articles and advertising to develop an image for their magazine. Successful magazines cultivate a distinct and loyal reading public. See what you can learn about the readers of a particular magazine by analyzing the magazine's image. Select three quite different mags, and ask yourself these questions about each:

1. What age group is this mag aimed at? Is it for men or women or teens or family? Is it for people in a specific profession?
2. What assumptions can you make about the economic level, social status, education, and political preference of the readers? What led you to make your assumption?
3. Why is the reader attracted to this magazine? Is the reader interested in thrift, in fantasizing and dreaming, or in the latest information on a specific topic?
4. How are the readers of this mag alike? What common experiences do they share?
5. What can you learn about readers' lifestyles?

Use a jot list to answer these questions. Brainstorm for characteristics of the readers of these mags. Try a short free writing describing the typical reader for each of the mags you have selected. Write your free writing in the first person as though you were the reader. Describe yourself in some detail: your age, what you look like, where you work, what you do with your free time, and why you buy this mag. Read these "reader profiles" aloud to your classmates. See if they can guess which magazine reader you are describing.

Advertising

Magazine advertising is big business. As you were thumbing through magazines to analyze their image and trying to picture the typical reader, you probably stopped more than once to look at an advertisement. Those ads are captivating. Readers can hardly avoid them. You may also have been aware that advertising differed from magazine to magazine. One magazine some students looked at had nine different floor-care products advertised, each claiming to make floors look their brightest. Sports magazines seemed to favor cars, cycles, liquor, and cigarettes.

Advertisements seem to dominate some magazines. One curious class counted pages in several magazines. One popular magazine had 66 pages of ads in their 112 page mag. Another had a whopping 120 pages of ads out of 190 total pages. There was even one with 130 out of 196. Clearly some magazines are more advertising than substance. No doubt some magazines are popular because of their advertising. There are magazines that are catalogues of new looks and fashions. Readers enjoy "shopping" their ads.

The price you pay for your magazine does not cover the production costs of that magazine. The profits come from advertising revenue. Magazines with large circulations can charge higher prices for their ads than those with fewer readers. The magazine advertising market is highly competitive, and the name of the game is "results." Studying advertisers' schemes in popular magazines may reveal some interesting things about our culture.

Appealing Ads

You're probably most familiar with appeals in the form of advertisements. Appeals slide in through humming radios, reach up from slick magazines, leap out from softly illumined screens, and loom down from larger-than-life billboards. Advertising appeals permeate daily life. With soft-sell and hard-sell approaches, appeals flatter, cajole, and seduce.

By now you've possibly learned more than you ever wanted to know about all this, but here's a quick review of ten standard advertising appeals.

Writer's Workbench 1

A Quick Guide to Advertising Appeals

1. The Down Home Approach.   Good ol' boys and good ol' girls are pictured. Plain folks frequently offer home spun wisdom.
2. The Crowd Appeal.   Known as the "bandwagon" approach. Insists that "everybody" is using the brand.
3. The Penny-Pincher Pitch.   Assures consumers that they can save money while spending.

4. <u>The Youth Appeal.</u>   Appeals to our youth-oriented culture. Even older people kick up their heels. Implies that the young-at-heart use the product.

5. <u>The Numbers Game.</u>   Statistics are used convincingly to show off the product's advantages. The statistics of one product are often compared to those of another.

6. <u>The Quality Appeal.</u>   Advertisers remind you that their product is synonymous with quality. Encourages you to stick with a known brand.

7. <u>The Attractiveness Ploy.</u>   Implies this brand can help consumers be more irresistible, more appealing to the opposite sex.

8. <u>The Snob Appeal.</u>   Shows their brand being used by the elite. Subtly suggests consumers can experience the advantages of luxury and wealth.

9. <u>The Star-Struck Appeal.</u>   Features popular stars, sports figures, or other prominent personalities who testify to the product's value.

10. <u>The Humorous Appeal.</u>   Seduces consumers through laughter. Frequently offers little information about the product itself.

While you may be able to recognize and manipulate these appeals, you may not be aware of how audience impacts the advertiser's pitch. No matter what the consumer's social status or economic niche is, humor can be an effective ploy. But the same type of humor will not reach every audience. Advertisers shape their message to suit consumers; they adjust appeals to hook a specific audience. You may want to refer to this guide for your next writing activity.

Uncovering Audience Strategies

Have you ever noticed that every year there's some new fad? Your parents may remember when irridescent polystyrene balls were popular. People attached them to their automobile antennas so that they could locate their cars amid the sea of vehicles in shopping malls. As you may guess, that fad died out once every parked car sported a glowing polystyrene ball. Ask your teacher about hoola hoops or pet rocks.

Advertisers call attention to these excesses of the human spirit—especially around gift-giving seasons. You no doubt remember the year everyone exchanged pocket calculators, t-shirts, gold coins, electronic games, and even ashes from Mt. St. Helens. Advertisers are quick; they rarely miss a trick.

What ads change as the audience changes? Which ads remain the same no matter who the intended audience? What do you make of that? Use this activity to spark your thinking. Follow each step.

A. In groups of three to five, brainstorm a list of current magazines directed at different audiences. It's a good idea to limit your list to popular magazines. Publications aimed at special interest groups tend to limit advertisements to products associated with that interest. (For example, ads for instructional software dominate *Media and Methods*, a magazine directed at educators.)

B. As a group, select at least three ads from three different magazine types.

C. Compare the ads in your groups. Ask a recorder to jot down specifics. Consider questions such as:

    1. How does the advertiser try to hook the audience?

    2. Do advertisers attempt to accommodate audience? How do they do this? (Look at advertising script, colors, scenery, models.)

    3. To what emotions, needs, or concerns does the ad appeal?

    4. How well does the advertiser know the audience? (Refer to your class chart.) Support your response.

D. Review your data. Compile your findings.

E. Pull together findings in a written form. Be certain all group members sign your findings.

F. Transform your class into a Consumer Advocate Council. Ask each group to present its findings to the Council. What are the implications for consumers? Do ads help or hinder the consumer's search for good products?

The Critic

Advertised products sometimes disappoint consumers. They may *subtly* suggest a dramatic change in your life if you purchase and use the advertised product. While advertisers rarely make such claims directly, their ads often suggest a better life. The projected message is, "If you use Brand X toothpaste, you can have two attractive girl/boyfriends hanging on your arm," or "If you use Brand Y shampoo, traffic will grind to a screeching halt while admirers lean out of their vehicles to whistle their approval." In reality Brand X may produce brighter teeth but not a brighter life. Brand Y may clean your hair but won't add sparkle to your life. Some unspoken promises in advertising just never materialize. Consumers who purchase such products hoping to improve their lives are left to wonder why they were so gullible.

Advertisements for movies, books, plays, and record albums can be equally disappointing. Have you ever found yourself in a theater watching a miserable movie billed as "so hilarious that you'll fall out of your seat laughing," but which in reality was so absurd that only your groans kept you awake? You sometimes leave such an experience mumbling phrases such as "rip off," "moronic," or "farcical." Even the recommendations of your friends are not always reliable. After you spend your money, you may realize that your friend's idea of high-level performance is not the same as your own.

Even though the opinions of others don't always match their own, the idea of hearing other people's views appeals to consumers. In fact there are several magazines devoted entirely to providing potential buyers with just those kinds of opinions and ratings: *Bookview*, a monthly which reviews hundreds of books; *Rolling Stone*, a monthly which reviews record albums, concerts, musicians, films, and books; and even *Consumer Reports* which reviews everything from peanut butter to movies to cars. A large number of popular magazines have a "review" section. A review is a critique. When critics review a form of entertainment, they give their criticisms of it. The reviews are often a mix of both positive and negative criticism.

Consumers tend to rely on reviews over advertisements. While ads are written by people paid to make that form of entertainment look good, reviews are written by critics—people with no vested interest in the success or failure of any form of entertainment. Sometimes reviews differ sharply from the advertised promise which attracts the paying audience. As in advertising appeals for products, advertisements for movies, TV programs, concerts, and record albums will assure you that "You can't miss it," "It's the greatest story of the decade," "It's nominated for an Academy Award," and "Don't be the only one who doesn't own this album." According to advertisements, there is no mediocre, tedious, monotonous entertainment. Because reviews are more objective, they are becoming increasingly popular with the public.

SPOTLIGHT

Reviews help consumers make informed judgments about whether they should spend their money or stay at home. Professional critics, people who earn their living by sharing their opinions and judgments, give consumers full benefit of their expertise. By viewing hundreds of films, reading thousands of books, or seeing a remarkable number of concerts, the critic cultivates a sense of value. Popular film critic Gene Shalit wrote this favorable review about the film *Ordinary People*.

Ordinary People

From the film's first moment you know you are on the threshold of something special. The baroque music adapted by Marvin Hamlisch sets the tone of a lush-lawned suburb and we are among ordinary people. They are so sensitively realized by Robert Redford that with this, his first film, he becomes an important director. *Ordinary People* is filled with a wringing pain, the dissolution of a family—a mother obsessed with affluence; a high school son obsessed with the drowning death of his brother; a father struggling to understand his wife and son. . . . You may squeeze your eyes, find your throat strangling, then feel the release of laughter. You will meet these people, know these people, remember these people, these ordinary people who are not so ordinary, in an extraordinary movie.

Gene Shalit

In this review, Mr. Shalit assures potential viewers that they can believe the advertisements for *Ordinary People*. The film, in his opinion, is excellent.

How does the writing "hook" your attention? What kind of support for his opinions does the author use? What do you notice about the language of his review?

Mr. Shalit's piece is an example of a well-written, succinct review. He speaks directly to his audience in an informal, yet precise voice. Good critic-reviewers make every word count. Magazine reviews are short— seldom longer than a paragraph or two and often shorter than 100 words—so reviewers must use their words wisely. Notice that Mr. Shalit's review is not a plot summary. The best reviews keep summary to a minimum. Reviewers suggest the barest outline of the story and instead devote their review to evaluative comments which help audiences make sensible, informed decisions.

Writer's Workbench 2

Reviewing

Your next writing challenge will be to write a review on some entertainment medium—a movie, a concert, an album, a play, or a book. Your review will be targeted for publication in a magazine whose intended audience will be your peers. In Chapter 11 you will publish your own class "mini mags." If your review is a piece you're proud of, you may want to submit it for publication. Here are some additional characteristics of a good review.

A good review is . . .

Honest. A review is one person's opinion. This gives reviewers maximum freedom to tell readers how they honestly feel. Honest reviews don't gloss over flaws or praise the unpraiseworthy. Truthful reviews examine the merits and demerits of a medium in precise language which accurately communicates the critic's views.

Fair. Negative criticism is not the same as an unwarranted personal attack on an artist nor is it unduly harsh or unfounded criticism. To be fair, critic-reviewers specify the problem, then support their criticism with evidence from the medium itself. Fair reviews evaluate a medium in light of its purpose. For example, the reviewer does not expect comedy in a serious drama.

Balanced. A balanced review is tempered. It gives neither wildly extravagant praise nor biting, vicious criticism. The mark of a balanced review is even-handed criticism. In such a review the language itself is balanced and precise.

Thoughtful. The thoughtful review shows evidence of careful consideration. In good reviews it is obvious that reviewers have done their homework. Reviewers often read the book, see the film, or listen to the album more than once. Good reviews replace haphazard or snap judgments with thoughtful evaluation.

Informative. Good reviews get to the point. Informative reviews are two-thirds evaluation and one-third summary. They provide the audience with information that will aid them in making informed decisions.

Memory Makers

By this time in your life you've probably logged a large number of movie, album, and television experiences. You may have chalked up quite a few books, too. Some of you may have attended numerous live concerts if you happen to live near a civic auditorium or a metropolitan center. Some of these entertainment media have touched you; others have long since slipped from memory.

For this activity you will try to recall these memorable entertainment experiences. In your Writer's Notebook make a jot

Getting
It
Down

list of entertainment happenings. List only those you have experienced first-hand. Write down those that stick in your mind because of an outstanding performance or a rotten one, or because of action-packed excitement, or because of an unbeliev-able special effects show. Spend about five minutes listing recent or memorable entertainment experiences.

SPOTLIGHT

Look at this jot list by a student.

Memory-Makers

TV Shows
CHIPS—I'm in love with Ponch!
Lou Grant—true-to-life, realistic stories
Diff'rent Strokes—fights stereotyping and prejudice; helps me keep an open mind
Mork And Mindy—great one-liners, impersonations by Mork
That's Incredible—Dangerous stunts

Albums by
Jackson Browne—a great poet as well as my favorite musi-cian
Earth Wind and Fire—great sound
War—albums leave me searching for peace and quiet!

Films
Ordinary People—I recognized my father in that film.
Breaking Away—my nominee for best movie

Books
Dairy of Anne Frank—moving story
A Teacup Full of Roses—depressing but it made me think
Being There—made me vow to read more, view less
1984—still a classic
After the First Death—sent cold chills down my spine . . . innocence turned evil; evil disguised as innocence.

Renee

Talking It Through

Share with a partner your list of best, worst, and so-so entertainment events. Talk through your list from start to finish. Tell your listener *why* you listed the entertainment extravaganza. Put your listener there. Let your partner see the same film you saw; allow your consultant to read the book through your eyes. Share the reasons behind your views. Discover the happenings you feel strongly about and the ones you're neutral toward. With the help of your consultant, select two or three review possibilities. Choose events you're knowledgeable about. Make sure that at least one of your choices allows you to experience it a second time. Remember that you will be looking for both the good and the less-than-spectacular features. Choose two or three events you'd feel comfortable reviewing. Switch roles and help your partner narrow his or her list.

A Closer View

As you discussed your rationale for feeling as you do, you may have noticed hazy spots or complete blanks in your memory. Fill in the gaps by taking a second, more critical look at the event you selected. Consider the book, film, or television show more carefully. Take a more detached, objective look this time. If your event happens to be the first and possibly only tour through your area by your favorite rock group, try a free writing.

Molding That Memory

In your Notebook develop your jot lists, using them to record impressions and collect support for your views. These suggestions may help you focus your scribbles.

People.   Scrutinize the performance of the characters in the book, the actors on the screen, or the musicians on stage. Do their performances reach you? What are the strengths of the performances? Where could they use some help? How do the performances compare to others in their field? Are there memorable lines spoken or sung? Write them down. Is there an unpardonable blunder? Explain what went wrong. What does the performance remind you of? Explore that.

Action.   Is there a story line? Is it believable? Why do you think so? Can you follow what is happening? Explain what baffles or fascinates you. Is the action fast-paced or sluggish? What can you compare the action to?

Appeal.   What touches you? Does anything put you off? Why? How? Does the event communicate honestly—clearly? Are you haunted by a scene, phrase, or person? Follow that. How did the event make you feel? Was the event worth the time and/or money? Why or why not?

Striking Feature.   When you think of the event, what stands out in your mind? Is there a distinguishing quality or style that makes the event unique? Is there an aspect so poorly handled that it detracts from the event?

Special Effects.   Add to your jot list anything not covered by the preceding categories. Think of both the good and the bad. Comment on technique, craft, language, or anything else that lingers in your mind.

Shaking Out Words of Criticism

Before you begin writing your review, you need to be armed with the ammunition of precise vocabulary. You have much of that language in your own head—all you need to do is some "word shaking." Word shaking is a brainstorming process for shaking words out of your head and onto a chalkboard. As a class, try shaking out a list of words you might use in writing your review. The larger your list, the better it is. When you have shaken as many words as possible, recopy the list and post it as a resource for writing.

What are some of the words you can use to give a favorable opinion of a performance? How about *refreshing, stimulating, engaging, delightful, effective, haunting, powerful, memorable*? Can you think of more?

What if you thought the performance was bad? How about *mundane, disappointing, unimaginative, tedious, monotonous, disastrous, tiresome, sleep-inducing*? Don't stop word shaking until you have emptied the words in your head onto the chalkboard.

Professional critics who write reviews are especially aware of the power and persuasion of the words they use. The reviewers must be concise, yet they must convince readers of their authority and fairness. Good reviewers use words that give the public insight into the entertainment being reviewed; their words must be accurate and direct.

Stretch your vocabulary; don't be satisfied with your first choice of words—look for words that are precise, powerful, and persuasive.

Free Writing a Review

Examine your three developed jot lists. Which list has potential? Which entertainment event would you enjoy reviewing? Which would your audience of peers like to see reviewed? Look at your jot lists and decide on the *one* event you feel comfortable writing about.

Getting
It
Down

With your developed jot list and word-shaking resource of precise words, express your views. Get out your Notebook and sharpen your pencils. Free write a review.

When you finish free writing, review the characteristics of a good review on pages 212–213. How does your review compare? Mull over ways to sharpen your review. Keep the review to no more than 150 words.

Writer's Workbench 3

Dropping Deadweight

Limiting your review to 150 words demands discipline. Ruthlessly stalk deadbeat words. If a word isn't pulling its weight, get rid of it.

Here are some words that can drag down your review.

Sleepers.   Avoid those words which are used so frequently that they tend to put readers to sleep: *good, exciting, nice, bad, boring, stupid, dumb.*

Weasel Words.   Avoid using qualifiers that suck the life out of effective writing: *very, somewhat, pretty, awfully.*

Peat and Repeats.   Avoid needless repetition. Gene Shalit's use of repetition in *Ordinary People*, page 211, is masterful. If repetition is effective, keep it in. If it isn't, get rid of it. Ask a consultant, if you're unsure.

Writer's Workbench 4

Revising the Review

The Hook

Good reviews are compact, intense little packages. A writer can't wait long to get the reader's attention. Good reviewers have mastered the quick opening line or "hook." Look at these effective opening lines:

Allen uses the rhetorical question to involve his readers quickly.

> Are you always putting yourself down? Are you always putting other people ahead of you? Do you often feel low? If you answered "Yes" to any of these questions, *Your Erroneous Zones* is the book for you.
> *Allen Posten, student*

This reviewer uses the sights and sounds of the movie to open the review.

Zap! Crackle! Crash! And all of a sudden you are careening through space to the dangers of a Black Hole.

Jane Henry, student

This reviewer uses a comparison for her opening line.

Watching *Raging Bull* is the cinematic equivalent of ten tough rounds in the ring: it never lets down, never stops pounding and mauling the audience.

Judith Sims, Ampersand

Look at the opening lines of your review. Does it grab the reader? How can you revise that opening to snatch the reader out of the doldrums and into your piece of writing? Experiment with several different openings.

Language

You've already been warned about sleepers, weasels, and repeaters. Check to be sure you have eliminated these culprits. The language of a good review is carefully chosen to create a particular feeling. Read this review by a professional writer Rex Reed:

Fort Apache, the Bronx, is a tough, disturbing, two-fisted look at life in a police precinct in the jungle called the South Bronx. The story is true and the precinct of the title is aptly named because it's like an armed fort. . . . Paul Newman plays a bedraggled cop from a family of policemen—divorced, without ambition, not really a hero—who sees things happening on the crime-filled streets around him he can't morally accept. When the nurse he's dating dies of a drug overdose, he goes on his own rampage to clean up the garbage. The results are brutal, violent and riveting. This raw film rips away the scar tissue from a diseased part of New York City few people ever see. It looks like World War II or III until you realize it's not a movie set, but the actual Fort Apache precinct and the real South Bronx. There's nothing romantic about it; nobody gets whitewashed. The cops don't come out with halos, neither do the poverty-stricken rats and hoods who live there, nor does the city of New York. There'll be lots of angry noise over this one, but when the smoke clears, you'll see Newman in his best role since the old "Hud" and "Cool Hand Luke" days. Warm, funny, cynical and rawhide-rough, Newman, at 56, is the stuff movie legends are made of.

Rex Reed

Point to effective uses of language in this review. How does the writer re-create the mood of the film? What words do you think the writer chose carefully? Work with the language of your review. Experiment with different words from the word-shaking list.

Clincher

Another indispensable element of a clever review is a creative closing line. Try to avoid the "It's wonderful!" or the trite "Don't miss it.", or the "It's horrible: save your money." Look at the concluding lines for ideas:

> ". . . In a season glutted with mediocrity and nice-tries, *Raging Bull* is an extraordinary film."
>
> *Judith Sims*

> ". . . Bring your tissues to this one; it's a real tear-jerker!"

> ". . . this is one of those avoid-paying-fifty-bucks-an-hour-to-hear-the-psychiatrist-tell-you-you're-fine books that's worth reading."

The clincher sums up your expert opinion without simply repeating what you've already said. Avoid the conventional platitudes "wonderful," "marvelous," and "neat." Work for a strong, fresh clincher.

Overall Effect

Checking It Out

Read your completed review aloud several times. Listen carefully. Are there any dead spots in it? What can you cut out or combine? Work to make your review as compact and powerful as you can. Remember, you are working to create an overall effect in your review.

Proofing

Getting It Right

Check carefully to see that all spelling and punctuation problems have been taken care of. Ask a consultant to read over your shoulder as you proof your review. Your teacher will rate your review on the basis of the following Checkpoint.

CHECKPOINT 5

	1	2	3	4	5

Hook   ×3=
Get a hook for this review.	Too slow starting. Reword that opening.	I'm hooked! Good opener.

Language   ×3=
Look out for sleepers, weasels, and repeaters. Back to the word-shaking list.	Imprecise words slipped in. Weigh word choices carefully.	Precise! Imaginative!

Support   ×5=
Opinions unfounded. Support with examples. Back to the jot list.	Some free-floating opinions. Nail down with examples.	Excellent examples. Your opinion is well-documented.

Clincher   ×3=
Was that it? Reread page 220 on the clincher.	Review slowly fades away. Rework clincher.	Creative closing. Good wrap-up.

Punctuation/Spelling   ×3=
Dust off your dictionary and Handbook. See me for help.	A few errors. Proofread more carefully.	No errors. Good work!

Overall Effectiveness   ×3=
Too much summary. Devote more space to evaluative comments.	Criticism is off balance. Temper the review.	Even-handed. Has audience appeal. Well-written.

Chapter 11

Getting Out the Mag

Magazines have long been an important market for professional writers. British novelist Charles Dickens got his start as a writer by selling his fiction to magazines by the page. American authors Edgar Allen Poe, Flannery O'Connor, F. Scott Fitzgerald, and Eudora Welty each began a literary career by publishing in magazines. Publishing has become extremely competitive and few first-line magazines accept unsolicited manuscripts from unknown writers. Beginning writers today look for publishing success in college and university literary magazines such as *Carolina Quarterly* and *Suwanee Review* and in hundreds of "little magazines" with such titles as *The Moonshine Review*, *Clown Wars*, and *Asphodel*.

The purpose of this writing book is not to turn everyone into a professional writer. The rigors of the publishing game are not for the faint of heart, but good writing needs and deserves an audience. You've been asked to share many of your earlier writings both in process and in final form with consultants and classmates. The real pay-off for serious writers is seeing their work in print. Like seeing your face on a television screen or hearing your voice on tape, seeing your writing in print is a vital confirmation that you really are a successful writer. "I know I'm a writer because it says right here, 'written by me.'"

This chapter on how to produce a magazine is designed to give each of you an opportunity to see your writing in print. Two things will become obvious as you work your way through this chapter. Producing a magazine requires careful planning and the cooperative effort of all, and seeing your own writing in print is a uniquely rewarding experience.

This chapter is organized as a step-by-step guide to magazine production. You may wish to read through the entire chapter to get an overview of the whole process before you begin the task. You will note that the process begins with planning and organization, moves to concerns about design, selection, and production, and concludes with details for reproducing your product to share with a wider audience.

Planning

Producing a professional-looking magazine with solid reader appeal will require the talents and cooperation of everyone in your class. The process is doomed to failure if the class follows the standard routine—a few people working like dogs, a few looking on in bemusement, and the remainder doing nothing. A magazine you are proud to have your name on needs contributions from everyone.

The initial tasks for producing a magazine involve some adjustment of the class routine. The suggestions in this chapter presume that your teacher will organize you into groups of five to seven members, with each group producing a separate mag. Your teacher may wish to modify this structure, but the steps will remain essentially unchanged.

Once you have been assigned to a group, you will assume a new identity. You are no longer just any old group of English students; you are a magazine staff. To help you feel more like a staff and to clarify lines of responsibility, begin your staff meeting by assigning and/or volunteering for the following positions:

1. Editor or Co-Editors.   Someone has to be in charge of this operation. The editor must oversee all aspects of the magazine's development. The editor makes tough decisions about what gets in and what gets left out. He or she arbitrates conflicting viewpoints of the staff and seeks to harmonize and bring the staff together. Most editors will find that shared decision-making and a democratic spirit contribute to the active involvement of all. Choose an editor or co-editors who will be comfortable in a leadership role and will respond with enthusiasm to the challenge of producing a magazine.

2. Art Director.   As you will soon see, eye-catching visuals are an important part of many mags. The art director's primary function is to supervise the overall design of the magazine and to direct and approve all visuals. This does not mean that the art director must be an artist-in-residence or a graphics-design expert. He or she should be someone who is enthusiastic about photography, drawing, cartooning, lettering, or graphics, and who is willing to assume responsibility for weaving these visuals throughout the magazine.

3. Proofreader.   You probably conjure up an image of a bald-headed old man with a green plastic eye shade low over his eyes, hunched over

pages of copy in a dimly lit room. Your proofreader need not be old or bald or even own an eyeshade, but he or she should be someone with a keen eye for detail and a thorough knowledge of the standard conventions of printed material. All staff members will be responsible for editing and proofing their own contributions, but the proofreader is responsible for the final copy of the magazine.

4. <u>Printer.</u>   The printer is responsible for the actual duplication process. He or she must work closely with the art director and the editor to insure that design and layout are practical and consistent with the magazine's formula. Someone with secretarial training or experience as a teacher's aide and who knows how to operate the school's duplicating equipment is preferable, but any reasonably interested student can learn the printing game.

5. <u>Binder.</u>   Collating pages and binding the final product is the last step in production. The binder is the first person to view the completed magazine. He or she checks each bound copy to be sure that pages are consecutive and that each magazine copy is complete and free of surface defects. The binder presents the bound copies to the editor and certifies their quality prior to distribution.

6. <u>Contributing Authors.</u>   In a sense all staff members are contributing authors, but there may be members of your group who see themselves primarily as writers. These staff members should be encouraged to spend most of their time reworking favorite pieces and drafting new pieces expressly for the magazine.

Publishing

Anyone who has ever worked on a school newspaper staff knows that the content of school publications must be closely scrutinized. Magazines should be free of offensive words and visuals. Taste and appropriateness supercede even concerns for audience appeal and peer approval. Your teacher will function as editor-in-chief with absolute power to suggest revisions and deletions. Teachers are directly responsible for anything that students publish under school sponsorship. To save you and your teacher embarrassment or frustration, respect your editor-in-chief's decisions.

Choosing a Theme

Your first staff task is to determine the kind of magazine you want to produce. You need to discuss thematic options and arrive at an amicable decision. A small, in-class magazine is easier to produce if you organize articles and graphics around a single topic. You might use "What's happening in . . ." as a way of beginning to consider options. Your staff might think about sports, popular music, school, teen fashions, heroes, people, the community, older citizens, perhaps even a futuristic "What will be happening. . . ." Target your magazine to an audience of your peers, both male and female. Choose your theme based on staff interests, knowledge, and experience. Take time at this point to discuss theme actions carefully. Try to select a theme on which all group members can agree.

FASHION & BEAUTY

58 Great 'TEEN Model Search
65 Put Your Looks Into Action
66 Patty Cherry . . . Drill Team
68 Eliska Krupka . . . Ballet
70 Sippy Woodhead . . . Swimming
72 Kim Stewart . . . Track
74 Time Out for Beauty
76 The Wading Game
78 Look Official! Dress for the Action
82 Suit Your Figure
100 Dear Beauty Editor

FEATURES

10 Too Tired? 10 Causes, 10 Cures
26 Action Report: Top Teen Athletes
33 Shape Up With a Splash
39 Get a Japanese Pen Pal!
42 Special for Nonjocks: Surviving the Fitness Fad
46 Fiction: Forever . . . a short story by Lynn MacDuff

'TEEN INQUIRER

51 Larry Manetti of "Magnum, P.I."
52 Celebrity Mailbox
53 Mariel Hemingway
54 Celebrities in Action
56 'TEEN Talks To: Lou Ferrigno
57 Hollywood Buzz

IN EVERY ISSUE

6 Horoscope
9 We Get
20 Rhyme & Reason
22 Dear Jill
25 Dear Jack
48 Entertainment Potpourri
63 Dear Doctor
94 Flea Mart

Building the "Formula"

Every magazine follows a certain formula from issue to issue which is based on its purpose—to make money, to spread ideas, to do a public relations job, to entertain, to offer solutions for problems, or to inform readers. The formula is the special mixture of articles, opinion, stories, and graphics.

Before you begin planning and putting your magazines together, take a look at the formula of a typical teen magazine (page 226). Read the table of contents and examine the formula of 'TEEN, a magazine which attempts to win teen-age readers. These readers want the latest "inside" tips and advice on achieving a self-confident, wholesome image. Such magazines consistently showcase pieces of writing which speak directly to teens on a variety of topics. One major teen magazine features articles every month on fashion, beauty, food, family relationships, friendships, and teen problems. These articles focus on new trends, the "how-to's," and helpful suggestions for smoothing your personal chaos into a livable survival. *Seventeen* magazine's monthly "mini mag" section often utilizes the interview as a means of sharing interesting people with readers. Look at this interview with a high school English teacher who won the nation's Teacher of the Year Award.

17-SECOND INTERVIEW
This teacher is in a class by herself

Beverly J. Bimes has been teaching English at Hazelwood East High School, in Hazelwood, Missouri, since 1968. But 1980 is special: She was named Teacher of the Year. She tells why students are her favorite subject.

Q. How were you chosen Teacher of the Year?

A. The faculty at my school chose me to represent them at the district level. Then I won the state-wide competition, then became one of four national finalists. Before one of us was declared the winner, our classes were observed, students and members of the community were interviewed, and we teachers had a videotaped interview.

Q. Why is your teaching so special?

A. I've learned how to create a nonthreatening classroom environment. I let my students know I care about them as people: A good teacher not only needs an excellent background in her subject, but she has to be a person who *cares*. And I'm dramatic. Once I taught a lesson in effective communication, and a male teacher and I played a husband and wife at the breakfast table who weren't communicating with each other. I wore a red fuzzy bathrobe and hair curlers. It's hard to feel threatened by that!

Q. How do your writing classes differ from other teachers'?

A. I devise a lot of simulated situations first. For example, I may ask kids to role-play different kinds of people who may be found in a shopping center, then I have them write about how each of them would react to an explosion at the center. This makes the learning experience active.

Q. How have students changed over the years?

A. They're more open now than when I first started teaching: I like that. For instance, as both an exercise in writing and in understanding, my students and I periodically exchange "telegrams"—urgent messages of 25 words or less. They help us communicate quite openly.

Q. How would you define a "Student of the Year"?

A. The same way I described a good teacher: one who cares. Students and teachers aren't so different—they need to grow and learn together.

Q. What's the best part of teaching?

A. The challenge of the classroom. No other job is as exciting, where you walk into a room full of 30 active minds. I have a poster hanging in my classroom that says, "The greatest use of life is to spend it on something that will outlast it." That's what teaching is: an investment in the future.

You may, of course, decide to produce a "specialty" magazine—one which focuses on a single topic rather than a single age group. The table of contents from *Runner's World* illustrates its focus (page 229).

In your magazine, include some pieces of opinion writing. Reviews on films, books, record albums, or show-business personalities may be used. Letters to the editor, editorials, or an advice column give you the opportunity to voice your carefully thought-out opinions.

An important part of any mag's fomula for reaching its intended audience is it graphics. Graphics are the visual appeals which include illustrations, photos, cartoons, special lettering, and advertisements. Look through magazines at home or in your school library to see the various ways these mags use graphics.

Feature articles may be a "people spot," a researched topic, an interview with someone famous or interesting, a sports story, a "how-to-do" article. Your magazine must include at least one feature article.

32 MEN AND WOMEN OF IRON by Jeanette Foster. Three hundred eighty-six participants tested their mettle in the world's most grueling endurance event — Hawaii's Nautilus International Triathlon.

36 SCIENCE SLOWS AGING by Sen. Alan Cranston. The California Democrat, who is also an outstanding masters runner, describes the strides being taken by science to slow the aging process.

41 THE FAD DIET GUIDE by Virginia DeMoss. The regular emergence of new fad diets has become almost as inevitable as death and taxes — and some can be nearly as unpleasant. A guide to help you through the treacherous waters of fad dieting.

48 THE BUDDY STRETCH SYSTEM by Jean Couch. Using a partner can make your stretching more effective and enjoyable.

52 RUNNING AS TRANSPORTATION by William Dunnett. The movement was fueled in New York City by a giant mass-transit strike. In the wake of that shutdown, increasing numbers of New Yorkers — and Americans in general — are hoofing it to work. A report on the run-to-work movement.

56 POSTURE by Dr. Ronald M. Lawrence. Proper posture is a vital component of relaxed, efficient running technique.

60 RW SPECIAL REPORT: ACTIVE SPORTSWEAR FOR THE RUNNER. In a short period, running wear has shaped up beautifully in the areas of comfort, function and fashion. As an important part of the sportswear industry, it has even taken on a new appellation: "active sportswear for runners."

71 A TRANSCONTINENTAL RECORD SEEMED COTTRELL'S DESTINY by Marcia B. Dowling. Stan Cottrell fulfilled a dream by running across the United States in record time.

108 ROAD TO SUCCESS: JACK LA LANNE by David Ryan Williams. America's father of fitness, at 66, sports the body of a fit 20-year-old. In a lively feature, La Lanne reveals the secrets to his eternally youthful appearance.

Most popular magazines include opinion writings such as letters, reviews, an advice column, and occasional guest editorials on some controversial or confusing issue. The following is an example of a guest editorial centering on the question of drafting women. This was written by an 18-year-old who raises some thought-stimulating questions.

Drafting Women: the Ultimate Equality?

This past summer, several million young Americans, born in 1960 and 1961, trudged—some of them reluctantly—to their local post office and registered for the draft, the first registration since 1975. That was just the beginning. In future years, all eighteen-year-olds will be required to file their name with their draft board.

Is there something wrong with this scenario? I think so: Half of the nation's eligible citizens were—and will be—exempt from registration simply because they are women!

I believe the time has come for us to recognize that men and women are equal under the law. I strongly believe that conscription violates certain basic human rights, and I don't find the prospect of war attractive or rational, but I do think it unjust that women—who are making rapid strides in business, industry, sports, and politics—should be exempt from the draft by virtue of their sex.

Not surprisingly, our nation is divided over this issue. Many people claim that women are not suited for military service because of their smaller stature or "emotional makeup." Yet some 150,000 women already capably serve in the U.S. armed forces, and that number is expected to reach 250,000 within the next five years. During World War II, thousands of women served this country in noncombat roles. In addition, women in countries like Israel have traditionally been drafted to serve in both combat and noncombat positions.

Still, the debate continues. Earlier this year, President Carter asked Congress for the authority to register women for the draft. In July, just days before registration began, three federal judges in Philadelphia ruled that because it excluded women, the Selective Service Act was unconstitutional. But the next day, a Supreme Court judge stayed that ruling!

Many politicians, military officials, and ordinary citizens—male and female alike—agree that the conscription of women raises questions that aren't easily answered. For example: Should women be sent into combat, or should they remain behind the scenes, thus freeing more men for battle? If a couple have children, which parent should be drafted? Such questions are serious ones, deserving of careful thought and consideration. But perhaps by examining these issues, we as a people will reevaluate our attitudes toward war in general. If women are drafted, America will have to worry about her daughters as well as her sons. Perhaps then, the prospect of war will seem less glorious, and our leaders will realize how very precious human life is—be it male or female.

I'm sure the controversy surrounding the conscription of women will continue in the years to come. No matter what arguments are raised, however, I think it's unrealistic for women to expect rights only in those areas which benefit them. **If we, as females, are to receive our fair share of all that is good in the world, we must also accept that which is not so desirable. Perhaps that is the ultimate equality.**

Stephanie Hayes

Another regular part of most teen mag formulas is the inclusion of a piece of fiction and a sprinkling of poetry in each issue. These contributions are often solicited from readers. The following poems are from 'TEEN.

Desk Writings

*Sitting in the worn desk
Of the English room,
I read the blurred messages
Of the day before.
The janitors tried to erase them,
Highly disapproving of desk
    writings.
"Who sits here?"
"I'm bored."
"I hate Brad Stevens."
"Did you know—" (too faded)
"Help me!"
And I wonder who
Would put their fears in writing,
Exposing their own souls
For unknown people to see?*
        *Kimberley Carter,
         Ontario, Can.*

Moving Day

The moving van is parked in front
Of our house.
I see our things being carried out
Coldly,
Impersonally,
By men in blue uniforms.
Don't they realize that
Slowly,
Piece by piece,
They're tearing my life apart?
Memories flood my mind . . .
The years I've spent here
Growing,
Learning,
Laughing,
Crying.
Bitterness fills my heart
When I think of leaving.
I stand alone
Amid empty rooms.
A tear
Rolls silently down my cheek.
One solitary drop—
Overflowing with emotion.

LuAnn Okrina, 17,
Rugby, N.D.

Along with the decisions you must make concerning the formula, you will need to consider the personality or mood that you wish the magazine to project. Many popular magazines seek to project a wholesome, positive, upbeat, and pace-setting image. The kinds of writing, illustrations, photos, page layouts, and typefaces all contribute to create a certain feeling—the magazine's personality. Your magazine may focus on a different dimension. Some possible moods you might consider are dignity, excitement, satire, youth, optimism, humor. You might also want to be informative, personal, revealing.

You may find that the personality of your magazine will grow as you are working with it—making editorial choices and selecting pieces of writing.

In addition to the formula and personality of the magazine, a third feature—layout—is an essential part of the planning; it should make the magazine attractive and readable. The layout is the *look* of the magazine: size, shape, arrangement of print and white space, pictures, and design. The Writer's Workbench on page 235 will give you some hints on layouts for your magazine.

Selection

Once you have a vision of the kind of magazine the staff wants, you're ready to begin the search for materials. The magazine staff, under the direction of the editor, is responsible for the magazine's content. You can find materials in three ways—by soliciting contributions from your classmates, by surveying your own Writer's Notebooks, and by creating the materials yourself. There are two ground rules:

1. Each staff member must contribute one piece of his or her writing.
2. Each magazine must contain at least one example from three of these four categories—a feature story, an opinion article, a fictional piece or poem, and graphics.

Look back at the formula section of this chapter (page 227) for suggestions on the kinds of materials included in each category. Follow these steps for the selection process:

1. <u>Solicit materials.</u>   Begin by inviting everyone in your class to contribute to your magazine. If you've taken time to hear each staff's decided-upon theme, it will be easy to solicit materials. These guidelines will keep you out of trouble:
    a. Accept all contributions regardless of how good or bad you think they are.
    b. Tell contributors that their materials will be carefully considered, but don't promise anyone that contributions will be published.
    c. Assure contributors that their materials will not be revised or edited in any way without their prior consent.
    d. Keep all your options open.
2. <u>Survey your Writer's Notebooks.</u>   Chances are that someone on your staff has already written a good piece related to the magazine's theme. Does anyone have an article that has promise, but that needs a little revision? Does reading through the Writer's Notebook give anyone inspiration for a new piece?
3. <u>Create your own materials.</u>   Your editor can determine the gaps in contributions and offer options to staff members. Volunteer for what you want to create, but be willing to work on other sections as well.

Once all the materials are in, you'll be ready to determine what will be in the magazine. As a staff, share contributions. Remember that good pieces can be edited if they're too long or reworked by the contributing author to reflect more closely the magazine's theme. Your editor will ask contributing authors to revise their materials, or he or she may offer to do that job for the writer. If authors do the revising themselves, editors can give broad suggestions, leaving the detailed decisions to contributing authors. If writers turn over their piece to the editor to revise, final decisions belong to the editor. In any case contributing authors have the option of accepting the editor's suggestions or of withdrawing their pieces from consideration.

When you review materials, keep your agreed-upon decisions about formula and personality clearly in mind. Evaluate contributions against these criteria. Make final decisions about inclusion by means of staff vote or editorial decree.

Production

Production involves the hands-on process of putting the magazine together. Producing the magazine includes shuffling materials into an eye-appealing layout, making sure that all materials have bylines or credits, compiling a table of contents, typing the magazine in its final form, proofreading the magazine, and designing a cover. After the magazine is checked by your editor, he or she submits the magazine to the editor-in-chief for final approval.

Writer's Workbench

The Layout

In the magazine business the word *design* can be either a verb or a noun. When you select a formula, personality, and look for your magazine, you design (verb) the magazine; you see it in your mind's eye. When you transfer that vision onto paper, you create the design (noun). Creating the design or magazine layout is a critical step. It gives you a chance to make mistakes without embarrassing consequences. If you make a mistake in the layout stage, you correct the error *before* the printer immortalizes your blunder.

The layout is a mock-up of your magazine pages. The layout pages, called dummy sheets, are lined off to indicate the exact page size. We suggest you use 8½ × 11-inch pages. Dummy sheets are often preprinted forms, but large sheets of graph paper work well. Line off 8½ × 11-inch spaces to represent actual pages. The space around that area may be used for notes or directions to the typist.

Here is a sample dummy sheet before layout.

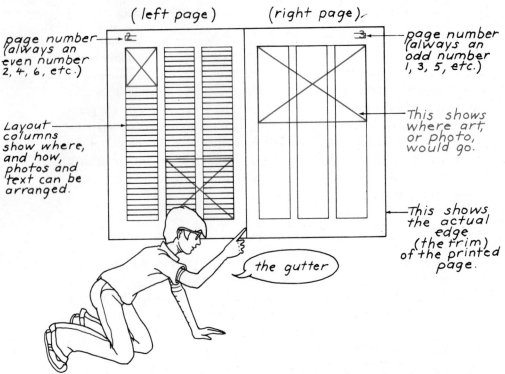

(left page)   (right page)

page number (always an even number 2, 4, 6, etc.)

page number (always an odd number 1, 3, 5, etc.)

Layout columns show where, and how, photos and text can be arranged.

This shows where art, or photo, would go.

This shows the actual edge (the trim) of the printed page.

the gutter

Laying out your materials is a time-consuming process but the result is a well-organized, visually appealing format, free of errors. The layout is a discovery process. Explore the possibilities of design. Enhance your magazine's formula, personality, and looks by some patient experimentation. Laying out your mag can be as simple or as complex as you wish. On the simplest level, the art director blocks out space for articles and visuals, and draws lines where print belongs. A more complex but worthwhile method is the paste-up. In the paste-up all print material is typed, then shuffled around until just the right arrangement emerges. Only when everything is just so are materials pasted.

Although experimentation and trusting your own intuitions will be the most reliable guide next to a design course, here are some pointers to keep in mind.

1. Organization.   Before you organize the magazine, gather your materials. You'll need pencils, erasers, rulers, dummy sheets, and the magazine's contents. Find a large, long work surface. A cafeteria table would be best, but a clean floor will do in a pinch. Arrange your dummy sheets in a row. Place all materials to be included beside each spread. A *spread* is two dummy sheets side-by-side. The spread represents the open magazine page as the reader sees it. Order your dummy sheets along the table in groups of spreads.

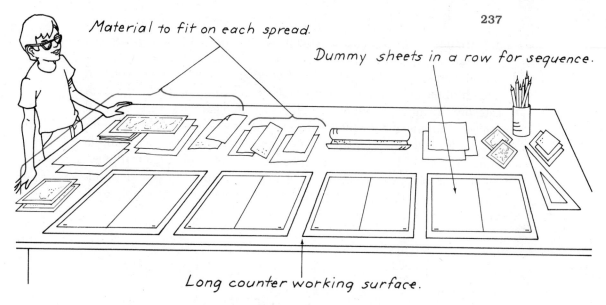

Material to fit on each spread.

Dummy sheets in a row for sequence.

Long counter working surface.

2. <u>Flow.</u>   Visualize your magazine as a continuous flow. Resist the temptation to work on one page at a time. Instead work from start to finish on each contribution. Think in terms of spreads. That forces you to see pages in horizontal units—just as readers see them. If an article runs three dummy pages, stick with it until you're satisfied with the arrangement.

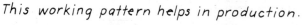

This working pattern helps in production.

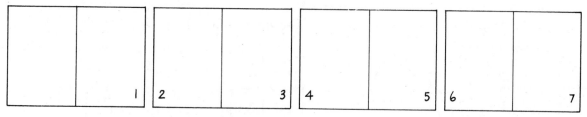

It would be better to think of them as flowing, folded space.

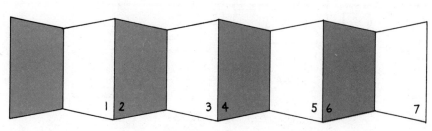

The reader sees them this way.

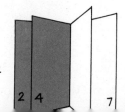

237

3. Arrangement.   Some arrangement decisions are common sense. For example, graphics illustrating articles belong on the same page or spread with those printed materials. Ordering materials is up to you and your art director. You may decide to cluster all contributions under each category—features, opinions, fiction/poetry, and graphics. Perhaps you'll opt for an arrangement which alternates examples of each. The possibilities are limited only by your imagination and your magazine's formula and personality. In many cases the content itself will suggest arrangement. In experimenting with arrangement, take time to consider contrasts. Sharp contrasts can often be effective. Here are some examples of arrangements which depend on contrast.

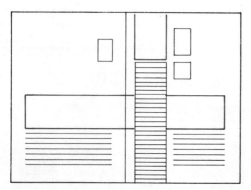

Small type contrasted with large type.

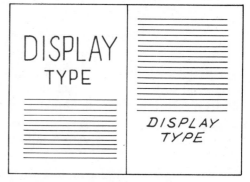

Regular type and display type

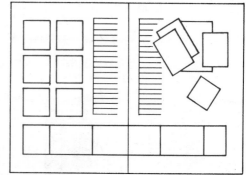

Horizontal / vertical

Regular / irregular

4. <u>Columns.</u>   There is no hard and fast rule for column width. Use your own judgment but be consistent with widths throughout. Wide columns suggest a quiet grace and a subdued quality, while narrow margins suggest insistence or urgency.

Stick with two or three columns for each page. On 8½ × 11-inch pages, four columns give a crowded appearance. Words tend to blend together; columns spill into each other. Unless you are purposely trying to create a frenzied, scrunched-up look, stick to two or three columns.

5. <u>Margins.</u>   Left margins should be perfectly even. By setting margin stops on your typewriter, you can be sure left margins will be absolutely even. Right margins are more difficult. Settle for rough approximations of even right margins. Keep your eye on the right margin as you type to be sure words don't go over into adjacent columns. One final word about margins: Leave extra room at the inside margin of all pages to accommodate stapling or other means of binding.

6. <u>Page Numbers.</u>   Assign page numbers to all pages, beginning with page one. All pages on the right contain odd numbers; pages on the left receive even numbers.

7. <u>Simplicity.</u>   It is far better to have a well-designed simple layout than a poorly executed complex one. Simplicity catches the reader's eye. It invites audience attention and saves wear and tear on frazzled nerves.

8. <u>Cover Design.</u>   The covers of professional magazines are designed to get you to buy the magazine. They may be designed with clever invitations to the material inside or they may be provocative or simply beautiful. Designing the cover for your magazine may be the most creative venture of your staff. You are limited by materials available and the personality and content of your magazine; but beyond that, anything goes.

Since you want your magazine to be handled and passed from reader to reader, choose a cover medium that is durable. Standard duplicating paper is too light weight to withstand much traffic. Some options you might consider include construction paper, file folders, card stock, tagboard or posterboard, plastic covers, shelf-paper over cardboard. Survey your school to see what's available first. Check with the art department and the school secretary. Do some investigative work before you run out and spend money. Good looking durable covers can be fashioned from inexpensive materials.

Develop several sketches of possible cover designs, soliciting advice and opinions from the entire staff. The name of your magazine should be displayed on the cover, with story leads or enticing printing suggesting what is inside the magazine.

You might consider silk screening or pasting a photograph on the cover. You may want to keep it simple, using colors and geometric designs. Printing may be done by hand, pasted on, or you may use some more imaginative method such as polystyrene printing. Carve your design on a sheet of polystyrene. Roll paint over the raised portion, and place your cover against the "inked" surface. You may use the same method with other materials, such as cork, linoleum, or wood blocks.

When your covers are finished and dry, you may wish to laminate them with clear plastic. See if your school media specialist has the equipment. Another alternative is to seal your finished cover with clear contact paper. This is sold by the foot at variety and department stores and is a satisfactory substitute for laminating. If you are using contact paper, lay your cover onto the sticky side of the plastic. Trim excess contact paper, and voilà!—a durable cover.

Reproduction: Printing

The reproduction of your magazine will be dictated by equipment available at your school. Most schools have ditto or mimeograph machines for inexpensive printing. Each machine requires slightly different stencils or masters, so be sure you have been briefed thoroughly on procedures before you begin.

Some schools have photocopy and heat transfer duplication equipment which can greatly simplify the printer's job, but these processes are more costly.

If your school has a graphic-arts department, a print shop, or offset or lithograph equipment, you might check with the person in charge. These printing processes can give your magazine a very professional look.

Since available equipment and policies regarding student use of school printing equipment vary widely from school to school, you should familiarize yourself with your own school regulations. Use school equipment carefully. Clean up when you have finished. Report any problems to the person in charge.

Collating and Binding

After you have the printed pages, scrutinize each one carefully. Check to see that the copy is sharp and free from any distracting marks or blemishes. Find a quiet place with lots of table space. Lay out your pages in consecutive order. Check and recheck page order. Make up one magazine at a time, walking from page to page. Before you staple or bind the magazine, make one final check to be sure no pages are missing, out of order, or turned the wrong way.

Bind the magazine with two or three staples along the left margin. If your cover is of heavy material, you may need a heavy-duty stapler. You might consider binding the stapled edge with plastic electrician's tape or colored plastic tape.

This final stage of production deserves the same care and concentration that you have given all other stages. Don't wait until the last minute. Take the time to do a first-rate job.

Process Checklist

Copy this checklist, and use it to keep track of your progress.
1. Planning:
   Magazine theme selected
   Staff roles assigned

2. Design:
   Formula and personality agreed upon
   General look or format envisioned

3. Selection:
   At least one piece contributed by each staff member
   Examples of at least three of the following: feature article, opinion article, fiction piece or poem, and graphics

4. Production:
Cover design, table of contents, credits
Layout completed
Final type proofed and ready for duplicating
Final copy approved by editor-in-chief

5. Reproduction:
Magazine reproduced in multiple copies, bound, collated, and ready for distribution

Take time to look at the Checkpoint at the end of this chapter to see how your editor-in-chief will evaluate your efforts.

CHECKPOINT 6

1	2	3	4	5

Audience Appeal   ×3=

It is not exactly clear who your audience is.

Some selections of questionable interest to your audience.

Interesting for both male and female.

Focus on Theme   ×3=

Theme is difficult to understand. More careful selection of articles would help.

Theme not fully developed.

Unified. All parts contribute to the whole.

Layout   ×5=

A bit haphazard. Did you work carefully on dummies? Back to the drawing board.

Take a few risks. See the Workbench on page 235.

Good design, and purposeful use of white space. Effective two-page spreads.

Visually Pleasing   ×3=

Cluttered, or distracting graphics. Keep it simple.

Neatly done. A more attractive cover and/or graphics would help.

Eye catching. Attractive. Inviting. Graphics effective.

Free from Error   ×3=

Too many errors. Needs careful proofreading.

A few errors mar an otherwise solid effort.

No errors. Well done.

Cooperative Group Effort   ×3=

No evidence of a good group effort.

Seem to have worked well together. A few freeloaders.

Cohesive, productive magazine staff.

Putting Your Writing to Work

Chapter 12

Describing and Summarizing

"Sue, have you been thinking some more about what you want to do after graduation?"

"I don't know for sure, Mom. I still think I might like to try being a flight attendant."

"That might be a good idea. I wonder how much money they make."

"I hear the pay is pretty good."

"Do you have to go to college or take some special courses to be a flight attendant?"

"I don't know. Guess I'd better find out, huh?"

Sue's conversation with her mother is like many that take place every day. Parents want their children to think of the future, and most want to help them find rewarding careers. Some offer advice. Most feel they should let their sons and daughters determine their own careers.

This chapter is meant to help you in two ways. It will help you find information about careers you might be interested in, and it will help you prepare a detailed description of one specific career which you think has potential for you. Since each member of your class will be writing a description of a job and sharing it with all of you, you will have access to many descriptions just in case you wish to investigate other possibilities.

This chapter works with the next in helping you look at possible occupations. While this chapter helps you look at jobs and career patterns, the next will help you look at yourself in a career. When you finish the next chapter, you will have completed a résumé—a summary of your qualifications for a particular occupation.

Preferences

What job possibilities have you thought of? Did you know there are more than ten thousand possible jobs? You have probably considered only jobs you know well, jobs friends or relatives hold, or ones you see in your community. What about all the others?

The *Dictionary of Occupational Titles* is a publication of the U.S. Government Printing Office. It contains a very complete listing of available jobs. Most school counselors' offices and many libraries have copies.

There are twelve major headings in the DOT, and they are listed here with short explanations. Perhaps this list will give you some ideas for occupations you have not considered before.

1. <u>Artistic.</u>   Appropriate if you have "an interest in creative expression of feelings or ideas. You can satisfy this interest in several of the creative or performing arts fields. You may enjoy literature. Perhaps writing or editing would appeal to you. You may prefer to work in the performing arts. You could direct or perform in drama, music, or dance. You may enjoy the visual arts. You could become a critic in painting, sculpture, or ceramics. You may want to use your hands to create or decorate products. Or you may prefer to model clothes or develop acts for entertainment."

2. <u>Scientific.</u>   Appropriate if you have "an interest in discovering, collecting, and analyzing information about the natural world and applying scientific research findings to problems in medicine, the life sciences, and the natural sciences. You can satisfy this interest by working with the knowledge and processes of the sciences. You may enjoy researching and developing new knowledge in mathematics. Perhaps solving problems in the physical or life sciences would appeal to you. You may wish to study medicine and help humans or animals. You could work as a practitioner in the health field. You may want to work with scientific equipment and procedures. You could seek a job in research or testing laboratories."

3. <u>Plants and Animals.</u>   Appropriate if you have "an interest in activities to do with plants and animals, usually in an outdoor setting. You can satisfy this interest by working in farming, forestry, fishing, and related fields. You may like doing physical work outdoors, such as working on a farm. You may enjoy animals. Perhaps training or taking care of animals would appeal to you. You may have management ability. You could own, operate, or manage farms or related businesses or services."

4. Protective.   Appropriate if you have "an interest in using authority to protect people and property. You can satisfy this interest by working in law enforcement, fire fighting, and related fields. You may enjoy mental challenge and intrigue. You could investigate crimes or fires. You may prefer to fight fires and respond to other emergencies. Or (you) may want more routine work. Perhaps a job in guarding or patrolling would appeal to you. You may have management ability. You could seek a leadership position in law enforcement and the protective services."

5. Mechanical.   Appropriate if you have "an interest in applying mechanical principles to practical situations using machines, hand tools, or techniques. You can satisfy this interest in a variety of jobs ranging from routine to complex professional positions. You may enjoy working with ideas about things (objects). You could seek a job in engineering or in a related technical field. You may prefer to deal directly with things. You could find a job in the crafts or trades, building, making or repairing objects. You may like to drive or to operate vehicles and special equipment. You may prefer routine or physical work in settings other than factories. Perhaps work in mining or construction would appeal to you."

6. Industrial.   Appropriate if you have "an interest in repetitive, concrete, organized activities in a factory setting. You can satisfy this interest by working in one of many industries that manufacture goods on a mass production basis. You may enjoy manual work—using your hands or hand tools. Perhaps you prefer to operate or take care of machines. You may like to inspect, sort, count, or weigh products. Using your training and experience to set up machines or supervise other workers may appeal to you."

7. Business Detail.   Appropriate if you have "an interest in organized, clearly defined activities requiring accuracy and attention to details, primarily in an office setting. You can satisfy this interest in a variety of jobs in which you can attend to the details of a business operation. You may enjoy using your math skills. Perhaps a job in billing, computing, or financial recordkeeping would satisfy you. You may prefer to deal with people. You may want a job in which you meet the public, talk on the telephone, or supervise other workers. You may like to operate computer terminals, typewriters, or bookkeeping machines. Perhaps a job in record keeping, filing, or recording would satisfy you. You may wish to use your training and experience to manage offices and supervise other workers."

8. Selling.   Appropriate if you have "an interest in bringing others to a point of view by personal persuasion, using sales and promotional techniques. You can satisfy this interest in a variety of sales jobs. You may enjoy selling technical products or services. Perhaps you prefer a selling

job requiring less background knowledge. You may work in stores, sales offices, or in customers' homes. You may wish to buy and sell products to make a profit. You can also satisfy this interest in legal work, business negotiations, advertising, and related fields found under other categories . . ."

9. <u>Accommodating.</u>   Appropriate if you have "an interest in catering to the wishes and needs of others, usually on a one-to-one basis. You can satisfy this interest by providing services for the convenience of others, such as hospitality services in hotels, restaurants, airplanes, etc. You may enjoy improving the appearance of others. Perhaps work in the hair and beauty care field would satisfy you. You may wish to provide personal services such as taking tickets, carrying baggage, or ushering."

10. <u>Humanitarian.</u>   Appropriate if you have "an interest in helping individuals with their mental, spiritual, social, physical, or vocational concerns. You can satisfy this interest by work in which caring for the welfare of others is important. Perhaps the spiritual or mental well-being of others concerns you. You could prepare for a job in religion or

counseling. You may wish to help others with physical problems. You could work in the nursing, therapy, or rehabilitation fields. You may like to provide needed but less difficult care by working as an aide, orderly, or technician."

11. Leading-Influencing.   Appropriate if you have "an interest in leading and influencing others by using high-level verbal or numerical abilities. You can satisfy this interest through study and work in a variety of professional fields. You may enjoy the challenge and responsibility of leadership. You could seek work in administration or management. You may prefer working with technical details. You could find a job in finance, law, social research, or public relations. You may like to help others learn. Perhaps working in education would appeal to you."

12. Physical Performing.   Appropriate if you have "an interest in physical activities performed before an audience. You can satisfy this interest through jobs in athletics, sports, and the performance of physical feats. Perhaps a job as a professional player or official would appeal to you. You may wish to develop and perform special acts such as acrobatics or wire walking."

Sue's idea for a career as a flight attendant may be a good one for her. It would be listed under item 9 in the list of occupational categories. Sue would probably find it useful to consider related jobs in this area such as waitress, cashier, hairdresser, social director in a hotel, or barber. Because this area involves an interest in serving others, she might also want to consider jobs under item 10, such as nursing, physical therapy, counseling, aide work in a hospital or retirement center, or social work.

Many sales positions (category 8) also require close one-to-one relationships. Sue should probably consider jobs in that category as well.

What other jobs are also in each of the twelve categories? In your *Writer's Notebook*, jot down at least five jobs under each of the twelve categories. When you finish, compare your list with those of your classmates. Add jobs to your lists as they come up in the discussion if they interest you.

Getting It Started

Discuss the jobs you have listed with some of your classmates. If a job a classmate has listed seems particularly interesting to you, ask him or her to give you additional information about it.

Checking It Out

After you have examined your list for interesting jobs, select five which you would like to explore further. They might all be in the same occupational interest group; they might be under different groupings.

Information Needed

What information might someone interested in applying for a job want? Among the possible questions might be: What are the qualifications for this job? What kind of work would I be doing? How much does the job pay?

SPOTLIGHT

You can get some of this information from the *Dictionary of Occupational Titles*. Here are some job descriptions from the DOT which illustrate the kinds of information included in that source.

099.227-010 CHILDREN'S TUTOR (dom. ser.)
Cares for children in private home, overseeing their recreation, diet, health, and deportment: Teaches children foreign languages, and good health and personal habits. Arranges parties, outings, and picnics for children. Takes disciplinary measures to control children's behavior. Ascertains cause of behavior problems of children and devises means for solving them. When duties are confined to care of young children, may be designated CHILDREN'S TUTOR, NURSERY (dom. serv.)

159.041-014 PUPPETEER (amuse. & rec.)
Originates puppet shows, designs and constructs puppets and moves controls of puppets to animate them for entertainment of audience: Writes or adapts script for use in puppet theater. Sketches designs for puppets based on script. Constructs hand, string, rod, and shadow puppets from materials, such as wood, papier-mache, styrofoam, and wires, using handtools and machine tools. Sews clothing for puppets by hand or machine. Animates puppets, using string, wire, rod, fingers or hands from position above, below, or at level with stage. Talks or sings during performance to give illusion of voice to puppets.

195.227-014 RECREATION LEADER *(social ser.)*

Conducts recreation activities with assigned groups in public department of voluntary agency: Organizes, promotes, and develops interest in activities, such as arts and crafts, sports, games, music, dramatics, social recreation, camping, and hobbies. Cooperates with other staff members in conducting community wide events and works with neighborhood groups to determine recreation interests and needs of all ages. Works under close supervision of RECREATION SUPERVISOR (profess. & kin.). Cooperates with recreation and nonrecreation personnel when in agency setting, such as settlement house, institution for children or aged, hospital, armed services, or penal institution.

207.685-014   PHOTOCOPYING-MACHINE OPERATOR (clerical)
Tends duplicating machine to reproduce handwritten or typewritten
matter: Places original copy on glass plate in machine. Places blank
paper on loading tray. Sets control switch for number of copies.
Presses button to start machine which transfers image of original
copy onto blank paper by photographic and static electricity process.
May clean and repair machine. May receive payment for duplicate
copies. Important variables may be indicated by trade name of machine tended.

379.267-010   WILDLIFE CONTROL AGENT (gov. ser.)
Controls animal population in geographical district and investigates
crop and property damage claims caused by wildlife: Conducts on-
site surveys to estimate number of birds and animals, such as deer,
pheasant, and mountain fox in designated areas and availability of
game food and cover. Recommends changes in hunting and trapping
seasons and relocation of animals in overpopulated areas to obtain
balance of wildlife and habitat. . . . Performs duties of wildlife agent
during hunting season. Gives talks to civic groups, school assemblies
and sports organizations to disseminate information about wildlife
and department policies.

Go through some of these job descriptions. How much of the information fits the facts you want to know about your job? Discuss the
information available in the DOT. What other sources will you have to
tap in order to find out what you need to know before you can make a
decision about that job? Look at the following list of items most often
found in a job description.

1. Personal requirements.   Are there special physical requirements
    such as super strength? Is special education or training necessary?
    Does the job call for a lot of mental ability, ability with words, with
    math?
2. Work performed.   What are the duties of persons who hold this
    job?
3. Rewards.   What salary is usually paid at the beginning? Does the
    pay increase with time, or is promotion to another job necessary in
    order to get a higher salary? Are there other rewards or benefits in
    addition to the salary?
4. Employment future.   Will there be openings in this field in the
    future, or will this job die as society advances?

5. <u>Advancement.</u>   What are the opportunities for promotion? What jobs might a person be promoted to?
6. <u>Work place.</u>   Where is this work done? What are the working conditions?
7. <u>Licenses or credentials.</u>   Are there special licenses or diplomas required? Is union or association membership expected or required?

Add to this list any other facts you would want to know about a job, and write your list in your Writer's Notebook. Share your additions with your classmates to be sure you have not omitted any important points. Add to your list as necessary.

Getting It Started

Collecting Information

Using the elements of a job description from this book and those you have added, make up a sheet like the following for each of the five jobs you have selected.

Getting It Down

Job Description Information

Personal requirements
Work performed
Rewards
Employment future
Advancement
Work place
Licenses or credentials
(Add to this list, if you wish.)

Sources

In order to gather fairly complete information about each of your five jobs, you will have to use several sources. While you may find complete information on a single job in one book, it is doubtful that you will find complete information for all your jobs there.

Brainstorm with your classmates possible sources of information for your job descriptions. Then list these sources in your

Writer's Notebook. Individuals who already hold such jobs are often a good source.

Writer's Workbench

Using Clauses, Phrases, and Single Words in Sentence-Combining

In an earlier Workbench, you combined sentences to include clauses, phrases, and single words. In this sentence-combining Workbench, you will use all three methods. If you are unsure of the clues, go back to the earlier Workbench on page 78.

1. Diets can cause problems.
   The problems are <u>fatal</u>.
   The problems are <u>associated with the heart</u>.
   The diet is <u>protein</u>.
   The protein is <u>liquid</u>.

2. The diet has caused patterns in three people.
   The patterns are <u>abnormal</u>.
   The patterns are <u>associated with a heartbeat</u>.
   The people were being studied by a team.   (who)
   The team was for <u>research</u>.

3. The three people developed the heartbeats.
   The people were women.   (who)
   The women's ages were 21, 29, and 49.   (, and whose ,)
   The heartbeats were <u>irregular</u>.
   They were on the diet.   (after)
   The diet was <u>liquid</u>.
   The women were on the diet <u>for forty days</u>.
   The forty days were <u>approximate</u>.   (-ly)

4. The diet ended.   (When)
   The patterns ceased.   (,)
   The patterns were <u>abnormal</u>.

SPOTLIGHT

Gathering Information

You have had a sample of an incomplete job description from the *Dictionary of Occupational Titles*. Interviews also present possible problems. Unless you structure your interviews carefully, you may come away with a lot of information you don't need and a lot of questions unanswered. The following is a transcription of a job description given by a ticket-taker in a movie theater. Notice how incomplete it is.

"I work in a place with two movie theaters. Taking tickets for one theater isn't so bad, but when you've got two you're responsible for, it's tough. We stagger the starting times so most of the people are in the one theater before we let them start coming into the other one. That makes it a little easier. And the manager helps me sometimes. But I'm usually on my own.

"I heard that thirty years ago people didn't come just at the beginning of a show, but they'd walk in anytime and then stay through the movie until the part where they came in. That would sure make it a lot easier for a ticket-taker.

"Basically, it doesn't seem like I do much. I just stand at the door and take tickets as people go by. But when you've got 400 people to get through a door in ten minutes, there's a lot of pressure. You've got to watch to see that nobody sneaks in. Boy, you'd be amazed at how many things people try.

"The old 'slide the phony under the good ticket' trick is still tried a lot. Lots of times when couples come through, one person will give me both tickets, usually one on top of the other. I've gotten to be able to feel the thickness of tickets so I know if there are two or not. But some people try to pass phony tickets that way. They make up a fake, using the same kind of paper as the tickets, cut just the same way as the tickets and even the same color. Usually there is some kind of printing on the fake, too. I've learned to look at *every* ticket. One guy had his whole family here one day and tried to pass off six phonies under one real ticket! The boss gives me a $10 bonus every time I catch a phony.

"There are kids who still try to sneak under the ropes when there's a crowd coming out. And some try to get in the fire doors, although the boss had alarms put on them last week, and that should stop that.

"My job gives me some free time so I can go up in the projection booth and watch the projectionist load the film. Things are pretty automatic up there, so there's not much to do except watch for problems.

"Some day I might want to try running a projector. They say that's one of the things every theater manager should be able to do just in case the projectionist gets sick or something. I want to be a movie theater manager some day. I really like the idea of bringing entertainment to people, and movies do that for us today."

Earl J.

What additional information should you get from this individual? Go through your list of information elements and write questions you could ask Earl which would give you the information you want about his job.

Gathering Information

Using the elements which you have noted in your Writer's Notebook and the sources you have brainstormed, complete a data sheet (page 255) for each of the jobs you have identified. Try to provide information for each of the elements for each job. Note the sources of your information so that you can return to them if you need additional information later.

**Getting
It
down**

SPOTLIGHT

A student completed a Job Description Information sheet for "Photocopying-Machine Operator" as follows:

Job Description Information

1. *Personal requirements.*   Must stand a lot (interview). Have to have some mechanical ability (*The Clerk's Handbook*). Can go to school at company's expense (interview).

2. *Work performed.*   Feed paper into machine, put blank paper in, fix machine when it doesn't work or call repair shop if too bad, write down number of copies and account to be charged (interview).

3. *Rewards.*   Pays minimum wage, no raises (interview). The only way to get more money seems to be by changing jobs. Mail clerk may be a possibility.

4. *Employment future.*   It looks like this job will be around for a while. The only change may be if machines change, and they'll probably still need operators (interview).

5. *Advancement.*   There don't seem to be opportunities for promotion, but if there is a lot of copying in a business, a person might be able to supervise all the copy machine operators (interview). Chances don't seem too good now.

6. *Work place.*   I saw seven copy machines being used, and all were in separate rooms close to business offices. One was next to the mail room.

7. *Licenses or credentials.*   None are required (interview).

Karen M.

Notice that Karen used information from an interview and from a visit to a place where a photocopying machine was being used. One printed source, *The Clerk's Handbook*, helped her to discover the skills necessary for doing the job.

Checking It Out

When you have finished your five Job Description Information sheets, share them with classmates. Have your classmates check to see that you have complete information so that they feel they know something substantial about the job after reading your notes. If the information is not sufficient, return to your sources and add material as necessary.

Making a Job Brochure

Getting It Down

From the five jobs you have researched, choose the one that interests you the most. It may be work you would like to do when you finish your education, or work you might do for the summer or during the school year. It is important that you choose what appeals to you.

What would a person want to know about a particular job? You have already gone through a process in which you have looked for information on at least seven areas, and you have added some important items to that list. Are there other more specific facts that you want to know about a job? Would you want to know in what part of the country or world you would have to live in order to have a particular job? Would you have to give up anything in order to take this job? What if the job requires a lifestyle quite different from the norm? Maybe you would like to know what things about this job make a person happy.

Put yourself in the "audience" for a few minutes. Jot down in your Writer's Notebook any facts that you would like to know about a job. Just use single words or phrases if you wish. Next, ask a classmate to go over your list to see whether it is complete, then add any necessary points.

Format.   Think about the format of an attractive brochure about a job. Put yourself in a potential employer's shoes as you think of this. You want your brochure to be attractive, telling prospective employees favorable facts about the company. You want the brochure to inform prospective employees accurately. You also want the brochure to attract top-notch applicants to the job.

Look for some brochures in your counselor's office or in businesses or employment offices in your community. Look at the formats. Perhaps you will choose one of those formats; perhaps you can improve on them.

Discuss this format decision with a classmate. Consider the image your brochure will convey, and decide on one you feel fits your imaginary company and the particular job that is available.

Copy.   Once you have decided on a format, prepare copy (written material) for the brochure. Keep two factors in mind as you write this brochure:

1. Your audience and the information they need,
2. The purpose of the brochure—to present an attractive image and a factual description of the job and the company.

Design.   In order to produce a brochure which meets these requirements, you will have to make it attractive. That means you will have to consider the possibility of art, of different sizes of print, and of spacing. Look at some examples of brochures and select the best features from them or, if you wish, be creative and make up something original. Just remember your audience and the purpose of the brochure.

~~~~~~

When you have roughed out your copy and your design, share your draft with a classmate or two. Get their reactions to your ideas. Have them consider the following:

**Checking
It
Out**

1. Does the copy answer the questions which an applicant might have about this job?
2. Does the copy present factual and complete information?
3. Is the design attractive? Does it relate to the copy?

~~~~~~

**Getting
It
Right**

Consider your classmates' reactions and make revisions as necessary. Then write or type your brochure, making sure you produce a clean, neat, attractive copy.

Sharing

Share your finished brochure with your classmates; display your brochures on a bulletin board if possible so that your classmates as well as students in other classes may profit from your research and writing. Your brochure might provide information which could make a real difference to someone. If you have chosen your job carefully, it could make a real difference to you.

SPOTLIGHT

Help Wanted

1. WATCHERS, Inc. is now hiring
professional security officers
Paid vacations
Free life insurance
Uniforms and training provided
Must have car and phone
Denver area positions
Many part time and weekend positions avail.
Apply at: 52 3rd St., Suite 81
Monday—Friday 9am—4pm

2. **PROMOTABILITY**
If you are looking for a spot that will lead to a career, now's your chance. $1200. plus to start, fee pd. with benefits that have no equal. Call Appleton, Inc. 882 Longfellow, 555-2222, Pvt. Empl. Agcy. No. 103.

3. **OIL COMPANY**
To $18,000 annual start
This energy related co. will train completely. This co. has doubled growth in 1 yr. Will start in yard. Good promotion. 632 Call 555-8741, Hillside, pvt. empl. agcy. In business 15 years

4. ASSISTANT, Full time, $5/hr
4546 A. Advox 8-8 Sm. Fee
Skills Referral Service 555-1982

5. DESK WORK-Light
No experience necessary, guaranteed hourly wage, full and part time openings. Full training program for anyone with a physical or emotional handicap or under a doctor's care. Call 9am to 9pm 555-6132

6. MAIL Carriers, part-time, ideal for homemakers & retired people, choose your own hours & area. Good pay. Car nec. 555-6186

7. SALES: used car. Apply 711 N. Lexington, experience & refs.

Look at the preceding want ads carefully. Which of them contains enough information to be helpful to a person looking for a job?

Ad #1 includes the name of the company seeking employees, the title of the position, benefits information (although no salary), basic requirements (car and home phone), area of work, work times available, and application instructions. All in all, it appears to be a rather complete request for job applicants. One thing, however, is omitted: The state in which this ad appeared requires all security guards and officers to be at least 21 years old!

Ad #2 is very interesting. It is an employment service ad, but it doesn't tell what kind of job is available. Look carefully at the ad and write notes in your Writer's Notebook about the facts that are missing from it. Clearly, it is not a very helpful ad. It may be a way the employment service company gets people to come in and file with them. (As you may know, employment service companies charge for finding jobs for their clients; these commissions are the way they make money.)

Ad #3 is interesting, but for another reason. Who do you think has been in business 15 years? It's not the oil company, but the employment agency that has a fifteen-year history!

Then there's #4. The company doesn't tell the reader what kind of assistant is needed. In addition, the pay is $5 per hour, full time.

And what kind of work would you expect a person hired in response to #5 would do? The ad only suggests that persons with handicaps or under a doctor's care will be trained to fit the job.

Then there's #6. Wouldn't one think this ad is from the U.S. Post Office? After all, the company says it is looking for mail carriers, and in the U.S., the U.S. Postal Service has a monopoly on letter services. But this is not the U.S. Postal Service. It's a small messenger service, and messengers must use their own automobiles to deliver their messages. Employees are on call 24 hours a day and are paid only when they are called. Payment is on a "per message" basis.

#7 is a straightforward help-wanted ad. This advertiser is looking for someone to sell used cars. The name of the company is not given, but the company's address is. The salary is not given, but the ad asks for experienced persons. Anyone who has sold used cars knows that most dealers operate on a commission basis, with a percentage of the selling price paid to the sales person whenever he or she sells a car.

Getting It Started

In your Writer's Notebook, jot down some things you would look for in a help-wanted ad. Look at the sample ads on page 262. Look for things you appreciate, factors that are missing or misleading.

Now, in your own local paper, look for help-wanted ads related to jobs you think are interesting. Are the ads in your paper more specific? Do they consistently provide information that would help you decide whether or not to apply for the jobs listed?

Writing a Help-wanted Ad

Getting It Down

Using the brochure developed in this chapter, write a help-wanted ad for your local paper. Remember that ads are paid for by the word—the fewer words, the cheaper the ad. Say what you have to say in the fewest words possible, but make your ad factual, honest, and attractive.

When your ad is finished, share it with a classmate. Have him or her go over it carefully, explaining exactly what he or she thinks your ad is looking for. Use your classmate's statements as a check to see whether you are communicating effectively.

    If your ad doesn't seem to be successful, discuss its problems with your classmate. What could be added? What could be cut? What needs to be made more specific?

**Checking
It
Out**

Rewrite your ad, making it the best you can produce. When you are satisfied with it, attach it to your brochure and make it available to the rest of your classmates.

**Getting
It
Right**

Chapter 13

Presenting Yourself

In this chapter, you will think and write about the future. The future can be a very distant, almost unreal place and time, but when *the* future suddenly becomes *your* future, the concept becomes much more real— sometimes exciting, often a little frightening.

Have you thought much about your future—especially your future when you complete school and begin work? In this chapter, you will focus on yourself and how you relate to jobs. You will look closely at your interests and abilities, and at how those characteristics fit various occupations. At the end of the chapter, you will have completed a résumé which you may use to present yourself to a possible employer.

Getting It Started

Plans often begin as daydreams. Take a few minutes to dream. Project yourself about ten years into your future. What do you see? Where are you? What are you doing? How do you look? What kind of lifestyle do you have? What kind of job do you have?

Close your eyes and think about these things for a short time. When you have a picture in mind, write in your Writer's Notebook thoughts about who you are, where you are, and what you are doing. These notes may be words, phrases, or sentences —even pictures—which will help your remember your pictures of yourself.

When you finish, go back to your writing and underline words and phrases that point out facts that are especially important about you and your future.

~~~~~~

Getting It Started

Next, think back over your past experiences. In your Writer's Notebook, jot down thoughts about your past. Concentrate on activities which you enjoyed, were successful at doing, and did frequently. For example, you may have helped coach a little-league sport, traveled often, or held a job. Jot down your thoughts about past experiences and state why they bring happy memories.

~~~~~~

Checking It Out

When you finish, go back and read over your notes. Underline words and phrases that signal your skills or abilities. For example, you might find that you write well, type well, ride a bicycle well, or that you listen carefully. Skills can be learned. Abilities are natural talents, such as artistic, musical, athletic, or social aptitudes.

~~~~~~

Getting It Down

Now, shift your thoughts from what you do well to things that are important to you. What comes to mind—money, friends, family, a lot of free time, independence, power? In your Writer's Notebook write down the five most important things you can think of, and also write a statement telling why you value each so highly.

Next, based on your past experiences and feelings about what is important to you, write several ideas you have about situations you want to be sure to *avoid* in the future. These may include specific jobs, certain types of people or places, or even climates. For example, if you do not like to spend a great deal of time outside, you would want to avoid work that would require you to be outdoors. If you have little or no athletic ability, you would want to avoid work which requires a great deal of physical agility.

~~~~~~

Writer's Workbench

Charting Your Interests

Using the information in your Notebook, complete the following three charts. You may wish to copy the charts into your Notebook, so that you will have a permanent record of your reactions to each.

Chart I Abilities

Requirements	I don't have this ability	Little strength in this area	Some strength in this area	One of my strong abilities
Problem-solving ability	1	2	3	4
Supervisory ability	1	2	3	4
Physical stamina	1	2	3	4
Precision	1	2	3	4
Ability to work with detail	1	2	3	4
Ability to work closely with the public	1	2	3	4
Creativity	1	2	3	4
Ability to work with others	1	2	3	4
Initiative	1	2	3	4
Ability to use tools or machinery	1	2	3	4
Ability to instruct	1	2	3	4

Chart II Job Location Preference

	Not for me	I doubt I'd like this	I might like this	Perfect for me
Outdoors	1	2	3	4
Indoors, generally in same location	1	2	3	4
Indoors, varied locations	1	2	3	4
Varied settings, both indoors and outdoors	1	2	3	4

Chart III Job Characteristics

	I couldn't stand a job like this	I'd do it, but I doubt I'd like it	I might like a job like this	I'd love a job like this
Repetitious	1	2	3	4
Varied	1	2	3	4
Competitive	1	2	3	4
Hazardous	1	2	3	4

You have looked at your abilities and your preferences for jobs. What about what motivates you in a job? What drives you to do a good job? What aspects of a job are more satisfying to you?

Complete the following questionnaire, writing your responses in your Notebook. If one of the items causes you to think about something that is especially important to you, jot down a note to yourself about the thoughts you had.

Why I Work

Use the following answers for the items in this questionnaire:

1 = Unimportant to me
2 = Not very important to me
3 = Somewhat important to me
4 = Extremely important to me

Read each item carefully. Then, from the preceding list, choose a number which fits your attitude about why you want to work.

1. ___ Friends.   I hope to find many friends wherever I work.
2. ___ Creativity.   I see work at a place where I can truly express myself in developing new ideas and new approaches.
3. ___ Security.   I think a job should provide the assurance that I will be able to continue work for my lifetime.
4. ___ Excitement.   I think work should be stimulating and exciting.
5. ___ Location.   I think my job should be in an area I really like, with a good climate and lots of opportunity for enjoying recreation or culture.
6. ___ Help society.   I want to use my job to make the world better.
7. ___ Individuality.   I want a job which permits me to work on my own.
8. ___ Contact with public.   I think a job should offer me many chances to deal with other people.
9. ___ Team work.   I want a job in which I can be a member of a team.
10. ___ Decision making.   I want a job in which I can make decisions.
11. ___ Help people in need.   I think the best job is one that enables me to help people who are in need.
12. ___ Supervise others.   I would like a job that would permit me to work up to being a supervisor.
13. ___ Physical.   I want a job that will offer me a physical challenge.
14. ___ Money.   I want a job that will give me a chance to earn a lot of money.
15. ___ Freedom.   I would like to have a job in which I call the shots concerning when I work.

"The secret of success in life is for a person to be ready when his opportunity comes."
Disraeli

**Getting
It
Down**

Being "ready" includes knowing who you are, what you want, and how to get what you want. Using the information you have collected about yourself, formulate ideas about several things you hope to accomplish in the future. Write these goals in your Notebook now. Your goal statements should reflect your abilities, your preferences, and your values.

SPOTLIGHT

Here is a sample of a simple goal statement written by a high school student.

> I'm the sort of person who likes to work by myself. I also would like to think that whatever I do would help others. I don't need a lot of money, but I do want to make enough to have an enjoyable life. I don't want to have to compete with others in my job. I just want to know what I have to do, and then have people leave me alone so I can get it done.
>
> *Melinda S.*

Melinda has laid out the kind of job she thinks she will be happy in. She used information from the "Why I Work" questionnaire and her Notebook as she wrote her goal statement. However, she does not appear to have thought through the kinds of work she might enjoy doing. The next activitiy will help her; it may also help you.

Exploring Work

Getting It Started

Are there some school subjects in which you do especially well? Sometimes success in school subject areas relates to possible success in certain work areas. Look at the following information and see if you can find areas of studies in which you are strong. Then, look to the right to find occupational areas which are related to those areas of study. Write the results in your Writer's Notebook.

Subject	*Occupation*
Agriculture	Agriculture, Forestry, and Fishery
Art	Education Performing Arts, Design, and Communications
Business education	Agriculture, Forestry, and Fishery Education Office Service

Distributive education   Sales

Driver education   Transportation
Health   Health
                          Scientific and Technical

Home economics   Agriculture, Forestry, and Fishery
                          Education
                          Service
                          Social Service

Industrial Arts   Agriculture, Forestry, and Fishery
                          Construction
                          Industrial Production
                          Mechanical and Repair
                          Performing Arts, Design,
                            and Communications
                          Scientific and Technical
                          Service
                          Transportation

Language arts   Education
                          Office
                          Performing Arts, Design,
                            and Communications
                          Sales
                          Service
                          Social Science
                          Social Service

Mathematics	Agriculture, Forestry, and Fishery
	Construction
	Health
	Industrial Production
	Office
	Performing Arts, Design, and Communications
	Sales
	Scientific and Technical
	Social Science
Music	Education
	Performing Arts, Design, and Communications
Physical education	Construction
	Education
	Health
	Service
Science	Agriculture, Forestry, and Fishery
	Education
	Health
	Industrial Production
	Office
	Scientific and Technical
	Social Science
	Transportation
Social studies	Education
	Office
	Performing Arts, Design, and Communications
	Service
	Social Science
	Social Service

Preferences and Job Characteristics

The following chart matches abilities, skills, and preferences with jobs. Several jobs have been entered on the chart to give you an idea of how the system works. Copy this chart in your Notebook and add the five jobs you researched in the last chapter.

Jobs

Postal Clerk	Police Officer	Librarian	Singer	Farm Laborer	Abilities and Preferences
					Problem solving ability
					Supervisory ability
					Physical stamina
					Precision
					Ability to work with detail
					Ability to work closely with the public
					Creativity
					Ability to work with others
					Initiative
					Ability to use tools or machinery
					Ability to instruct
					Located outdoors
					Located indoors, generally in same location
					Located indoors, varied locations
					Located in varied settings, indoors and outdoors
					Repetitious
					Varied
					Competitive
					Hazardous

**Getting
It
Down**

You and Jobs

Consider what you know of yourself; then consider what you know about several jobs. Now try a match. Are there any jobs you have listed which fit you just right? Are there any which come close?

Choose a job which you think might be appropriate for you. Then write a paragraph or two in your Notebook explaining why that job seems to be a good one for you. You might include some possible problems you might have in the job, but be sure that a reader would understand that you and the job have a reasonable chance of getting along.

Next, do the same for a job that clearly is not suitable for you. Of course, there may be some characteristics of the job which fit you, but a reader should be able to see that you and the job are not compatible.

SPOTLIGHT

Michael, a high school student, wrote the following paragraphs in response to this assignment.

I think I would like to work as a farm laborer. I have always liked working outdoors, and I have a lot of physical strength and stamina. My experience in sports shows that I can get along well working with others. I might get bored doing the same thing all the time, but I think as I learned more about farming, my boss would probably assign me different jobs. I can work with machines pretty well, and I might even be able to repair machines for the farm. I'm a little clumsy sometimes, and I'll have to be extra careful when I'm working with farm machinery, but I don't think that needs to be a problem as long as I'm aware of it.

The last thing on earth I'd like to be is a librarian. I've always had trouble with detail, and I just can't see myself giving numbers to books, checking out books, and putting books back on shelves after people have used them. I wouldn't like working inside all the time,

either. I need air and sunshine. I just can't see anything more boring than playing nursemaid to a bunch of books. Talking to people and helping them find books wouldn't be so bad, but the other work would kill me.

Michael K.

When you have finished Getting It Down (page 276), share your writing with a classmate. Does he or she think you have been honest with the job and with yourself? How do you feel? Do you think you have given both you and the job a fair treatment?

Checking It Out

A Paper Portrait

Getting It Started

Vital Statistics.   For the next ten minutes, write all you can about yourself in your Writer's Notebook. Begin by recording your name, your birth date, your social security number, the state of your health, and any other vital statistics you feel are necessary. Include all the schools you have attended. Also, list any educational experiences you have had other than those in school, such as basketball camp, gymnastics instruction, or a Great Books course you have taken.

Experience Preferred.   An important part of who you are is what you have done and what you can do. Use your Notebook to describe the kinds of work experiences you have had. Mention any jobs you have held and describe the type of work you did in each. Did you acquire any skills while you were working? List any activities you have participated in (paid or unpaid) that might qualify as work-type experiences. For example, if you tutored a classmate in math, list tutoring and describe what you did during that experience. Perhaps you taught a church-school class. If so, list it. Think hard, and list as many experiences as you can.

Putting in a good word.   Who is in a position to know about your skills and the kind of person you are? Would these persons also be willing to pass along the "good word" about you to others? In your Notebook, list all of the people, other than classmates, who are in a position to be able to assess your skills and the kind of person you are. List each person's name and describe how that person knows you and your abilities. You might include teachers, past employers, friends who are adults, clergy, or others who know you well.

SPOTLIGHT

Look back over the notes you made during your "Paper Portrait." Which pieces of information would interest an employer considering you for the job you wrote about earlier? Underline key pieces of information.

The Résumé

Résumé is a French word meaning "summary" or "short history." It is an autobiography written according to a specific form, organized in categories, and condensed into one or two pages. It is also one of the most important pieces of writing you will ever complete.

A well-written résumé is often your entry card to a job interview. It may also accompany an application to a college to help you make a positive impression. On the other hand, a poorly-written résumé can spoil your chance to "get your foot in the door."

There was a time when the process of getting a job or being admitted to a college was less complicated. In those times, it was possible to be granted an interview on the spot. Those days are generally gone. Today, a well-written résumé is the first step toward making a favorable impression and getting an interview. Much of the information you have been collecting during your work in this chapter will form the basis for your résumé.

Résumés are often quite different from one another, yet they all contain the same basic information. Look at the following résumé written by a high school student.

RÉSUMÉ

Sherri Bymers   Born August 21, 196___
670 Arbutus Street   Health excellent
Marian, Colorado 80498
(303) 555-1818
Social Security Number 333-77-3183

Job Goal: To become an assistant librarian

Education
     Sophomore at Marian High School
     Major areas of academic interest: English, social studies
     Grade average: A− (includes junior high school work)
School Activities
     President of sophomore class
     Editor of class literary magazine
Work experience
     Volunteer, Marian High School Library
     Read stories to children, Marian Public Library, three summers
     Playground assistant, Marian City Recreation, one summer
     Child care several times a week for the past three years

Personal background

I have lived in Marian for the past five years. Prior to that time, I lived with my family in Noble, Missouri. My family and I have traveled through the central part of the United States and have been to Mexico once. My interests include reading, writing poetry, and writing short stories.

References (with permission)

Ms. Leota Colson, librarian, Marian High School, 448 Broadway, Marian, Colorado 80498. Phone (303) 555-8879.

Ms. Janice Schultz, English teacher, Marian High School, 448 Broadway, Marian, Colorado 80498. Phone (303) 555-8879.

The Rev. Harrison Conway, Pastor, First Presbyterian Church, 1830 Maple St., Marian, Colorado 80498. Phone (303) 555-2784.

Notice how the information presented in this résumé fits Sherri's job goal—getting an assistant librarian's job. What specific items did Sherri include which suggest that she is very interested in a library job? Discuss these with your classmates.

Sherri has "built a case" for herself in her résumé. She had two major factors in mind as she prepared this document: the purpose (to get a job as an assistant librarian), and her audience (a prospective employer). Notice that even her references are chosen carefully to fit her audience and purpose. A prospective employer can get specific information concerning what Sherri knows about working in a library from the school librarian— someone she has worked for as a volunteer. Sherri's English teacher can provide information about Sherri's verbal ability and her academic talents. Sherri's pastor can provide character references and discuss Sherri's ability to work with people in a community setting.

~~~~~~

Getting It Down

A History of You in 500 Words or Less, or The Résumé

Using thoughts collected in previous activities, write a résumé. Be sure to design it so that it presents you in your very best light for a specific job and to an audience you feel is typical of prospective employers. Remember, your résumé is a *selective summary* of your life. Its purpose is to present you in an appealing way and to illustrate that you are qualified for a specific position. Make careful decisions about what should and should not be included in your résumé.

Include the following basic categories:

Career or job goal: type of work or specific job you are interested in. Use the information you have about yourself and jobs to help you make this decision.

Personal information: name, address, social security number, phone.

Educational background: schools attended and dates if completed; diplomas, certificates, or degrees.

Employment and experience: include all related employment experience, paid and unpaid; include names of companies and individuals you worked for if your work was extensive.

References: names, titles, addresses, and phone numbers of at least three people, carefully chosen to present a picture of you as a capable person with reliable character. You can expect your potential employer to contact these individuals if he or she is serious at all about hiring you.

Optional categories:

Honors or awards: offices held, academic honors, athletic honors, music honors, if they apply at all to the job or to making a good image for you.

Interests or hobbies: especially if they are related to the job or help make you an attractive applicant.

Extracurricular activities: especially if they are related to the job or help make you an attractive applicant.

Affiliations: clubs and organizations you belong to, especially if they support you as a strong individual or if they relate specifically to the job.

Your résumé should be only one page long and should be typed. (When you need to cut material, keep your audience and purpose in mind.) Spelling, punctuation, mechanics, and typing must be perfect. Remember, this single piece of paper can mean the difference between your getting an interview and being completely ignored. Messy, non-specific résumés tend to get thrown in the trash. Make sure yours rises to the top of the pile.

**Checking
It
Out**

When you have completed the rough draft of your résumé, share it with a classmate or a group of students. Have them go over it with a fine-toothed comb, checking for things you should have included, making suggestions about any parts that should be cut, and fixing up the mechanical aspects of your writing. See the Checkpoint on page 287 for help, too.

**Getting
It
Right**

When you have input from your classmates, do your own re-checking. Then rewrite your résumé as necessary. When you are satisfied with your work, type it in the most attractive form you know. Remember, this single piece of paper represents *you* to a potential employer.

SPOTLIGHT

Now that you are armed with a well-written résumé, how will you use it to open some of those doors of opportunity?

Sherri, the student whose résumé appears on pages 279 and 280, saw the following advertisement in the Help-Wanted section of her local newspaper.

Library Assistant. Part time. Exp. required.
Work with children's section to start. Apply
Sally Paton, Marian Public Library, 9–4 daily.

She was interested. At least on the surface this appeared to be an ideal job, since she needed a part-time job while she was in school.

Sherri's first step was to check her résumé to be sure it contained all the information required by the ad. Clearly it did. Next she drafted a *cover letter* to accompany her résumé.

This is the cover letter she wrote:

```
                                    670 Arbutus Street
                                    Marian, CO 80498
                                    May 10, 198___

Ms. Sally Paton
Marian Public Library
930 Broadway
Marian, CO 80498


Dear Ms. Paton:

    I would like to be considered for the job of
library assistant which you advertised in the paper
on May 8.

    I have worked as a volunteer for Ms. Colson at the
Marian High School Library for nearly a year now. I
have also worked as a reader for children in the
Public Library for three summers. As you can see, I
have some library background, both in school and
public libraries, and I believe I would serve well as
a library assistant.
```

I am enclosing my résumé and would be happy to
provide any additional information you might request.
I may be reached at 555-1818 after 3 p.m. on weekdays
or at the Marian High School Library (555-8879) from
10-11 a.m. on Mondays, Wednesdays, or Fridays.

Please feel free to contact the references listed
on the résumé should you wish to.

May I have an interview at your convenience?

                                        Sincerely,

                                        Sherri Bymers

                                        Sherri Bymers

Notice how Sherri establishes a *point of contact* with the employer in the first paragraph. She immediately states what the letter is about. She doesn't bother with comments about the weather, or how nice the public library is, or how good she is. She gets right to the point.

In the second paragraph, she lists some of her most important qualifications for the job. She does this to *arouse the employer's interest*. She is careful to show how her experience fits the job.

Sherri's cover letter *mentions that she is including her résumé*, and *asks for an interview*. She also notes the phone numbers where she may be reached at various times, since that specific information is not on the résumé.

In one sense, the cover letter is a summary of a summary (the résumé). It serves to highlight the parts of the résumé that especially fit an applicant's qualifications to a specific job.

Help Wanted

Getting It Started

Use the Help-Wanted section of your local newspaper to locate an advertisement for a job opening you might be interested in. Clip the ad.

Now, compose a cover letter for your résumé in which you apply for the job described in the ad. Remember, a cover letter is a business letter and should follow business-letter style. Check Sherri's letter if you have questions about this form.

When you have finished the draft of your letter, ask a parent or another adult to read your résumé and your cover letter. Ask for comments including the following:

1. Does the résumé contain all necessary information to present a complete and favorable impression of skills and abilities?
2. Are there unnecessary bits of information which should be cut?
3. Has the résumé been written with a prospective employer in mind?
4. Is the résumé organized in a clear and logical form?
5. Are the best references listed?
6. Is the letter in proper business form?
7. Does the letter specify the job being applied for and how the writer heard of the opening? Does it arouse interest? Does it mention that a résumé is included? Is an interview requested?
8. Are there spelling or mechanical errors in the letter?
9. Would readers have a positive impression after reading the letter and the résumé?

Based on the comments you received from the person checking your résumé and cover letter, and after checking the criteria on page 287 which will be used to evaluate them, prepare the final draft. When you are satisfied that the résumé is logically organized, impressive, written with a prospective employer in mind, is an accurate, concise summary of who you are, and is neat and correct, turn it in.

When you are satisfied that the cover letter is the best you can write, that it fits both the job and the résumé, and that it is written with the employer's needs clearly in mind, put it in final form and hand it in.

Be sure to submit the want ad with the cover letter and the résumé to aid your teacher in doing his or her evaluation.

Your résumé and cover letter will be evaluated using the criteria in the Checkpoint on page 287.

Summary

When you write to present yourself, you may be writing for many different purposes and audiences. As you think back over your work in this chapter and Chapter 12, consider the following questions:

What have been the major facts I have learned about putting myself in writing?

What have I learned about tailoring my description of myself to an audience?

What have I learned about designing my message to fit a specific purpose?

CHECKPOINT 7

1	2	3	4	5

Résumé as a summary of your autobiography.   ×4=

Too long or too short. See me for help condensing.	Necessary information given, but you either left out details or told too much.	Information carefully selected and summarized.

Organization of your résumé.   ×3=

Poorly organized and confusing. See me for help.	You're on your way. Sharpen the organization.	Great! Your résumé is organized logically and is easy to follow.

Cover letter includes all necessary information.   ×3=

You left out several important bits of information.	You left out one important detail.	Complete in all respects.

The impression made by your résumé and cover letter; sense of audience.   ×3=

Not too appealing or interesting. The employer probably wouldn't call you back.	Close; remember to think in terms of what is appealing to an employer.	Your letter should catch the employer's attention. You know just what an employer is looking for.

Use of correct business letter and résumé form.   ×3=

Incorrect form. Review pages 279–280, 283–284.	One error. Proofread more carefully.	Correct form.

Appearance of your résumé and cover letter.   ×2=

Untidy. Do again.	Looks fair.	Looks great on the page and is spotless.

Mechanics (spelling, capitalization, punctuation).   ×2=

Many errors; review Handbook sections carefully.	One or two errors. Be more careful.	Perfect! Congratulations.

Chapter 14

Responding to Literature

I was dribbling down the court with ten seconds on the clock. I got into position for my shot. At five seconds, I let it go. The ball swished through the basket, and we won 59-60.

Naomi J.

It was the applause that woke me up to the reality that I was the one the principal had introduced. I had won the scholarship! As I walked slowly to the middle of the stage, I looked down to see my mother and dad crying tears of joy. I had made it.

Kevin L.

I hadn't really wanted to go on this blind date, but my friend had insisted with "This will be the best date you've ever had." So I agreed. We were waiting in the living room when suddenly a dream stepped through the door. "This is a blind date?" I thought to myself.

Gale M.

These are fantasies reported by three high school students. They relate to things that are important to the individuals reporting them—Naomi the basketball player, Kevin the scholar, and Gale the romantic.

These fantasies are probably like some you have. You may dream a good deal about something you would like to have come true in your life. Your fantasies may concern the present or the future.

"Feels Like Spring" is a story about a fantasy that comes true—at least in the end, we are led to believe that it is in the process of coming true. As you read the story, think about your own fantasies—those which have come true and those which have not.

Feels Like Spring

I stop at the corner drugstore for a breakfast of doughnuts and coffee. I eat fast because I'm a little late, and then I race to the subway station and gallop down the steps to catch my usual train. I hold on to the strap and make believe I'm reading my newspaper, but I keep glancing at the people crowded in around me. They're the same ones I see every day. They know me and I know them, but we don't smile. We're strangers thrown together accidentally.

I listen to them talk about their troubles and their friends, and I wish I had someone to talk to, someone to break the monotony of the long subway ride.

As we approach the 175th Street station, I begin to get tense again. She usually gets into the train at this station. She slips in gracefully, not pushing or shoving like the rest, and she squeezes into a little space, clinging to the pole and holding on to an office envelope that probably contains her lunch. She never carries a newspaper or a book; I guess there isn't much sense in trying to read when you're mashed like that.

There's a fresh outdoor look about her, and I figure she must live in New Jersey. The Jersey crowd gets in at that stop. She has a sweet face with that scrubbed look that doesn't need powder or rouge. She never wears make-up except for lipstick. And her wavy hair is natural, just a nice light brown, like the color of poplar leaves when they turn in the fall. And all she does is hold on to the pole and think her own thoughts, her eyes clear blue and warm.

I always like to watch her, but I have to be careful; I'm afraid she'll get sore and move away if she catches me at it, and then I won't have anyone, because she's my only real friend, even if she doesn't know it. I'm all alone in New York City, and I guess I'm kind of shy and don't make friends easily. The fellows in the bank are all right, but they have their own lives to lead. Besides, I can't ask anyone to come up to a furnished room; so they go their way and I go mine.

The city is getting to me. It's too big and noisy—too many people for a fellow who's all by himself. I can't seem to get used to it. I'm used to the quiet of a small New Hampshire farm, but there isn't any future on a New Hampshire farm any more; so after I was discharged from the Navy, I applied for this position in the bank and got it. I suppose it's a good break, but I'm kind of lonesome.

As I ride along, swaying to the motion of the car, I like to imagine that I'm friends with her. Sometimes I'm even tempted to smile at her, not in a fresh way, but just friendlylike, and say something like "Nice morning, isn't it?" But I'm scared. She might think I'm one of those wise guys and she'd freeze up and look right through me as if I didn't exist, and then the next morning she wouldn't be here any more and I'd have no one to think about. I keep dreaming that maybe someday I'll get to know her. You know, in a casual way.

Like maybe she'd be coming through the door and someone would push her and she'd brush against me and she'd say quickly, "Oh, I beg your pardon," and I'd lift my hat politely and answer, "That's perfectly all right," and I'd smile to show her that I meant it. Then she'd smile back at me and say, "Nice day, isn't it?" and I'd say, "Feels like spring." And we wouldn't say anything more, but when she'd be ready to get off at 34th Street, she'd wave her finger a little at me and say, "Good-bye," and I'd tip my hat again.

The next morning when she'd come in, she'd see me and say "Hello," or maybe "Good morning," and I'd answer and add something like "Violets ought to be coming up soon"—something like that to show her I really know a little about spring. No wisecracks, because I wouldn't want her to think that I was one of those smooth-talking guys who pick up girls in the subway.

And, after a while, we'd get a little friendlier and start talking about things like the weather or the news, and one day she'd say, "Isn't it funny? Here we are talking every day and we don't even know each other's names." And I'd stand up straight and tip my hat and say, "I'd like you to meet Mr. Thomas Pearse," and she'd say very seriously, "How do you do, Mr. Pearse. I want you to meet Miss Elizabeth Altemose." She'd be wearing those clean white gloves girls wear in the spring, and the other people around us would smile because people in the subway are so close to you that they just can't help sharing a little of your life.

"Thomas," she'd say, as if she were trying out the sound of it.
"What?" I'd ask.
"I can't possibly call you Thomas," she'd say. "It's so formal."
"My friends call me Tommy," I'd tell her.
"And mine call me Betty."
And that's the way it would be. Maybe after a while I'd mention the name of a good movie that was playing at the Music Hall and suggest if she weren't doing anything in particular—

And she would come right out with, "Oh, I'd love it." I'd knock off a little earlier and meet her where she worked, and we would go out to dinner somewhere. I'd ask some of the men at the bank for the name of a good restaurant. And I would talk to her and tell her about New Hampshire and maybe mention how lonesome I got, and if it's a really nice place and it's quiet and cozy, maybe I'd tell her how shy I was, and she'd be listening with shining eyes and she'd clasp her hands and lean over the table until I could smell the fragrance of her hair, and she'd whisper, "I'm shy too." Then we'd both lean back and smile secretly, and we'd eat without saying much because, after all, what's there to say after that?

We'd go to the Music Hall and I'd get reserved seats and we'd sit there, relaxed, enjoying the movie. Some time during the picture, in an exciting part, maybe her hand would brush against mine, or maybe I'd be shifting my position and my hand would touch hers accidentally, but she wouldn't take it away and I'd hold it, and there I'd be in the middle of eight million people, but I wouldn't be alone anymore; I'd be out with my girl.

And afterwards I'd take her home. She wouldn't want me to travel all the way out. "I live in New Jersey," she'd say. "It's very nice of you to offer to take me home but I couldn't ask you to make a long trip like that. Don't worry, I'll be all right." But I'd take her arm and say, "Come on. I want to take you home. I like New Jersey." And we'd take the bus across the George Washington Bridge with the Hudson River flowing dark and mysterious below us, and then we'd be in New Jersey and we'd see the lights of small homes and we'd stop in one of those little towns, Englewood, Leonia, Ridgewood—I looked them up on a map, wondering which one was hers—and she'd invite me in but I'd say it was too late and then she'd turn to me and say, "Then you must promise to come for dinner this Sunday," and I'd promise and then—

The train is slowing down and the people are bracing themselves automatically for the stop. It's the 175th Street station. There's a big crowd waiting to get in. I look out anxiously for her, but I don't see her anywhere and my heart sinks, and just then I catch a glimpse of her, way over at the side. She's wearing a new hat with little flowers on it. The door opens and the people start pushing in. She's caught in the rush and there's nothing she can do about it. She bangs into me and she grabs the strap I'm holding and hangs on to it for her life.

"I beg your pardon," she gasps.

My hand is pinned down and I can't tip my hat, but I answer politely, "That's all right."

The doors close and the train begins to move. She has to hold on to my strap; there isn't any other place for her.

"Nice day, isn't it?" she says.

The train swings around a turn and the wheels squealing on the rails sound like the birds singing in New Hampshire. My heart is pounding like mad.

"Feels like spring," I say.

Milton Kaplan

Think of a fantasy you once had or one you have on and off now. Maybe you see yourself as a great athlete or as a popular singer mobbed by your cheering admirers. You may see yourself as a successful business executive, managing millions of dollars and thousands of people, or maybe you see yourself creating a silver necklace that is so beautiful you can't bring yourself to sell it.

Getting It Started

You may think of a fantasy about you and someone else. Perhaps you fantasize about a girl or boy you wish you had the courage to ask for a date. Your fantasy may be very much like Tommy's. Maybe your fantasy could even come true!

Getting It Down

Write your fantasy in your Writer's Notebook. Leave out names if you wish, since this will be read by some of your classmates, and you may not wish to make every detail of your fantasy public.

Checking It Out

Now share your fantasy writing with a classmate. As you read each other's writing, think about things you have in common when you fantasize. Do you have similar thoughts, or are your fantasies very different?

How do your fantasies compare with Tommy's in "Feels Like Spring"? Have you ever fantasized about something that eventually became a reality? If so, how did things work out?

Do you think Tommy's fantasy has a chance of working out in reality beyond the point at which the author ends the story? If this situation were real, what do you think would happen next?

You probably base your thoughts on your own experiences. If you have had fantasies come true, you may be optimistic and feel that Tommy's may also come true. If your fantasies never seem to come true, you may be pessimistic and feel that Tommy will be disappointed in his next conversation with his dream girl.

Talk with your classmates about how your experiences affect the way you view this story. As you discuss the story, think about experiences that influence your feelings about other stories that you read.

Why You React to Stories

Most readers base their reactions to stories on their own experiences. If they learned to like ". . . and they lived happily ever after" stories when they were children, they may like advanced forms of the same stories later. If their fantasies and personal experiences turn toward sports, they may like sports stories. If they are interested in science, they may like science fiction or nonfiction.

What types of stories do you like to read? Do you like love stories, science fiction, adventure?

~~~~~~

In your Writer's Notebook, make a list of the subjects you like to read about in stories. As you do this, think of the stories or books you have read recently that you have especially liked.

Now think about the kinds of television programs you like to watch. Do you like television programs with the same subjects as the stories you read? Expand your list in your Writer's Notebook to include subjects of the television programs you like.

When your list is as complete as you can make it, ask yourself these questions:

1. Why do I like to read about and watch these subjects?
2. What is there in my experience that makes these subjects interesting to me?

Jot down some notes to yourself in your Writer's Notebook as you think about these questions.

Getting It Started

~~~~~~

Now, select one kind of story that you especially like, and think about some very specific reasons you have for liking that sort of story. Write a short paragraph in which you explain to a classmate why you like that kind of story.

Getting It Down

~~~~~~

When you have finished your draft, ask a classmate to read and react to your paragraph. Do you and your classmate like similar kinds of stories? Do you have similar reasons for liking them? Is the reason you gave for liking certain stories solid? Is it honest?

After you have read your classmate's paragraph and he or she has read yours, discuss your preferences and your reasons for them. After your discussion, think about what you have written. Have experiences formed your preferences for what you read and

Checking It Out

watch on TV? If they have not, what factors do you believe have shaped your likes and dislikes?

〰〰〰〰〰〰〰〰〰〰〰〰〰〰〰〰〰〰〰

**Getting
It
Started**

Now go back to "Feels Like Spring." Did you like the story? If you did, think about why you liked it. What experiences have you had that would make you feel pleasure when you read this story?

Did you dislike the story? If you did, consider why you didn't like it. Have you had experiences which would make it difficult to like such a story?

〰〰〰〰〰〰〰〰〰〰〰〰〰〰〰〰〰〰〰

**Getting
It
Down**

Write a paragraph for your teacher in which you explain why you liked or disliked "Feels Like Spring." Remember that you must give reasons for your preference, and that those reasons should come from your own experiences.

〰〰〰〰〰〰〰〰〰〰〰〰〰〰〰〰〰〰〰

SPOTLIGHT

The following reaction to "Feels Like Spring" was written by Alan, a student in a midwestern high school.

> I didn't like "Feels Like Spring." Life just isn't like that. I can't stand that romantic junk. Here I am, trying to learn to be logical and think things through, and I have to read junk like this! When I was little, I used to dream about stuff. None of it ever came true. I like to read real things, stuff that is really life. How are we going to learn to think when we have to read stupid stories like that?
>
> *Alan T.*

Alan told why he didn't like the story, and his attitude certainly comes through in the paragraph. He clearly prefers stories that fit his version of reality, a version which differs from the one presented in the story. We certainly know what Alan's biases are after reading his paragraph.

Is your paragraph clearer than Alan's? Perhaps it is more specific. Read through your writing and check to see that you have been as specific as you can be. Make changes in your writing if necessary.

Ask a classmate to react to your paragraph. Use the following questions to guide that reaction:

1. Does the writer indicate whether he or she likes or dislikes the story?
2. Is the reason for liking or disliking clearly given?
3. Is there a specific experience or collection of experiences given which make the author's preference believable?
4. Is the author's voice strong and genuine in this writing?

Checking It Out

Rewrite your paragraph based on your classmate's reaction. Then copy it over, checking to be sure there are no mechanical errors, and give it to your teacher. Your teacher will use the previous questions for evaluation.

Getting It Right

SPOTLIGHT

Knowing About a Story

Knowing that you like or dislike a particular writing and knowing the reasons for your preference are very important to understanding literature. However, there are many other things that are also important.

In order to understand literature, you need to get beneath the surface of the writing and see how the author has worked with words and ideas to communicate with the reader. In "Feels Like Spring," it is important to understand how the author uses *point of view*.

Mr. Kaplan never says, "Tommy was a really nice guy who rode the subway and fantasized a lot." Yet we know that and much more when we read the story. How do we know about Tommy? We know because Tommy tells us about himself. Mr. Kaplan has chosen to have Tommy tell the story. When one of the characters tells the story, we say that the story is written in the *first person*.

The author chose *first person* as his *point of view* for this story. Point of view refers to the relationship between the teller of the story and the characters in the story. If the teller of the story is one of the characters, as in "Feels Like Spring," the author tells the story from a first-person point of view.

The other option an author has is to tell the story from a *third-person* point of view. If Mr. Kaplan had chosen this point of view, the story might have begun something like this:

> Thomas stopped at the corner drugstore for a breakfast of doughnuts and coffee. He ate fast because he was a little late, and then he raced to the subway station and galloped down the steps to catch his usual train.

Compare these sentences to those at the beginning of the story. Can you see that Tommy is telling the story in "Feels Like Spring," while someone else tells the story in the changed sentences?

An author writing in the *third person* tells a story as if he or she were looking down on the action and reporting what the characters were

doing. An author using *first person* tells the story through the voice of one of the characters.

~~~~~~

To see the difference point of view can make in a story, form a group of four, and rewrite "Feels Like Spring" using a third person point of view. Each of you should take approximately one-fourth of the story to rewrite.

**Getting
It
Started**

~~~~~~

When you finish, read your rewritten sections aloud for your entire group to hear. As you listen to the reading, follow Mr. Kaplan's story in your text. Think about the following questions as you listen to the reading:

**Checking
It
Out**

1. What kinds of changes had to be made in the language of the story as the shift from first to third person was made?
2. What differences are there in tone between first and third person? Is the story more formal with one than the other? Is it more personal with one than the other?
3. Does the shift from first- to third-person point of view make this story less effective? If you think so, can you give reasons for your opinion?

When you have completed your reading, talk about the differences between the use of first and third person in this story. (You may be so used to third person—most stories are told from that point of view—that you were uncomfortable with the first-person form when you first read the story. After you have worked with the story, are you more comfortable with first person?)

Try to think of times when first person might be a better choice than third person. Think of the role of the narrator (the person who tells the story) and its effect on choice of point of view. Think of the tone of the story (informal, formal, serious, comical, sarcastic, factual) and how that influences an author's choice of point of view.

Look for stories in a literature book or go to your library and get a collection of short stories. Then find examples of first- and third-person points of view. Talk with your classmates about circumstances in which authors choose one or the other.

~~~~~~

**Getting
It
Down**

In your Writer's Notebook, write some notes to yourself about first- and third-person point of view. Comment on what the terms mean, how they are used, and when they are used.

SPOTLIGHT

Using Quoted Material

In the next assignment, you will use material from "Feels Like Spring" to write a short paper. When you take material from another person's work, you must give credit to that author for the material you use. There are some very specific, simple rules to follow when using quoted material.

1. In a short paper, with no bibliography, give the author's name and the title of the publication so that a reader can easily identify where the material came from.

2. Place quotation marks around the quoted material. For example:

> Milton Kaplan's first sentence in "Feels Like Spring"—"I stop at the corner drugstore for a breakfast of doughnuts and coffee"—tells us that the story is written in the first person.

3. If the quoted material is especially long (more than a few lines), you may indent the material from the margins of your page. It is not necessary to put quotation marks around material that is indented. For example:

> We meet Tommy's fantasy friend early in Milton Kaplan's "Feels Like Spring." We see that she is someone he admires very much. The author helps us like her, too.
>
> As we approach the 175th Street station, I begin to get tense again. She usually gets into the train at this station. She slips in gracefully, not pushing or shoving like the rest, and she squeezes into a little space, clinging to the pole and holding on to an office envelope that probably contains her lunch. She never carries a newspaper or a book; I guess there isn't much sense in trying to read when you're mashed like that.

4. If you leave out material in a sentence, use ellipses (. . .) in place of the words you omitted. For example:

> Milton Kaplan tells us early in "Feels Like Spring" that Tommy feels strongly about his fantasy friend. "I always like to watch her . . . because she's my only real friend, even if she doesn't know it."

5. If you use another person's material without placing quotation marks around it (or indenting it, in the case of long quotations) and mentioning the author's name and the title of the publication from which you took it, you are calling another person's writing your own. This is called plagiarism. You certainly wouldn't want someone else passing off your writing as his or hers! Give other writers the same courtesy.

In formal research papers, you must be much more specific in this respect. ● Pages H-48–62 in the Handbook contain helpful information about using quoted material in more formal papers.

Now think about Mr. Kaplan's choice of the first-person point of view for this story. What specific elements such as use of language or expression of the narrator's emotions and feelings can you point to that make the first person a good choice for this story? When you used third person, what did the story lose?

Getting It Started

Look for specific sections of the story which illustrate your reasons for thinking first person was a good choice. Then write a short paper explaining to your teacher why you think first person was a good point of view for Mr. Kaplan to use in this story.
Keep the following in mind as you write:

Getting It Down

1. Have I shown that I know what the first-person point of view is?
2. Have I quoted material from the story to support my position?
3. Does the evidence I have chosen really support the use of the first-person point of view in "Feels Like Spring"?
4. Have I chosen a writing style that fits my audience—my teacher?
5. Have I kept my own voice in my writing? Would my teacher know that this was my paper even if my name were not on it?

6. Have I given credit to Mr. Kaplan by mentioning his name and by using quotation marks or indenting all material taken from his story?

Checking It Out

Before you turn in your paper, have a classmate check it for you. Be sure he or she reads it with the six questions in mind, just as you did when you wrote the paper. Get an honest reaction from your classmate, and change your writing if you feel the criticism is on target. Be sure to check your draft carefully yourself, just in case your classmate missed something important.

Getting It Right

Check your draft for mechanical errors before you copy it over. Then, prepare your final copy and turn it in. Your teacher will evaluate your paper using the same six questions you used to guide your writing and revision.

Seeing Character

Another important element of a short story is its characters. An author uses the characters to build the story. Without characters, there would be no story. As the characters interact with each other, as they encounter obstacles and overcome them or fail to overcome them, the story unfolds.

Getting It Started

Think about Tommy in "Feels Like Spring." What sort of a character is he? Do you like him?

Use the following scales to help you form an opinion of Tommy. Choose a number on each scale which represents how you feel about this character. For example, if you feel Tommy was a real villain, a character who was really nasty, choose a "5" on the *Kind, Cruel* scale.

Write your choices in your Writer's Notebook; be sure to make a choice for each scale. Remember, you are selecting numbers which represent the character Tommy in the story, "Feels Like Spring."

Kind	1	2	3	4	5	Cruel
Strong	1	2	3	4	5	Weak
Pleasant	1	2	3	4	5	Unpleasant
Relaxed	1	2	3	4	5	Tense
Honest	1	2	3	4	5	Dishonest
Forceful	1	2	3	4	5	Hesitant
Attractive	1	2	3	4	5	Unattractive

~~~~~~

Checking It Out

When you finish, join a group of classmates and talk about your selections. Do you agree on your feelings about Tommy? Are there some points of serious disagreement? If you disagree, discuss your reasons for this. Do you have different feelings about Tommy than some of your classmates have? Does your like or dislike for the story cause you to see Tommy in different ways compared to your classmates who feel the opposite?

~~~~~~

Getting It Down

Now, in your Writer's Notebook, write the first scale

Kind   1   2   3   4   5   Cruel

and circle your choice of the numbers. Then, go to the story and find at least three specific words, phrases, or incidents which support your choice. Be careful to find specifics which illustrate the overall impression Tommy makes in the story.

Write your words, phrases, or summaries of incidents below the rating scale.

Sandy, a student in California, selected a "2" on the scale. The evidence she cited was as follows:

"I like to imagine that I'm friends with her . . ."
"And, after a while, we'd get a little friendlier and start talking about things like the weather or the news . . ."
". . . maybe I'd tell her how shy I was . . ."

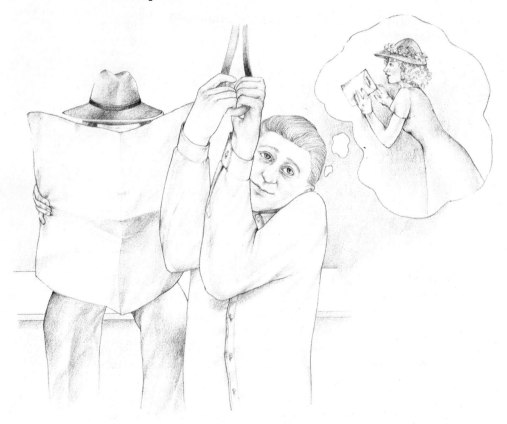

Do your conclusions on the first scale agree with Sandy's? Or do you have a completely different sense of Tommy? Many interpretations are possible on this scale. However, often when we read a story, our own experiences are so powerful that we ignore the words of the author. Look for what the author wanted you to believe about Tommy, not what you want to believe about him. You may find that you will need to change your feeling about him when you begin to look closely at the story.

Be sure the evidence you have selected is representative of the whole story, and not just a word or two pulled out of context. For example, you may have chosen a "5" on the *Kind, Cruel* scale, indicating you felt Tommy was a very cruel person. By taking a few words or phrases out of context, you might provide evidence such as this:

". . . I keep glancing at the people crowded around me."

". . . we don't smile."

". . . I begin to get tense again."

Anyone who has read the story would know that Tommy is *not* a cruel person. Anyone taking quotations such as these to support a feeling that Tommy is cruel would be making the story *say* something it doesn't. Be careful to select evidence that represents the *story's* feeling, not merely something you have made up.

When you have finished the first scale and have found words, phrases, or incidents to support your selection of a point on the scale, do the same for each of the remaining ones. Remember to check carefully to see that your first impression agrees with what the story actually says. Look for evidence that will help you form an impression. Try not to let your own experiences influence your impression too much. Concentrate on the impression the author creates.

After you have finished providing evidence for each of the scales, join a group of classmates and compare notes. See if your ratings are closer than before. See if the evidence you have selected is similar to that selected by your classmates.

Checking
It
Out

By this time you should have a fairly solid image of Tommy as a character. Now, think carefully about one or two major feelings you have about him. You might look back at the seven scales you completed to see whether they will provide help, or you may have though of other impressions as you studied Tommy while you were searching for characteristics.

Getting
It
Started

Write a simple sentence stating your feeling about Tommy. You might write, "Tommy is a very tense person," or "Tommy is lonely."

Getting
It
Down

**Checking
It
Out**

When you have written your statement, share it with a classmate. Discuss the reasons for your choice of impression. Did you choose the impression because it is the overwhelming, most important impression the author communicates in the story? Did you choose your impression because you always look for that particular characteristic in a person?

Next, discuss evidence in the story that you might use to support your statement. Think about the quotations you took from the story to provide evidence for your choices on the scales. Use the same process and look for evidence to support this impression. Jot down ideas for evidence in your Writer's Notebook.

Discuss your selections with a classmate and check to see whether you have chosen evidence that supports your impression and remains faithful to the story. If your classmate spots problems, discuss the difficulties and get help in selecting more appropriate evidence.

You have formed an impression that you feel is an important statement about Tommy, the main character in "Feels Like Spring." You have looked for and found evidence from the story to support your position. Now it is time to put your words into a composition.

**Getting
It
Down**

Write a short paper in which you persuade your teacher that your impression is an important aspect of Tommy's character.

As you write, keep these things in mind:

1. Have you clearly stated your impression?
2. Have you used the best evidence from the story to support your position?
3. Have you arranged your evidence so that it persuades your reader that your impression is important?

4. Have you written this paper to your teacher? Can you clearly see the difference between this writing and a paper you might write for someone else?
5. Does your voice come through in the writing?

When you have completed your first draft, look through your writing and review it carefully. Be sure you can answer yes to each of the preceding questions.

When you are reasonably sure of your writing, ask a classmate to read it and make suggestions for improvement. He or she should read it with the above questions in mind and make suggestions based on them. Ask your classmate to be honest with you, no matter how critical he or she may be, but also ask your classmate to suggest how you should change your material to make it more effective.

After your classmate has offered suggestions for change, look at the Checkpoint on page 309. These criteria will be used when your teacher evaluates your paper. As you can see, they match the preceding questions with the addition of *mechanics*.

Checking It Out

Now, using your classmate's suggestions and your own thoughts about how you might improve your paper, make any appropriate revisions. When you have finished your revision, go back over the paper carefully and catch any mechanical errors—usage, spelling, punctuation mistakes—you may have made. Be sure to correct them in your draft so you won't miss them when you prepare the final copy.

Getting It Right

If you wish, have your classmate go over your paper one more time just to be sure you are on target. If you have chosen not to include some of the items he or she suggested earlier, talk with him or her and explain your decision. Then ask your classmate whether yours was a wise choice. Talk about the changes you made as well as those you did not make.

Checking It Out

**Getting
It
Right**

After this final conference, you may decide to make some changes. Be sure you are convinced the changes will make your paper stronger before you agree to make them.

When you have your draft in good form, copy it over and turn it in.

A Quick Try on Your Own

You have gone through a carefully guided process as you studied Tommy, the main character in "Feels Like Spring." It involved examining your own feelings about the character, then using scales to help you look carefully at several parts of Tommy's character. Then, you looked at the story itself for words, phrases, or incidents which you used as the basis of an impression.

When your impression was formed, you looked for quotations from the story to support that position. Using the impression and the material from the story, you wrote a paper in which you persuaded your teacher that your impression was important and honest.

**Getting
It
Down**

Write a paper in which you give an impression of Betty, Tommy's dream girl. Using material from the story, provide evidence that your impression is an important and honest one. Write this paper for your teacher.

**Checking
It
Out**

Use classmates to assist you when necessary. If you wish to develop some scales to help in this process, do so.

**Getting
It
Right**

Since this paper is similar to the one you wrote about Tommy, you may use the same Checkpoint to guide you (page 309).

CHECKPOINT 8

1	2	3	4	5

Is the impression stated clearly?   ×4=

No. Make your statement more obvious.

Not clearly enough. You're probably not sure of your impression.

Yes.

Has the best evidence been used to support the impression?   ×4=

No. You have missed some excellent evidence.

Your evidence is generally good. However, there is better material in the story.

Yes.

Is the evidence arranged persuasively?   ×4=

No. Read through your paper and see if you can work out a more powerful sequence.

Your sequence is not as persuasive as it might be, but it is quite effective.

Yes.

Is the audience obvious in the way the paper is written?   ×3=

No. I couldn't tell whether this was written for a special audience. Think about special words you might use, or special things you might say.

Sometimes the audience is really addressed, sometimes not. Look for weak areas and change them.

Yes.

Is the author's voice apparent in the paper?   ×3=

The writing seems sterile, not the work of a person. Let your voice come through.

There are some excellent points in the paper where I can hear your voice. Make it come through it all.

Yes.

Mechanics.   ×2=

Problems in this area interfere with understanding. Use your Handbook.

This could be more perfect, although it has no serious problems. Be careful.

An outstanding technical job.

Chapter 15

Looking Ahead

What lies ahead for you? You have personal goals you hope to reach; you have ideas you hope to adhere to; you have dreams you hope will come true.

SPOTLIGHT

"You can't have your cake and eat it, too."
Jane was taking stock one day. "I'm doing pretty well in competition in high school swimming. The coach said yesterday I might be able to make a college swim team! I'm really excited!"

"Have you narrowed down your list of colleges?" asked her father.

"I guess I'll base my choice on whichever one has the best team." replied Jane.

"What about your plans to go into some kind of research, maybe in biology," said her father.

"Well, I want that, too," said Jane.

"Don't forget you'll have to pay some of your own expenses when you go to college. That means you'll probably have to have a part-time job," said her father.

"Everything's so complicated. I want to go to a good college. I want to keep on competing in swimming. I want to work toward some kind of research career. And then I want to travel, too. I just want too many things, I guess," said Jane.

Jane's problem is a common one for all of us. We have many dreams we would like to see come true. We have many abilities we would like to develop. We have many interests we would like to pursue. But usually we can't do everything we want to do.

Sometimes developing a decision grid can help us see what things we can do and which we can't. Look at a grid of Jane's decision problem.

Jane has five concerns: college, competitive swimming, travel, part-time work, and a career preparation in biological research. These concerns are placed along both axes of the grid.

The vertical axis (along the left-hand side of the grid) forms the first element of a question; the horizontal axis forms the second. The first question goes like this: "If college is most important, what about competitive swimming?" The next question is, "If college is most important, what about travel?" and so on through all intersections of the grid.

This grid gives Jane information to help her make decisions about her future. As you can see, she is going to have to set some priorities for herself. The elements she decides are most important will influence her decisions more than those she feels are less important.

**Getting
It
Started**

Think of at least four concerns that are important in your future plans. Try to choose ones similar to those Jane selected, decisions which you will have to make in the next year or so.

When you have identified your concerns, make a grid and complete the blanks, just as Jane did.

**Checking
It
Out**

Share your grid with a classmate and get a reaction. Have you been honest? Have you looked at all the possibilities? Are there other concerns you should have included?

Then show your grid to a parent or an adult friend. Ask him or her to react just as your classmate did. Let the adult's experience form his or her reaction. Are you being realistic? Are there other concerns which are more valid than those you have listed?

After you have reactions from a classmate and an adult, sit back and think about your grid. What information does it give you? What compromises will you have to make? Can you set priorities now that will shape your future?

Decision Grid	College	Competitive Swimming	Travel	Work Part time	Research Career
College	X	Conflict with study and classes	Possible only during vacation periods	Problems with full-time study; could take 6 years	Strong research department needed
Competitive Swimming	Need a scholarship; college must have competitive swimming	X	Problems with practice; could practice in hotel pools	May not have enough time for practice if I work too much	Research courses are tough; there may not be enough time for swimming or going to meets
Travel	Might consider "year abroad" type programs	Could practice at various places; what about meets?	X	Serious interference with a traditional job	Could travel to places where research is being conducted
Work Part time	Might take 5-6 years for degree	Enough time for practice and meets if I have job?	Travel would require me to change jobs often or find seasonal work	X	Might be able to get a job in a laboratory or a hospital
Research Career	College must have strong programs in science	Tough courses require time for preparation, long labs	Might have to travel only in the summers	There may not be enough time for even part-time work	X

This whole process may be frustrating to you. Things are not clean and unambiguous. They are messy, and you probably see some hard decisions that need to be made.

Think about the topic, "Making Hard Decisions About the Future." Jot some notes to yourself in your Writer's Notebook, notes you will be able to use as you write on that topic.

~~~~~~

**Getting
It
Down**

Now rough out a draft of a few paragraphs on "Making Hard Decisions About the Future." Your audience is yourself. Your reason for writing is to react to the process of future-oriented decision making.

~~~~~~

SPOTLIGHT

When given this assignment, Jane wrote the following:

This is the most frustrating thing I've ever done. I have so many things I want to do. I just can't decide which ones are most important. I've always known I couldn't do everything I wanted, but this is ridiculous. If I want to work in research, I have to go to a college where there's a strong major in that area. But what if they don't have a competitive swim team? I'll have to give all that up! But I know if I give up on the research career so I can swim, I'll be sorry. I can't swim for a living.

I don't know whether I'm a good enough swimmer to get a scholarship. At least that would make it so I wouldn't have to do any part-time work during college. But what if I had to work *and* be on the swim team! That would be a disaster. I couldn't take any courses, I'd be so busy.

And then there's travel. I always thought I'd like to travel, at least to Mexico, after I got out of high school. I've always liked going with my folks to different towns and the mountains and the beach. It looks as if I may have to give that up. There's no justice!

Jane P.

Jane used her writing to express some of her frustration about planning for the future. Perhaps you did, too. Share your draft with a classmate. Do you have similar feelings, or do you feel good about the decisions you have to make? Perhaps you have already made your decisions for the future, and the exercise was an easy one. If so, your classmates will probably envy you!

**Checking
It
Out**

Just what will the future hold for you? The world has always had prophets. Today's prophets are economic forecasters, weather forecasters, and even population forecasters. The one characteristic these present-day prophets have in common is that they base their predictions on what has happened in the past. They study their particular areas very closely and, based on what happened in similar circumstances in the past, they predict what will happen in the future. It is not always correct, of course, but this technique has proven quite successful.

**Getting
It
Started**

Perhaps you should do some prediction about your future. First, it might be good to place yourself in history.

In your Writer's Notebook, draw a line similar to the following one. Be sure to include the dates, and try to get them in similar places on your line.

1900	1950	2000	2050

Now, let's get a little history about you. Enter the following information on the time line:

1. the birth dates of your grandparents
2. the birth dates of your parents
3. your birth date
4. a date 25 years after your birth date which you will label "the birth date of my first child"
5. a date 25 years after that date which you will label "the birth date of my first grandchild"

The purpose of this chart is to enable you to see yourself in the middle of a family history, with two generations behind you and two ahead. It is also important for you to think about the way the world was during your early lifetime. As you study the time line, think briefly about events which have happened in the world, the nation, your community, your school, and your family so far during your lifetime.

History is very important in determining how we see things. Some social scientists feel that the prevailing attitudes and beliefs of society when a person is 10 to 15 years of age form the basis for that individual's attitudes through the remainder of his or her life. Certainly, everyone would have to admit that experience does have a major influence on our attitudes.

Using your time line, identify the period when your grandparents were 10 to 15 years old. Write those dates in your Writer's Notebook. Then, find a classmate who has similar dates for his or her grandparents, and talk about that period of time. Was the time during the "Roaring Twenties"?—the "Great Depression"? —the "War years"?

Together, jot down things you know about the time when your grandparents were 10 to 15 years old. If you do not know much about that period, go to your library or a history book and find out some facts about people's experiences then.

Now identify the period when your parents were 10 to 15 years old. Write those dates in your Writer's Notebook as well. It may be that the same classmate you worked with before has relatively similar dates for parents; if so, continue working with him or her. If not, find another partner.

What characterizes the time when your parents were 10 to 15 years old? Was the world in a depression?—in a war?—in a post-war period?—in an economic boom?—in a recession?—in a time of social unrest?

Jot down things about the time when your parents were 10 to 15 years old. Again, if necessary, go to the library or a history book for additional information.

If possible, interview your parents and grandparents about the time they were 10 to 15 years old. Get additional information about the time, but primarily try to determine what might have helped shape their attitudes toward themselves, life, social institutions, government, human relationships, family, and other important elements.

SPOTLIGHT

Henry, whose parents were born in 1940, asked them questions such as these:

1. You were 10 years old in 1950, just before the Korean War. By the time you were 15, the war was over. Did you worry about having to go to war?
2. Do you think the war had an effect on your attitudes? How did you feel about not really winning? Do you think that had an effect on your ideas about the possibility of success? Do you think it affected your attitudes about government?
3. Do you remember when President Truman stopped General Mac Arthur from entering China with his army? How did you feel about that? What do you think about that decision now? Was it a good decision? Do you think we learned anything from that experience?
4. Do you think your experiences during that time helped to shape your feelings? Can you think of some things you learned then that might have carried over into the way you feel today?

Henry's questions show that he knew something about the time when his parents were 10 to 15. He asked questions that probed, since he knew that his parents might not even be aware of how the period influenced them. He jogged their memories by bringing up important events of the time.

He also asked them whether that time in their lives was important and whether some things they learned had influenced them. These are not easy questions for people to answer, because sometimes those influences have been so subtle that they are not even aware of any effect. But by persistent questioning, you will often find some influences that people will recognize.

Getting It Started

Jot down your feelings about the effect of this important period on your parents or grandparents. See to what extent their attitudes have been shaped by those years. Then talk with your classmates about the influence time can have on shaping one's future attitudes.

Your Future

If history has an important role in shaping the attitudes of others, perhaps it has with you as well.

Getting
It
Down

At the top of separate pages in your Writer's Notebook, write the following titles: Events, Prevailing Attitudes, and Mood.

On the first page, list as many significant *events* as you can that happened during the period between your tenth and fifteenth birthdays. (Significant, in this case, means events which might influence the way you feel about things in the future. Significant events could be personal, such as having your money stolen; they could relate to a group of friends, such as being accepted into a group that was important to you; they can also relate to family; of course, you should not leave out state, national, and world events which could influence you.)

On the second page, list what you felt to be prevailing *attitudes* around you during that time. Think about family attitudes; think about attitudes in school; think about community, state, national, and world attitudes that seem to be important. These attitudes can be about how individuals are treated, what seems to make a person important, the value of group relationships, the importance of institutions, rights of people, the importance of family relationships, and many others.

On the third page, write what you feel the *mood* of the time was. You may feel the mood of the time was optimistic. If so, name the reasons in a few sentences. You may feel the mood of the time was pessimistic. Explain why you feel this to be so.

This item is very important. If you have trouble deciding on the mood of the time, ask yourself this question: Did most people in this time feel there were better, brighter days ahead, or did they feel things were going downhill? Once you have answered the question, try to support your answer with some evidence as you answer "Why?"

Since you and your classmates probably share the time when you were 10 to 15, your class should enjoy a rousing discussion about the factors which may help shape your individual attitudes. Talk about these times with your classmates. See if you agree on the significant events, the prevailing attitudes, and the general mood

Checking
It
Out

of the time. Don't feel you have to come to a common solution, but do listen to evidence which every member of your class brings up. It may be that you have a narrow view of this time and need to consider it more broadly. It may be that you have an inaccurate view of the time, or you may be right on target.

**Getting
It
Right**

After your discussion, you may wish to add to or change what you have written in your Writer's Notebook about this time. Do not make any changes if you were not convinced by the class discussion. You are looking at an important time in *your* life, and your experiences are what are most important. Remember, though, that many things outside your immediate reach can influence you, too. Add them if you feel comfortable doing so.

It is important for an individual to think about and say what is important to him or her in life. Many people go through life never having set down what is important for them, and never knowing what principles actually shape their feelings and mold their actions.

**Getting
It
Down**

Your next writing assignment is to write a statement of the things that are important to you. Write about religion, social justice, opportunity, economics, government, family, success, national stature, anything which you feel is important enough to write about. Give your paper a title such as, "Important Things" or "This I Believe" if you wish.

SPOTLIGHT

Thomas Jefferson, writing the Declaration of Independence, wrote something similar to what you will write, except that he wrote it for an entire country. These are his words:

We hold these truths to be self-evident; that all Men are created equal, that they are endowed by their Creator with certain inalienable Rights, that among these are Life, Liberty, and the pursuit of Happiness. That, to secure these Rights, Governments are instituted among Men, deriving their just powers from the consent of the governed; That whenever any Form of Government becomes destructive of these ends it is the Right of the People to alter or to abolish it, and to institute new Government, laying its foundation on such Principles and organizing its Powers in such form, as to them shall seem most likely to effect their Safety and Happiness.

〰〰〰〰〰〰〰〰〰〰〰〰〰〰〰〰〰〰〰〰〰〰〰〰〰〰〰〰〰〰〰〰〰〰〰

**Checking
It
Out**

When you finish a draft of your statement, share it with one of your classmates. Get an honest reaction to the following points:

1. Is the statement honest? Does the author really believe it?
2. Is the author's voice present?
3. Does the statement deal with real and important issues?

〰〰〰〰〰〰〰〰〰〰〰〰〰〰〰〰〰〰〰〰〰〰〰〰〰〰〰〰〰〰〰〰〰〰〰

**Getting
It
Right**

After you have a reaction, rewrite your statement as necessary, put it in final form, and give it to your teacher.

〰〰〰〰〰〰〰〰〰〰〰〰〰〰〰〰〰〰〰〰〰〰〰〰〰〰〰〰〰〰〰〰〰〰〰

Writer's Workbench

Uncued Grouped Sentence-Combining Activities

In the sentence-combining activities that you have done so far, you have been given cues for combining sentences using clauses, phrases, and single words. For this Workbench, you will not be given cues, but it will be up to you to decide how you will combine the group sentences.

Stereotype

1. He comes to school.
   His hair is styled.
   The style makes him more handsome.

2. He wears a shirt.
   The shirt is neatly pressed.
   He wears jeans.
   His jeans are clean.

3. His feet are covered.
   He wears socks.
   The socks are white.
   The socks are for sports.
   He wears shoes.

The shoes are for tennis.
The shoes are expensive.

4. His walk is purposeful.
Confidence exists.
The existence is in every stride that he takes.

5. He attends all of his classes.
His attendance makes him a favorite.
The favorite is of his teachers.

6. He practices athletics.
He works hard.
This impresses people.
The people are cheerleaders.

7. The crowd cheers.
The cheers are for him.
The cheers are at all games.
The cheers are because he scores.
The scores win the game.

8. He never smokes.
He never drinks.
This is according to his coach.

He is an all-around athlete.

SPOTLIGHT

Writing for the Future

Sometimes we remember something important that a person did for us or told us which became a major influence in our lives. Chaim Potok, in his book *The Chosen*, writes of such an experience.

I came back to my room and found my father standing in the doorway that led to his study. He had a bad cold and was wearing a woolen sweater and a scarf around his throat. This was his third cold in five months. It was also the first time in weeks that he had been home at night. He had become involved in Zionist activities and was always attending meetings where he spoke about the importance of Palestine as a Jewish homeland and raised money for the Jewish National Fund. He was also teaching an adult studies course in the history of political Zionism at our Synagogue on Monday nights and another adult course in the history of American Jewry at his yeshiva on Wednesday nights.

He rarely got home before eleven. I would always hear his tired steps in the hallway as he came in the door. He would have a glass of tea, come into my room and chat with me for a few minutes, telling me where he had been and what he had done that night. Then he would remind me I didn't have to do four years of college all at once, I should go to bed soon, and he would go into his study to prepare for the classes he would be teaching the next day.

He had begun taking his teaching with almost ominous seriousness these past months. He had always prepared for his classes, but there was a kind of heaviness to the way he went about preparing now, writing everything down, rehearsing his notes aloud—as if he were trying to make certain that nothing of significance would remain unsaid, as if he felt the future hung on every idea he taught.

I never knew when he went to sleep; no matter what time I got to bed he was still in his study. He had never regained the weight he had lost during the weeks he had spent in the hospital after his heart attack, and he was always tired, his face pale and gaunt, his eyes watery.

He stood now in the doorway to his study, wearing the woolen sweater, the scarf, and the round, black skullcap. His feet were in bedroom slippers and his trousers were creased from all the sitting over the typewriter. He was visibly tired. . . .

"You'll be working late tonight, *abba?*"

"Yes."

"You're not taking care of yourself, you know. Your voice sounds awful."

He sighed again. "It is a bad cold," he said.

"Does Dr. Grossman know you're working so hard?"

"Dr. Grossman worries a little bit too much about me," he said, smiling.

"Are you going for another checkup soon?"

"Soon," he said. "I am feeling fine, Reuven. You worry like Dr. Grossman. Worry better about your schoolwork. I am fine."

"How many fathers do I have?" I asked.

He didn't say anything, but he blinked his eyes a few times.

"I wish you'd take it a little easy," I said.

"This is not a time to take things easy, Reuven. You read what is happening in Palestine."

I nodded slowly. . . .

He sat on the bed, lost in thought. We were quiet for a long time. Then he stirred and said softly, "Reuven, do you know what the rabbis tell us God said to Moses when he was about to die?"

I stared at him. "No," I heard myself say.

"He said to Moses, 'You have toiled and labored, now you are worthy of rest.'"

I stared at him and didn't say anything.

"You are no longer a child, Reuven," my father went on. "It is almost possible to see the way your mind is growing. And your heart, too. Three years ago, you were still a child. You have become a giant since the day Danny's ball struck your eye. You do not see it. But I see it. And it is a beautiful thing to see. So listen to what I am going to tell you." He paused for a moment, as if considering his next words carefully, then continued. "Human beings do not live

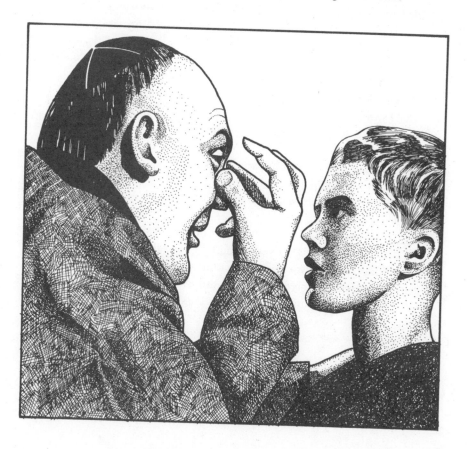

forever, Reuven. We live less than the time it takes to blink an eye, if we measure our lives against eternity. So it may be asked what value is there to a human life. There is so much pain in the world. What does it mean to have to suffer so much if our lives are nothing more than the blink of an eye?" He paused again, his eyes misty now, then went on. "I learned a long time ago, Reuven, that a blink of an eye in itself is nothing. But the eye that blinks, *that* is something. A span of life is nothing. But the man who lives that span, *he* is something. He can fill that tiny span with meaning, so its quality is immeasurable though its quantity may be insignificant. Do you understand what I am saying? A man must fill his life with meaning; meaning is not automatically given to life. It is hard work to fill one's life with meaning. *That* I do not think you understand yet. A life filled with meaning is worthy of rest. I want to be worthy of rest when I am no longer here. Do you understand what I am saying?"

I nodded, feeling myself cold with dread. That was the first time my father had ever talked to me of his death, and his words seemed to have filled the room with a gray mist that blurred my vision and stung as I breathed.

My father looked at me, then sighed quietly. "I was a little too blunt," he said. "I am sorry. I did not mean to hurt you."

I couldn't say anything.

"I will live for many more years, with God's help," my father said, trying a smile. "Between my son and my doctor, I will probably live to be a very old man."

The gray mist seemed to part. I took a deep breath. I could feel cold sweat running down my back.

"Are you angry at me, Reuven?"

I shook my head.

"I did not want to sound morbid. I only wanted to tell you that I am doing things I consider very important now. If I could not do these things, my life would have no value. Merely to live, merely to exist—what sense is there to it? A fly also lives."

I didn't say anything. The mist was gone now.

Getting It Started

Your final assignment is to send a message of your own to a child. Think of the impact of the father's message in *The Chosen*. Your message will be important to you, and it will be important to the child to whom you will send it. You have the raw material in the statement you wrote about the things that are important to you. All you lack is a specific audience.

You will write to someone you've never met. In fact, no one has ever met this person, for the child hasn't been born yet. This person exists in the future. This person is *your* child, a son or daughter you may have some day. You placed this child's birth date on your time line.

In a way, you have met this unborn child every day of your life, for the child is partly you. But in another way, you have never met this child, for this is a unique individual, one of a kind. You have an important message to give him or her. What you do and say can help shape this child's point of view of the world.

What message do you have to convey to your child? Make it an important one, something that can help that boy or girl come to grips with reality and still live a fulfilling life.

You may write your communication to this unborn child in the form of a letter, a short essay, or even in a parable or short-story form. Just be sure the message is clear and that it is honest.

Getting It Down

Check through your rough draft carefully. Be sure this writing is the best you are capable of. Be sure your voice comes through clearly and that any reader will see that you mean what you say.

Checking It Out

Copy over your final draft and turn it in. Your teacher will return the paper after evaluation so you may keep it. You may wish to give it to a son or daughter some day.

Getting It Right

Acknowledgments

Grateful acknowledgment is made to the publishers, authors, or copyright holders for permission to use and adapt the following materials in this book:

G.Q. Magazine: Review of *Fort Apache, the Bronx* by Rex Reed. Copyright © 1981 by G. Q. Magazine, Inc.

Holt, Rinehart and Winston, Publishers: From *The Starship and the Canoe* by Kenneth Brower. Copyright © 1978 by Kenneth Brower. Reprinted by permission of Holt, Rinehart and Winston, Publishers, New York; From *A Rumor of War* by Philip Caputo. Copyright © 1977 by Philip Caputo. Reprinted by permission of Holt, Rinehart and Winston, Publishers.

Milton Kaplan: "Feels Like Spring" by Milton Kaplan. © copyright 1952, by Milton Kaplan.

William Morrow & Company: "The Adolescent Boy" from *Growing Up in New Guinea* by Margaret Mead. Copyright 1930, 1958 by Margaret Mead. By permission of William Morrow & Company.

National Geographic Society: "The Tallgrass Prairie: Can It Be saved?" by Dennis Farney; "The World of the American Indian" by Jules Billard © National Geographic Society, Washington, D.C.

New Directions: "Visit to Grandpa's" Dylan Thomas, *Portrait of the Artist as a Young Dog.* Copyright 1940 by New Directions Corporation. Reprinted by permission of New Directions.

Peachtree Publishers, Ltd.: Excerpt from "The Class of '64," In *Kathy Sue Loudermilk, I Love You* by Lewis Grizzard, Atlanta, Georgia: Peachtree Publishers, Ltd., 1979, pp. 57–58. (Peachtree Publishers, Ltd. 494 Armour Circle, N.E., Atlanta, GA 30324)

Runner's World Magazine Co.: From *Runner's World*, May, 1981, p. 3, Runner's World Magazine Co., 1400 Stierlin Rd., Mountain View, CA 94043.

Shaftesbury Publishing Company: From *The Book of Merlyn* by T.H. White. The University of Texas Press. Copyright © 1977 by Shafesbury Publishing Company.

Gene Shalit: Review of *Ordinary People,* © Gene Shalit © 1981 LHT Publishing, Inc. Reprinted with permission of the author and Ladies' Home Journal.

Simon & Schuster: *The Chosen.* Copyright © 1967 by Chaim Potok reprinted by permission of Simon & Schuster, a division of Gulf & Western Corporation.

'TEEN Magazine: "Desk Writings," "Moving Day," Table of Contents, from 'TEEN magazine, May 1981.

Triangle Communications Inc.: "This teacher is in a class by herself," "Drafting Women: The Ultimate Equality?" Reprinted from *Seventeen* ® Magazine. Copyright © 1981 by Triangle Communications Inc. All rights reserved.

Writer's Handbook

Special Problems in Writing

Most writers operate with a "first-things-first" method. They get their ideas down on paper and then worry about following the conventions of spelling, punctuation, and usage. We certainly suggest you do the same. The sections which follow are here to help you with problems you might encounter when you revise your rough draft. There are several sections, each serving a special purpose.

The following table of contents indicates the areas covered and the pages on which assistance may be found.

Usage

USE OF PRONOUNS

The following examples provide models which should guide you in the proper use of pronouns. Refer to the sample sentences and find one which is similar to the sentence you are concerned about. Then see how the pronouns have been used and make sure that your sentence uses the pronouns similarly.

Subject

___ liked the movie.	___ and ___ liked the movie.
I	I I
We	We we
You	You you
He	He he
She	She she
They	They they
It	It it

Direct Object

The kangaroo chased ___.	The kangaroo chased ___ and ___.
me	me me
us	us us
you	you you
him	him him
her	her her
them	them them
it	it it

Predicate Pronoun

The winner is ___.	The winners are ___.
was	were
I	we
you	you
she	they
he	

H-5

Object of the preposition

The fight was with ___.

- me
- us
- you
- her
- him
- them
- it

The fight was between ___ and ___.

me	me
us	us
you	you
her	her
him	him
them	them
it	it

Possession

___ running impressed the judges.

My
Your
His
Her
Their
Its

Indirect Object

The faculty sent ___ the book.

- me
- us
- you
- him
- her
- them
- it

The faculty sent ___ and ___ the book.

me	me
us	us
you	you
him	him
her	her
them	them
it	it

SUBJECT-VERB AGREEMENT

A verb must agree in number with its subject. A singular subject takes a singular verb; a plural subject takes a plural verb.

That *man owns* the store.   (singular subject and singular verb)
Those two *women own* the store.   (plural subject and plural verb)

Past tense verbs are the same in singular and plural except for forms of the verb "be."

it *missed*, they *missed*   I *looked*, we *looked*
he *shared*, they *shared*   he *was*, they *were* (changes for
                               a form of the verb "be")

Compound subjects joined by *and* take a plural verb, whether the subjects are singular, plural, or mixed:

Sue and her father *cook* delicious family meals.
The actors and actresses *need* more rehearsals.
Only three students and one teacher *want* to come along.

The number of the verb is not affected by words or phrases between the verb and its subject:

A *resolution* of these problems *is* vital.
Diplomacy, as well as intelligence, *is* crucial.
The *construction* of more skyscrapers *is* unavoidable.

The following pronoun subjects use a singular verb: anybody, anyone, each, either, everybody, everyone, neither, one, no one, someone, somebody:

Does anybody want to learn? *Each* of the boys *has* money.
No one cares enough. *Someone has* to accept the responsibility.

The following pronoun subjects use a plural verb: both, few, many, several:

Both Larry and Tony *are* excellent divers.
Many are supportive of the administration's stance.
Several of the teachers *were* angry.

The following pronoun subjects use either a singular or plural verb depending on the meaning of the sentence: any, all, most, none, some:

Some of the merchandise *was* stolen.

Some of the dresses *were* stolen.
All of the fruit *is* ripe.
All of the bananas *are* ripe.
None of the construction *is* completed.
None of the buildings *are* completed.

Whether the subject precedes or follows the verb, the verb must agree with its subject in number:

Has anyone seen Jim?
The *assignment was* scribbled on the chalkboard.
On the chalkboard *was* scribbled the *assignment*.
Here *comes* the *sun*.
Here *come* the football *players*.

Singular subjects joined by *or* or *nor* use a singular verb; when a singular and a plural subject are joined by *or* or *nor*, use the verb that agrees with the nearer subject:

Either the *lawyer* or the *witness is* lying.
Either the *lawyer* or the *witnesses are* lying.
Neither the *students* nor the *teacher knows* how to balance the equation.

A collective noun used as a subject takes a singular verb when the subject refers to a unit. If the subject refers to the individuals of a group rather than to a unit, use a plural verb:

The *audience is* thrilled with the performance.
The *audience are* clapping their hands wildly.
The *number* of car accidents *increases* each year.
A *number* of teachers *are* retiring in June.

When the subject of a subordinate clause is a relative pronoun (which, that, who), the number of the verb agrees with the antecedent.

He spread a <u>rumor</u> *that was* unforgivable.
He spread <u>rumors</u> *that were* unforgivable.
Sue is a <u>person</u> *who loves* music.
Sue is one of those <u>people</u> *who love* music.

Plural subjects which indicate amount, distance, or other singular units of measure require singular verbs:

A hundred *dollars is* a lot of money.
1,000 *miles seems* like a long drive.
Three *inches* off the bottom *makes* the skirt a lot shorter.

VERB TENSE

Do not mix present, past, and future time within a passage.

Mr. Browning had been my friend for years. When I was a little girl he even took me horseback riding a few times. After I was saddled onto the horse, he <u>looks</u> at me and <u>says</u>, "I wish I had a little girl like you for a daughter."

The underscored verbs are present tense. Past tense should have been maintained by using the following verbs . . . he *looked* at me and *said*,"

When statements either occur in the present or are "timeless" (meaning true in both the present and the past), use the present tense even though the rest of the sentence or paragraph uses the past.

Dr. Williams believed that Albert Einstein, who uncovered the principles of relativity and expanded on other laws of physics, <u>is</u> the first and foremost scientific genius of all time.

Use the present participle to indicate an action or state of being that occurs at the same time as the main verb:

Glancing carefully from side to side, Eleanor *led* Jeramie across the street.

Being the eldest, Sue *felt* responsible for her younger sister.

Use either the past participle or the perfect participle to indicate an action or state of being that occurs before the time of the main verb:

Left alone by her wealthy husband's sudden death, my client naturally distrusted her flock of sudden admirers.   (past participle)

Having completed the exam early, Jim went outside for some fresh air.   (perfect participle)

Concerned by her son's sudden unwillingness to communicate, Mrs. Frank sought the help of a psychologist.   (past participle)

ACTIVE AND PASSIVE VOICE

An *active* voice verb expresses an action performed by the subject. A *passive* voice verb expresses an action performed upon the subject.

Active Voice

Passive Voice

action
His bat struck the ball.

action
The ball was struck by his bat.

Use the active voice, which is more immediate and lively, whenever possible in narrative and descriptive writing.

When the doer of the action is unknown or when the direct object (the receiver of the action) is of more interest than the doer of that action, use the passive voice.

On the way to the airport, I stopped at my bank's special services window and *was given* travelers' checks for cash.

THE IMPERATIVE

When giving directions, avoid shifting between the imperative and other verb forms.

Correct:

Before you go to bed, *turn* off the sprinkler, *cover* the plants, and *turn* off the lights.

Incorrect:

Before you go to bed, *turn* off the sprinkler, *cover* the plants, and *you need to turn* off the lights.

PLACEMENT OF MODIFIERS

Avoid "dangling" introductory phrases and clauses that do not sensibly and clearly modify a word in the main clause.

Strong:

Overcooked and tough, the meat was inedible.

Dangling Modifier:

Overcooked and tough, I could not eat the meat.   (*Overcooked and tough* mistakenly appears to modify *I*.)

Strong:

Straining under a load of books, he caught his toe on the edge of the step.

Dangling Modifier:

Straining under a load of books, his toe caught on the edge of the step.   (*Straining under a load of books* seems to modify *toe*.)

Strong:

After I graduated from high school, my mother bought me a new car.

Dangling Modifier:

After graduating from high school, my mother bought me a new car. (*After graduating from high school* seems to modify *mother*.)

RUN-ONS AND FRAGMENTS

Be careful not to fuse two or more sentences together without using either a conjunction or the proper punctuation. Here are sentence-combining exercises which show how two simple sentences can be joined in different ways.

1. Joining with *and, but,* or *or*
    The apples were green_x   (, but)
    The oranges were red.
    >   The apples were green, but the oranges were red.

2. Joining with a *semicolon*
    The apples were green_x   (;)
    The oranges were red.
    >   The apples were green; the oranges were red.

3. Joining with *a semicolon followed by a conjunctive adverb*
    The apples were green_x   (; however,)
    The oranges were red.
    >   The apples were green; however, the oranges were red.

A fragment is an incomplete sentence or a group of words that is not complete. Usually it lacks either a complete verb or a subject. Be sure not to let a fragment stand alone, as if it were a sentence. Here are a few examples of sentence fragments:

>   The reason being that I was too tired to stick around.
>   Although I could have done the job better than the person she hired.

There are two easily identifiable types of sentence fragments: the phrase fragment and the subordinate clause.
    Do not separate either a phrase or a subordinate clause from the sentence.

The Phrase Fragment

Complete sentence

>   My parents' new townhouse is on the east side of a small Wisconsin lake in a wooded area full of ravines.

Fragment

> My parents' new townhouse is on the east side of a small Wisconsin lake. *In a wooded area full of ravines.* (Prepositional fragment)

Complete sentence

> As I drove by her house, I saw Jean struggling to push a clunky old lawnmower across a lawn overtaken by weeds.

Fragment

> As I drove by her house, I saw Jean. *Struggling to push a clunky old lawnmower across a lawn overtaken by weeds.* (Participial fragment)

The Subordinate Clause Fragment

Complete sentence

> Although I won't be able to attend next Monday's meeting, I will attend Thursday's session.

Subordinate clause fragment

> *Although I won't be able to attend next Monday's meeting.* I will attend Thursday's session.

Complete sentence

> When the rains come and the breeze is warm, it feels like spring.

Subordinate clause fragment

> *When the rains come and the breeze is warm.* It feels like spring.

Punctuation and Capitalization

COMMA

The comma (,) is the most frequently used punctuation mark within the sentence. When used effectively, it can make lengthy sentences easy to understand. When used carelessly, it can cause your reader to miss the point of your writing. The following examples show you how commas are used by many writers. Emphasis is placed on the kind of materials that you will be writing in school.

Commas Between Items in a Series

Three or more words, phrases, or clauses used together in a sentence make up a series (*words*, *phrases*, or *clauses* in this very sentence make a series of words). The commas help you use a shorthand form of repeating part of a sentence several times. Look at the following example:

The Great Hall was decorated with paper flowers.

~~The Great Hall was decorated with~~ streamers.   (,)

~~The Great Hall was decorated with~~ two giant gazeboes.   (, and)

> The Great Hall was decorated with paper flowers, streamers, and two giant gazeboes.

The commas allow you to say three things about the decorations in the Great Hall without repeating "The Great Hall was decorated with" three times.

In this next sentence, the phrases in the series are expanded and moved to another position.

Paper flowers ~~decorated the Great Hall.~~

Streamers of twisted crepe paper ~~decorated the Great Hall.~~   (,)

and Two giant gazeboes surrounded by green plants decorated the Great Hall.   (, and)

> Paper flowers, streamers of twisted crepe paper, and two giant gazeboes surrounded by green plants decorated the Great Hall.

A series ordered with commas can be made of single words:

Nouns

Jim placed in the semi-finals competition.

Jose placed in the semi-finals competition.   (,)

, and   Michelle placed in the semi-finals competition.   (, and)

Jim, Jose, and Michelle placed in the semi-finals competition.

Erica likes pickles on her sandwich.

Erica likes mustard on her sandwich.   (,)

, and
Erica likes sprouts on her sandwich.   (, and)

Erica likes pickles, mustard, and sprouts on her sandwich.

Adjectives

The streamers made the gym look like a Fourth-of-July celebration.

The streamers were red.

The streamers were white.   (,)

, and
The streamers were blue.   (, and)

The red, white, and blue streamers made the gym look like a Fourth-of-July celebration.

If you add words that modify red, white, blue, and streamers, use the same two commas.

The red, white, and blue streamers made the gym look like a Fourth-of-July celebration.

The red was brilliant.

The white was chalky.

The blue was royal.

The streamers were crepe.

The <u>brilliant</u> red, <u>chalky</u> white, and <u>royal</u> blue <u>crepe</u> streamers made the gym <u>look</u> like a Fourth-of-July celebration.

A series ordered with commas can be made of simple sentences:

The clouds appeared.

   The wind came up.   (,)

, and   The rains fell for hours.   (, and)

The clouds appeared, the wind came up, and the rains fell for hours.

A series ordered with words such as <u>and</u>, <u>or</u>, or <u>nor</u> does **not** need commas.

Neither   Wind kept New Year's Eve motorists off the roads.   (Neither)

nor   Snow kept New Year's Eve motorists off the roads.   (nor)

nor   Ice kept New Year's Eve motorists off the roads.   (nor)

Neither wind nor snow nor ice kept New Year's Eve motorists off the roads.

Commas Between Pairs or Items

Two clauses are usually combined with commas even if the items are already joined with a conjunction such as <u>and</u>, <u>but</u>, <u>yet</u>, <u>or</u>, <u>nor</u>, or <u>for</u>.

Long independent clauses need commas:

This arrangement would be more convenient for me.

, but   You must consider the others in the group.   (, but)

This arrangement would be more convenient for me, but <u>you</u> <u>must</u> consider the others in the group.

Short independent clauses do **not** need commas:

You go ahead.

and   I'll come later.   (and)

<u>You</u> go ahead and I'll come later.

Dependent clauses in pairs do **not** need commas:

When   The trees begin to bud.   (When)

and   The ice melts.   (and)

It will feel like spring.   (, then)

When the trees begin to bud and the ice melts, then it will feel like spring.

Paired phrases of any length are not separated from each other by commas:

Adverb Phrases:

mopping
While   Burt ~~mops~~ up the mess in the kitchen.   (While ——-ing)

answering
and   Burt ~~answers~~ the phone with his free hand.   (and ——-ing)

,   Burt had his first misgivings about having his own apartment.   (,)

While mopping up the mess in the kitchen and answering the phone with his free hand, Burt had his first misgivings about having his own apartment.

Verb Phrases:

We looked around everywhere.
but   ~~We~~ couldn't find him   (but)

We looked around everywhere but couldn't find him.

Adjective Phrases:

The ball was quite large.

and
~~The ball was~~ somewhat deflated.   (and)

The ball was quite large and somewhat deflated.

Noun Phrases

The Sulphur Street gang met at noon.

their
and   ~~The Sulphur Street gang's~~ uptown rivals met at noon   (and)

The Sulphur Street gang and their uptown rivals met at noon.

Commas After Introductory Items in a Sentence

It is sometimes effective to set the stage for your readers with an introductory item before you give them the content of your sentence. When you do so, use a comma to set off the introduction from the main part of the sentence. If you don't, you might confuse your readers.

Introductory Words

> Above, the thick clouds began to disperse and let the sun peek through.
>
> Somewhere, somehow, we've got to get to the bottom of this.

Introductory Phrases

> By the way, Jim was looking for you.
>
> As a matter of fact, I am pretty tired of listening to you complain about school.

Introductory Clauses

> When you finish playing, the piano needs to be dusted.

Commas Before and After Items That Interrupt Sentences

Appositives

Words, phrases, or clauses in apposition are nouns that follow another noun in the sentence; appositives further explain or identify or restate the noun that they follow. Notice how the appositives interrupt the flow of the sentences they are in and add needed information.

Words

> Lena Wilson played the piano in the concert.
>
> ~~Lena Wilson is~~ a student. (, —,)
>
> Lena Wilson, a student, played the piano in the concert.

Phrases

> Pierre is returning to Paris next week.
>
> ~~Pierre is~~ our foreign exchange student. (, —,)
>
> Pierre, our foreign exchange student, is returning to Paris next week.

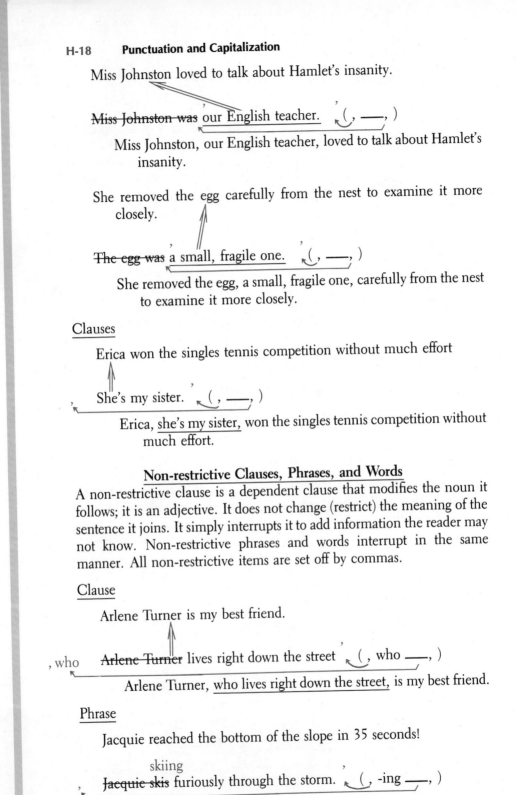

Miss Johnston loved to talk about Hamlet's insanity.

~~Miss Johnston was~~ our English teacher.   (, ——,)

> Miss Johnston, our English teacher, loved to talk about Hamlet's insanity.

She removed the egg carefully from the nest to examine it more closely.

~~The egg was~~ a small, fragile one.   (, ——,)

> She removed the egg, a small, fragile one, carefully from the nest to examine it more closely.

Clauses

Erica won the singles tennis competition without much effort

She's my sister.   (, ——,)

> Erica, she's my sister, won the singles tennis competition without much effort.

Non-restrictive Clauses, Phrases, and Words

A non-restrictive clause is a dependent clause that modifies the noun it follows; it is an adjective. It does not change (restrict) the meaning of the sentence it joins. It simply interrupts it to add information the reader may not know. Non-restrictive phrases and words interrupt in the same manner. All non-restrictive items are set off by commas.

Clause

Arlene Turner is my best friend.

, who   ~~Arlene Turner~~ lives right down the street   (, who ——,)

> Arlene Turner, who lives right down the street, is my best friend.

Phrase

Jacquie reached the bottom of the slope in 35 seconds!

skiing
, ~~Jacquie skis~~ furiously through the storm.   (, -ing ——,)

Jacquie, skiing furiously through the storm, reached the bottom
of the slope in 35 seconds!

Words

Fido chased Fluffy away.

Fido is unfriendly.   (, ——,)

Fluffy is friendly.   (, ——,)

Fido, unfriendly, chased Fluffy, friendly, away.

Nouns of Direct Address

Sometimes you may interrupt your sentence to address your readers
directly. You may simply want to get their attention or you may want to
convince them of your seriousness. Set off their names with commas.

We are proud to present, ladies and gentlemen, "The Greatest Show
on Earth!"

You can be assured, Carol, of the money by the end of the month.

Parenthetical Expressions

Parenthetical expressions are words or phrases used to explain, emphasize, or qualify a statement. Some common parenthetical expressions are:
as a matter of fact, consequently, however, for example, for instance, I
believe (think, hope), indeed, moreover, on the other hand, therefore.

He is, I believe, the only person who can do the job well.

Jim did say, however, that he would think it over before making his
final decision.

The house next door, as a matter of fact, is for sale right now.

I can't wait around this town for two more weeks; consequently, we'll
have to make the decision this week.

Embedded Questions

Short questions within a sentence are set off with commas as well.

Team A is the stronger of the two.

Don't you agree?   (, ——,)

Team A is, don't you agree, the stronger of the two?

Phrases Used for Emphasis

A sleek limousine pulled into the driveway.

A limousine was hardly the car I expected   (, —— ,)

A sleek limousine, hardly the car I expected, pulled into the driveway.

Speaker Tags in Direct Quotations

"I am not the only student who thinks so!"

" She argued.   (," —— ,")

"I am not," she argued, "the only student who thinks so!"

"Those will have to do until I can afford new radial tires."

" Jim mumbled,   (," —— ,")

"Those will have to do," Jim mumbled, "until I can afford new radial tires."

Commas in Certain Conventional Situations

Items in dates and addresses:
   On Monday, February 5, 1981, the building was destroyed.
   He has lived at 1500 Park Avenue, New York, New York, since August, 1956.

The salutation of a friendly letter and the closing of any letter:

   Dear Nancy,   Dear Father,   Love,   Sincerely,

Degrees and titles that follow names:

   Joseph Lytle, Ph.D., authored the Preface to the book.
   James Johnson, Jr., will talk on endangered species of birds in Newfoundland this Sunday.

SEMICOLON

There are three primary uses for semicolons in more formal papers:

<u>Independent Clauses without Conjunctions</u>

Walter started walking toward the car.

;   Nothing would make him turn back.   (;)

Walter started walking toward the car; nothing would make him turn back.

<u>Independent Clauses with Certain Conjunctions</u>   (for example, <u>for instance</u>, <u>however</u>)

The bell rings at 11:30.

; however   It has been late before today.   (; however,)

The bell rings at 11:30; however, it has been late before today.

<u>Between Word Groups Containing Commas</u>

The paper was full of humor.

,   ~~The paper was full of~~ life.   (,)

, and   ~~The paper was full of~~ happiness.   (, and)

; but   Its punctuation ~~was horrible.~~   (; but)

,   Its spelling ~~was horrible.~~   (,)

were
, and   Its capitalization was horrible.   (, and)

The paper was full of humor, life, and happiness; but its punctuation, spelling, and capitalization were horrible.

COLON

There are four uses for the colon in writing:

<u>At the Introduction of a list of items</u>

Our guidebook recommended the following items.

:   ~~It recommended~~ a knife.   (:)

,   ~~It recommended~~ a compass.   (,)

~~It recommended~~ a small backpack.   (,)

~~It recommended~~ some edibles.   (,)

~~It recommended~~ a canteen.   (,)

~~It recommended~~ matches.   (,)

~~It recommended~~ a sweater.   (,)

, and   ~~It recommended~~ a camera.   (, and)

Our guidebook recommended the following items: a knife, a compass, a small backpack, some edibles, a canteen, matches, a sweater, and a camera.

At the Introduction of a Formal Statement or Address

The world will never forget Theodore Roosevelt.

or   ~~The world will never forget~~ his famous words.   (or)

:   "Walk softly and carry a big stick."   (;)

The world will never forget Theodore Roosevelt or his famous words: "Walk softly and carry a big stick."

After an Independent Clause that is explained by a second clause

Clothing isn't made the way it used to be.

:   Seams tear easily.   (:)

,   Zippers break.   (,)

, and   Fabric isn't very durable.   (, and)

Clothing isn't made the way it used to be: seams tear easily, zippers break, and the fabric isn't very durable.

Certain Conventional Situations

Salutation of a formal letter:
Dear Sirs: Gentlemen: Ladies: To Whom It May Concern:

In noting time:
1:15 a.m.   12:30 p.m.

Biblical references and other bibliographical references:
John 19:57   James 9:1   Hebrews 2:7   Proverbs 34:50
Boston: Allyn and Bacon, Inc.

APOSTROPHE

You may use the apostrophe (') for three different purposes in writing: it can signal possession (Erin's book), plurals (I made two A's.), or an omission of letters (aren't for are not, we've for we have).

Possession

To show possession for one person or thing (any singular noun), place the apostrophe and then an s after the noun or indefinite pronoun ('s).

The opinion was written on the board.

The opinion belonged to the teacher   ('s)

The teacher's opinion was written on the board.

The taxi came to a screeching halt.

The taxi belonged to Gus   ('s)

Gus's taxi came to a screeching halt.

Other Examples: brother's gloves, Caroline's hat, the elephant's trunk, Rawl's grocery, Mr. Comb's glasses, bus's brakes, everybody's loss, anybody's guess, someone else's problem

To show possession for several people or things (any plural noun), place only an apostrophe after the noun   (') . . .

The swimming pool is now empty.

The swimming pool belongs to the girls.   (')

The girls' swimming pool is now empty.

If the plural form does **not** end in s. Plurals such as deer, children and women are made possessive by adding 's.

deer's,   children's,   women's

When two or more nouns possess something individually, indicate the possession (according to the rules above) for each noun.

The departments are on different floors of the store.

~~One department is for~~ men.   ('s)
                    's

~~Another department is for~~ women.   (and ___'s)
                  and   's

The men's and women's departments are on different floors of the store.

When words indicate joint possession, indicate possession (according to the preceding rules) for only the last noun.
The records were the hit of the party.

The records belonged to Jose and Marguerita.   ('s)
                                         's

Jose and Marguerita's records were the hit of the party.

Other examples: the cat and dog's dinner time,
                   mom and dad's vacation

When using a personal pronoun to replace any possessive noun, do **not** add an apostrophe.
The dress was two sizes too large for me.

The dress belonged to Evelyn.   (her)
                  her

Her dress was two sizes too large for me.

Other examples: his gloves, its profit, their mis-
          take   (Don't confuse the possessive pronoun, its with
          the contraction of it is—it's. They are easy to mix up.)

Plural

To indicate the plural of numbers, symbols, letters of the alphabet, and words referred to as words, use 's.
How many is three 3's and four 4's?
Count the +'s and the −'s in this equation.
Occasion is spelled with two c's.
Try to cut down on the number of and's and but's in your paragraph.

Omission of Letters

We have only just begun.   ('ve)   We've only just begun.
There is no doubt about it.   ('s)   There's no doubt about it.
You have not told everything.   (n't)   You haven't told
                                                    everything.

DASH

The dash is used somewhat as the comma is. It is more appropriate to use a dash than a comma . . .

when the shift in thought is *sudden*
   I hope that next time he has the sense to—but perhaps, we should
      first hear what he has to say for himself.

or when the interruption in the sentence is especially abrupt
   He could have—and indeed should have—been a bit more consider-
      ate.
      Other examples: His goal—if you can even call it a goal—
         should have been to get himself out of debt.

or when the series ordered by commas is long and possibly confusing
   You should use sections—the table of contents, chapters with
      headings, tables and graphs, appendixes, and references—to
      make your research paper easy to read.

HYPHEN

Use a hyphen between syllables to divide a word at the end of a line.
   regis-/ter
   oppor-/tunity
   indica-/tive

Be sure to leave more than one letter of a divided word at the end of or at the start of a line.
   e-/lope (faulty)   (Put the entire word on the next line.)
   speed-/y (faulty)   (Put the entire word on the line.)

When there is a prefix or a suffix, divide the word just after the prefix or just before the suffix.

    inter-/dependent   (not in-/terdependent)

    merri-/ment   (not mer-/riment)

    sub-/ordinate   (not subor-/dinate)

    elusive-/ly   (not elu-/sively)

Often, a good place to divide a word is between double consonants.

    run-/ning

    Missis-/sippi

Use hyphens when two or more words combine to form a modifier.

    a would-be movie star

    a well-kept beard

    a don't-care-if-you-do attitude

If the first word of the modifier unit is an adverb ending in *ly,* do not use a hyphen.

    a neatly dressed woman

    a poorly worded sentence

Hyphenate compound numbers from twenty-one through ninety-nine, and fractions.

    Thirty-three years old hardly makes you old!

    A one-fourth portion goes to charity; the other three-fourths is needed to pay back expenses incurred.

Use a hyphen to avoid confusion or between awkward letter combinations.

    re-collect   (collect again; prevents confusion with recollect meaning *to remember*)

    semi-interesting   (avoids awkwardness of *semiinteresting*)

PARENTHESES

Parentheses indicate another kind of interruption in a sentence. When the interruption includes material most people already know, but some may not, use parentheses.

    Mayor Daley (Chicago) had more political control than any other mayor in the country.

The make-up of carbon dioxide molecules (see Diagram B) consists of two atoms of oxygen and one of carbon.

The film *Gone with the Wind* (1939) was aired on television recently.

Sen. Percy (R., Ill.) was re-elected by a narrow margin.

All other punctuation near the parentheses must come after and not before them. When a parenthetical item is added to a clause that ends with a comma, extend the comma beyond the parenthetical information.

The ghost of Hamlet's father commanded Hamlet's friends to "swear by the sword" (the sword itself was, ironically, symbolic of the cross), forbidding them to tell anybody about his appearance.

BRACKETS

Use brackets to enclose explanations within quoted material when the explanation is not part of the quotation.

Mr. McDonough calmly addressed the audience with these words: "I am honored by it [the nomination for presidency], and if elected I will do my utmost to carry out the awesome responsibilities of this honored position."

Use brackets to enclose explanations within parentheses when the explanation is not part of the material in parentheses.

The molecular structure of more complex molecules is harder to understand. (See page 219 [Chart A] for detailed breakdowns of five complex molecules.)

THE PERIOD

Use a period to follow a statement or a command.

The trees shivered in the cold.

Please keep the noise down.

Use a period after abbreviations.

Dr.   Mr.   Mrs.   Ms.   Nov.   B.C.   Ave.

Abbreviations of various governmental agencies and social, professional, or business organizations are **not** followed by periods.

NATO   UNICEF   CIA   HEW

IBM   dbs (decibals)   mph (miles per hour)

Avoid abbreviating common words in ordinary writing.

Unclear:
Two new mfg. cos. were just built on Co. Blvd. last Oct., just next door to my two bros., Chas. and Jim.

Clear:
Two new manufacturing companies were just built on Colorado Boulevard last October, just next door to my brothers, Charles and Jim.

Indirect questions are followed by a period.
She asked whether I wanted to come.
We wondered how much longer we should wait.

Polite requests in formal business letters are followed by a period.
Will you please send me ten extra copies and bill me for them.

THE QUESTION MARK

Use a question mark to follow a question.
Do you want to come?
How much longer should we wait?

A question mark should be placed inside quotation marks **only** if the quotation itself is a question.
"Do you think you'll come?" he asked me.
BUT
Who said, "All the world's a stage . . ."?

THE EXCLAMATION POINT

Use an exclamation point after statements expressing strong, excited feeling.
Wow! What a dress!
"Cut it out!" he yelled at me sharply. (Note the period after *sharply* and the exclamation mark within the quotation marks.)

ELLIPSES

Use three periods to show where words have been omitted within a quotation; use four periods where words have been omitted at the end of a sentence or where two or more sentences have been omitted.

> I pledge allegiance to the flag . . . and to the republic . . . with liberty and justice for all.

> Speak properly and in as few words as you can, but always plainly, for the end of speech is not to make a show but to be understood. . . .

> Be reserved but not sour . . . cheerful, not light. . . .

QUOTATION MARKS

Use quotation marks before and after a person's exact words. If you aren't quoting a person exactly, you needn't use quotation marks at all.

> She told us to think about our attitude.

If the person's words ask a question, state a command, or simply make a statement, use the appropriate end punctuation inside the second quotation mark.

> I asked, "Why don't you go along?"

When a person's words are interrupted with a quotation stem (said mother, replied George), place a comma and quotation mark before and after the stem.

> "How would you feel," asked Mother, "if Aunt Ruth didn't even mention your birthday?"
> "Leave me alone," I shouted, "before I lose my temper!"

If you use a semi-colon which is not a part of the quotation, place it outside the quotation marks.

> Father said, "I don't want to discuss it at all"; unfortunately, Mr. Rogers thought it was an important matter and refused to drop it.
> He grumbled, "They just don't make clothes the way they used to"; from the looks of what he was wearing, I knew what he meant!

If the sentence is a question, but the quotation is not, place the question mark outside the quotation marks.

Didn't you tell Mark, "Forget it"?
You said to me, "Forget it!" didn't you?

Use quotation marks before and after words referred to as words.

Don't use "but" or "and" at the start of a sentence.
I tried to explain to the psychiatrist my hostility against the world and against the "dopes" that controlled it.

Use quotation marks before and after titles of songs, short stories, short poems, essays, articles, and subdivisions of books (chapters, subheadings, etc.).

"Georgia On My Mind" is Ray Charles' most popular tune.
E.E. Cummings "In Just Spring" is my favorite poem.
I read a fascinating article entitled "Computer Art" in yesterday's newspaper.

BUT

No quotation marks are used for the title of a poem of book length.
Walt Whitman's *Leaves of Grass* is an American classic.

Begin a new paragraph each time a speaker changes.

"I can't wait until Christmas," Jamie babbled, "and school's out for awhile."
"I know what you mean," Sarah sighed wishfully. "I think I'm going skiing for the week between Christmas and New Years."
"Too bad it's not summer vacation coming up," Ralph intervened. "I have a good job this summer!"

When you quote the same person for more than two paragraphs, use quotation marks at the start of each paragraph and at the end of the final paragraph.

"I'll never forget that vacation, because everything seemed to go right.
"First, the weather was perfect. The sun was out every day, the snow was fresh, light, and powdery, just the way I like it. The slopes weren't even crowded. I remembered how sunburned my nose was at the end of the first day.
"Then Sue and Deborah came up. On Sunday morning we all went cross-country skiing, out away from the crowds into some of the back country. All of us worked up a sweat and laughed a lot. At one

point, we even ran into a herd of elk and took some great photographs."

"Photographs?" Jim interrupted. "Do you have them here?"

Extensive quotations are indented five extra spaces from both the left and right margins (ten spaces if beginning a new paragraph) and single-spaced, even if the rest of the paper is double- or triple-spaced. Leave an extra line above and below the indented quoted material to separate it clearly from the rest of the copy. No quotation marks are necessary.

"However that may be," Taylor related, "neither the President nor Secretary of Defense Robert McNamara gave objective review to Westmoreland's operations." Townsend Hoopes further states:

> The Pentagon simply lost sight of the truth that protection for the people against Viet Cong terrors had to be achieved by means that did not themselves alienate the people by causing heavy casualties and wanton physical destruction.

Use single quotation marks to enclose a quotation within a quotation.

"What do you mean by saying, 'Put the news peg in the upper lefthand corner of the first page'?" I asked Mrs. Weber.

CAPITALIZATION

Capitalize the first word in any sentence or in any quoted sentence or fragment.

Everyone agreed that the rooms needed painting. "Do you think that we'll have time to do them next week?" asked Charles.

BUT

"Do you think," asked Charles, "that we'll have time to do them next week?" [Note: "that" is *not* capitalized since it is a continuation of the direct quotation beginning with "Do you think . . .]

Traditionally, the first word in each line of poetry is capitalized. In modern poetry, while this observance is still common, it is **not** a hard and fast rule.

I think that I shall never see
A poem lovely as a tree . . .

Capitalize proper nouns.

Capitalize the names of persons.

Miles Davis   Picasso   Hamlet   Charles Dickens   Mr. McDonald   Mrs. MacDuff   John O'Brien

Capitalize geographical names, including:

Cities, counties, states, countries, continents

Atlantic City, New Jersey, Boulder County, Canada, Europe

Bodies of water

Atlantic Ocean, Black Sea, Lake Michigan, Mississippi River, Beaver Pond, Chipmunk Creek

Islands, peninsulas, straits, canals, beaches, mountains

Hawaii, Florida Peninsula, Strait of Gibraltar, Panama Canal, Daytona Beach, Grand Tetons, Longs Peak

Streets, specific buildings

Broadway, Main Street, Birch Boulevard, Fifty-ninth Street, Highway 119, Sears Tower, White House, Conrad Hilton Hotel

Parks, forests, dams, canyons, valleys

Yellowstone National Park, Pike National Forest, Hoover Dam, Poudre Canyon, Beaver Valley

Recognized parts of the country or world

the North, the Middle East

Note: The words *north, south, east,* and *west* are *not* capitalized when they refer to directions, but *are* capitalized when they refer to sections of the country.

Drive *east* from Colorado for 1,000 miles and you will be in the *Middle West*.

Capitalize the names of ships, boats, planes, trains, awards, and monuments:

S.S. Titanic, the Lucille (name of boat), the Blue Angels, Olympic Gold Medal, the Statue of Liberty

Capitalize the brand names of consumer products—do **not** capitalize any common nouns which may follow the brand name:

Seven-Up, Crest, IBM typewriter, Volkswagon Rabbit, Jay's potato chips, Butternut bread, Sunkist oranges

Capitalize the names of specific rooms and other nouns followed by a numeral or letter;

Room 607   School District 12   Chapter 8   Diagram B

Capitalize the names of school classes—however, the words *freshman, sophomore, junior, senior* are not capitalized when they refer to either a student or a year:

Jim Stone is valedictorian of the *Senior Class*.

They were a fine group of *Seniors*.

Sue is a *junior* this year.

Al's grade point average rose dramatically his *sophomore* year.

Capitalize the names of specific business firms, and governmental, scholastic, professional, and social organizations or departments

Business firms

United Airlines, Xerox Corporation, Sperry Rand, Inc., Flatirons Theatre, Fred's Cafe

Governmental, scholastic, and social organizations

Congress; Department of Health, Education and Welfare; United Nations; French Club; American Honor Society; Phi Beta Kappa; Lions Club, Shriners, Pep Club; Photographic Society of America

Institutions

Harvard University, Lawrence College, Glenbard East High School, Ford Foundation, Institute for Peace Studies, Language Arts Department

Capitalize the names of nationalities, races, and religions

American, French, Oriental, Caucasian, Protestant, Moslem, Catholic, Jewish

Capitalize the names of specific deities or prophets and possessive pronouns or nouns referring to those deities

God, Christ, Buddha, Mohammed, John the Baptist, Zeus, Apollo, Simon Peter

God gave the world *His* only *Son*.

Capitalize proper adjectives, but not the common nouns that follow them.

America, American *people*   Canada, Canadian *winters*
Elizabethan *drama*, Gothic *architecture*, Renaissance *literature*

Capitalize the names of events

Capitalize historical events and periods of time

World War I, Civil War, Battle of Bunker Hill, Dark Ages, Iron Age, the Renaissance

Capitalize special events

the Super Bowl, the Olympics, the World Series

Capitalize political or religious holidays

Fourth of July, Memorial Day, Christmas, Easter

Capitalize calendar items including the days of the week and the months of the year

Book Week, National Secretaries' Week, Sunday, April

Do **not** capitalize the names of seasons unless personified.

I can't wait for spring.

BUT

There was Spring, tripping in all dressed in green with flowers in her hair.

Capitalize specific titles of persons

Capitalize the title of a person when used preceding a name

Superintendent John Knolls   Reverend Philips

Dean Williams   General Eisenhower

Capitalize a title either used alone or after a name only if referring to a high government official or in order to show special respect.

Hello, Reverend   What next, Coach?   President Roosevelt

Jim Withers, president of the Senior Class

John Daley, ex-Mayor of Chicago (**Note:** the prefix *ex-* is not capitalized.)

the Senator

BUT

a committee of six senators

the Chief of Police

Vice-President Johnson (Two capitals are required only when referring to the Vice-President of a nation.)

Capitalize the first word and all important words in titles of books, short stories, poems, plays, periodicals, articles, documents, songs, films, and works of art. Articles (*a, an, the*) and conjunctions and prepositions of fewer than five letters are not capitalized unless they are the first word in the title.

Have you ever read the *Chicago Tribune?*

"Snows of Kilimanjaro" is, perhaps, illustrative of Hemingway at his best.

I Never Promised You a Rose Garden is the story of the rehabilitation of a precocious, teen-age schizophrenic named Deborah.

The award-winning film, "One Flew over the Cuckoo's Nest," was aired for the first time on television in 1979.

Capitalize the titles of academic subjects only if they refer to languages or specific course titles.

French, Spanish, English, History II, Algebra I, American Poetry, Advanced Placement English

BUT

home economics, history, algebra, chemistry

Capitalize words showing a family relationship when used with a person's name or in place of that person's name, but **not** when preceded by a possessive.

> my *u*ncle, his *a*unt, Uncle Remus, Aunt Sally,
> my *c*ousin Ralph, my *s*ister Ruth
> I told my *m*other all about it.
> *BUT*
> I told Mother all about it.

Always capitalize the pronoun "I."

> *I* know what *I* know when *I* know it.

UNDERLINING (ITALICS)

Underline (or use italics) for titles of books, periodicals, names of ships, and works of art. Do not underline or italicize *a*, *an*, or *the* preceding a title unless it is part of the title.

> *The Scarlet Letter* by Hawthorne
> Have you read the *Wall Street Journal*?
> My favorite painting is *Portrait of an Artist's Son* by Renoir.
> The *Titanic* is a well-known ship.

Underline (or use italics) for words, numbers, letters, and figures referred to as such.

> The number 6 looks like the number 9 upside down.
> The word *and* is the most common conjunction.

Underline (or use italics) for foreign words or phrases.

> She always used the words *c'est la vie* when something problematic
> but unavoidable happened.

Commonly Confused Words

The following words are commonly confused. Sometimes the problem is with spelling; sometimes it is with meaning.

accept/except	I accept your settlement offer except for the part on the first page.
advice/advise	I advise you to take my advice and be careful.
affect/effect	The smell affects me so much I feel sick. What effect does it have on you? Could you effect a change in the ventilation?
already/all ready	John has already gone. My friends, are you all ready to go?
alter/altar	We can't alter the past. The altar was covered with flowers.
altogether/ all together	I don't altogether dislike the taste. The flavors are blended all together in the drink.
angel/angle	A triangle has three angles. Much early art portrays angels as babies.
assent/ascent/ ascend	Will your parents assent to your making the ascent? Don't ascend without their permission.
bath/bathe	I decided to bathe in the warm bath water.
bear/bare	The only kind of bear I have seen is a bare bear.
berth/birth	She gave birth to a baby in the berth of a Pullman car.
bore/boar	Bore holes in the tree and attach the fence. That will keep the boar away. However, without any excitement, the country may bore you.
born/borne	Where were you born? They have borne their troubles well.
brake/break	Step on the brake lightly. These glasses I'm holding break easily.
capital/capitol	Springfield is the capital city where they voted on capital punishment. It takes lots of capital to start a business. The Capitol building is in Washington.
cite/site/sight	He cited Shakespeare in his paper. The site of our new home has not been picked yet. A beautiful sight greeted us when we saw the lovely valley.

cloths/clothes	There are six new wash cloths under the pile of clean clothes in the linen closet.
coarse/course	The wool shirt felt coarse against my skin. The plane followed a straight course. Chicken Kiev was the main course. I signed up for the course in Latin.
consul/council/ counsel	I called the British consul in Rome to get help. Jeremy was elected to the school council. I tried to get counsel from the best lawyer in town. She agreed to be my counsel.
desert/dessert	The Sahara Desert is huge. Grandpa would never desert the family. We had chocolate mousse for dessert.
diary/dairy	I once wrote in my diary about my experiences milking cows at my uncle's dairy.
dissent/descent/ descend	Did your parents dissent when you asked them if you could make the descent? You didn't descend in spite of their dissent, did you?
formerly/formally	She was formerly Miss America. She formally addressed the group.
forth/fourth	Go forth to battle in the fourth company of infantry.
its/it's	The cat licked its paws. It's too late now.
later/latter	I'll see you later. I'll choose the latter of the two.
lose/loose	Don't lose your temper. I have to tie up some loose ends.
moral/morale	You have to have strong moral character to keep your morale high these days.
miner/minor	My father was a coal miner. A sixteen-year-old is considered a minor in some states. I have one minor objection.
muscle/mussel	There are many mussels at our beach. The athlete has very strong muscles.
pair/pare	Please pare a pair of apples.
past/passed	Grandma lives in the past. We drove right past your house. I passed up a great opportunity.
peace/piece	I feel at peace in the mountains when I have a big piece of pie.
personal/ personnel	I don't want a personal involvement. I took the job because I liked the personnel working there.
plane/plain	They hired four planes to spray herbicides. She had a plain dress on. The settlers traveled across the plain.
precede/proceed	I will precede you as you proceed down the aisle.

presence/presents	She had a mysterious, self-contained presence. We opened our presents on Jim's birthday.
principal/ principle	Greed was his principal motivation. Who is principal of the school? He has strong principles.
prophecy/ prophesy	Does the prophet prophesy? Or is his prophecy just a lot of words?
quiet/quite	Be quiet. I'm quite sure we'll go.
rain/reign/rein	The king began his reign in a heavy rain; it was pouring so hard his horse would barely respond to the rein.
sheathe/sheath	Sheathe your sword in its sheath.
stationary/ stationery	The seats were stationary and couldn't be moved. I received a letter on perfumed stationery.
straight/strait	We went straight through the Strait of Gibraltar on our ship.
than/then	I am taller than he. If he puts on elevator shoes, then he'll be taller.
their/they're there	It's all their fault. They're waiting at the club. Put the flowers over there. There are three of us.
to/too/two	Give it to me. He is too young for me. I'm coming, too. Here are two of my best recipes.
waist/waste	She has a 24-inch waist. Do you know what we should do with nuclear waste?
weather/whether	We're going whether the weather cooperates or not.
wholly/holy	The group was wholly in agreement. The saint was holy.
whose/who's	Whose hat is this? Who's responsible here?
your/you're	This is your copy. You're too young to drive.

Lie and Lay

Lie means "to recline" or "to be in a horizontal position." The verb *lie* is intransitive; it never takes an object. *Lay* means "to put or place something down in a resting position." The verb *lay* is transitive; it requires an object.

I think I'll *lie* down.   (intransitive)

Lay the book on the table.   (transitive; *book* is the direct object)

Below are the principal forms of these verbs:

Present	Present Participle	Past	Past Participle
lie	lying	lay	lain
lay	laying	laid	laid

Lie down. I *am lying* down. Five minutes ago, I *lay* down for a nap. Perhaps they have *lain* down for a while.

Lay the book on the table. He *is laying* the book on the table. He *laid* the book on the table. I *have laid* the book on the table.

Sit and Set

Sit means "to assume an upright position." *Sit* is almost always an intransitive verb; it rarely takes an object. *Set* means "to put or place something down." *Set* is a transitive verb; it usually requires an object.

Sit down on the sofa.   (intransitive)

Set the packages down on the table.   (transitive)

Below are the principal forms of these verbs:

Present	*Present Participle*	*Past*	*Past Participle*
sit	sitting	sat	sat
set	setting	set	set

Sit down over there.

He *is sitting* on the floor. He *sat* on the floor.

We *have sat* here waiting for you for hours.

Set the packages on the table. Jane *is setting* the groceries on the front steps.

They *set* the boxes on the floor. We *have set* the larger boxes on the floor.

Rise and Raise

Rise means "to go up" or "to get up." It is intransitive; it never takes an object.

Raise means "to force something to move upward." *Raise* is transitive; it takes an object.

What time does the sun *rise*?

Can you *raise* the flag?

Below are the principal parts of these verbs:

Present	*Present Participle*	*Past*	*Past Participle*
rise	rising	rose	risen
raise	raising	raised	raised

Rise to your feet. He *is rising* to his feet. The crowd *rose* during the Pledge of Allegiance. The moon *has risen* at sunset for the last five days. *Raise* the flag. The janitor *is raising* the flag. Two students *raised* their hands. I *have raised* my hand three times in the last five minutes.

A List of Frequently Misspelled Words

The following list includes many of the words in English which are thought to be difficult to spell. You can solve many spelling problems by checking this list or a dictionary.

A

abbreviate
absence
abundant
accelerator
accidentally
acclimated
accommodate
accompanied
accompaniment
accomplishment
accumulate
accuracy
achievement
acknowledgment
acquaintance
acquire
adequately
adolescent
advantageous
aerial
aggravate
allegiance
allusion
amateur
among
analysis
analyze
angel
angle
annihilate
anonymous
answer
anxiety

anxious
apologetically
apparatus
apparent
appearance
appreciate
appropriate
arctic
argument
arrangement
ascend
ascent
assent
association
atheistic
athletic
attendance
audience
auxiliary
awkward

B

bachelor
ballet
bankruptcy
barbarian
bath
bathe
bear
beggar
beginning
behavior
beneficial
benefit

benefited
berth
bibliography
birth
biscuit
blasphemy
boar
bore
boulevard
boundaries
breath
breathe
brilliant
buffet
buoy
bureau
business
busy

C

calendar
campaign
candidate
captain
carburetor
caricature
catalogue
catastrophe
category
cellar
cemetery
certain
changeable
characteristic

choose
chose
circumstantial
colossal
column
committee
communist
comparative
compelled
competent
competitor
completely
complexion
compulsory
conference
confidentially
connoisseur
conscience
conscientious
consciousness
consistent
controversial
criticism
criticize
curiosity
curious
curriculum

D

dairy
decadent
deceitful
decision
definite

descend
descendant
descent
describe
description
desirable
despair
desperate
devise
diary
different
dilapidated
dilemma
diligence
disappear
disappoint
disapprove
disastrous
disciple
discipline
discrimination
dissatisfied
dissent
dissipate
divide
divine
doesn't
dormitory

E

ecstasy
efficiency
eligible
eliminate
embarrass
emperor
emphasize
endeavor
enthusiastically
environment
equivalent
especially
espionage
exaggerate
exceed
excellent

exceptionally
exhaustion
exhibition
exhilaration
existence
extraordinary
extremely
exuberant

F

familiar
fascinate
fascism
February
feminine
foreign
forfeit
forth
forty
fourth
frantically
freight
fulfill
fundamental

G

gaiety
galaxy
gauge
generally
government
governor
grammar
grammatically
grievous
guarantee

H

handsome
harassment
height
hereditary
hindrance
holy
hospital

horizontal
humorous
hygiene
hypocrisy

I

illusion
imaginary
immediately
incidentally
incredible
independent
indispensable
inevitable
influential
ingenious
initiative
innocent
intellectual
intelligence
interesting
interpretation
interrupt
irrelevant
irresponsible

K

kerosene
knew
knowledge

L

laboratory
larynx
legitimate
leisure
liable
library
license
lightning
liquor
literature
livelihood
loneliness
luxurious

M

magnificence
maintenance
manageable
maneuver
marriage
martyr
mathematics
meant
mediocre
melancholy
melodious
merely
miniature
minute
mischievous
misspell
moral
morale
mortgage
mosquito
municipal
murmuring
muscle
mussel
mysterious

N

naive
necessity
neither
neurotic
nickel
ninety
ninth
noticeable
nuclear

O

obedience
occasion
occurred
omission
opinion
opportunity

optimistic
orchestra
original
outrageous

P

pageant
paid
pain
pamphlet
pane
parallel
paralysis
parliament
particularly
pastime
peasant
penicillin
permanent
permissible
perseverance
persistent
perspiration
persuade
phenomenon
physically
physician
picnicking
playwright
pneumonia
politician
possess
practically
precede
preference
preferred
prejudice
presence
prestige
presumption
prevalent
privilege
probably
procedure
proceed

prominent
pronunciation
propaganda
prophecy
prophesy
psychiatrist
psychoanalysis
pursue

Q

quantity
quietly
quite

R

rain
rebellion
receive
recognize
recommend
reference
rehearsal
reign
rein
religious
remembrance
reminiscent
remittance
repetition
representative
respectful
responsibility
restaurant
rhyme
rhythm

S

sandwich
satisfactorily
saxophone
schedule
secretary
seize
separate

sergeant
sheath
sheathe
siege
significant
similar
sophomore
souvenir
speak
specifically
specimen
speech
sponsor
straight
strait
strictly
stubbornness
succeed
success
superintendent
supersede
surprise
surroundings
susceptible
syllable
symbolic
symmetrical
symphonic
synonymous

T

tariff
temperament
temperature
tendency
thorough
together
tolerance
tomorrow
tortoise
tragedy
transcend
tries
truly
twelfth

typical
tyranny

U

unanimous
undoubtedly
universal
unmistakable
unnatural
unnecessarily
unscrupulous
until
usually

V

vaccine
vacuum
valuable
variation
various
vegetable
vehicle
vengeance
versatile
vigilant
village
villain
vinegar

W

weather
Wednesday
weird
whether
whisper
whistle
wholly
withhold

Y

yacht
yawn

Spelling Helps

VISUALIZING

One of the most successful techniques for remembering the spelling of a word is to see the word in your "mind's eye." If you have this ability, you will be able to retrieve a correct spelling easily, and you will be able to spot misspelled words, too. Most visualizers look at the word on a page, then look away and try to "see" the word in their memories.

MNEMONIC TECHNIQUES

Some people remember correct spellings by developing "hints" which are based on some characteristic of the words they are to spell. The following examples are presented so that you can see how the process works. Only a few of these "hints" are presented, since the best way to use this process is for you to develop your own. Use the examples here as suggestions; then, make up your own tricks to help you remember.

absence	I will "c" you at the end. absence
accompanied	An "a" is accompanied by two "c's" in this word. *acc*ompanied
captain	Don't let it *rain* on the cap*tain*.
describe	There is a *scribe* in de*scribe*.
excellent	There is a prison *cell* in ex*cell*ent.
fundamental	*Fun* is *mental*.
independent	Put a *dent* in indepen*dent*.
knew	The "k" is new.
paid	How is it that *I* always get involved when something is to be *paid*?
parliament	Can there be a *liar* in a par*lia*ment?
pronunciation	A *nun* always has good pro*nun*ciation habits.
speak	Give him an "*a*" and let him spe*a*k.
succeed	It takes double letters to su*cc*eed.
vegetable	Your vege*table* is waiting at the *table*.
Wednesday	We hope to *wed* on *Wed*nesday.

SELECTED SPELLING RULES

IE or EI

Use <u>I</u> before <u>E</u> except after <u>C</u> for the long "<u>E</u>" sound.

believe	priest	<u>after C</u>
fiend	relieve	ceiling
grievance	retrieve	conceit
niece	shriek	deceive
piece	thief	receive

Learn the exceptions to this rule by memorizing this nonsense sentence (Note the spelling of each word):

Neither financier seized either species of weird leisure.

Use <u>E</u> before <u>I</u> when the sound is not a long "<u>E</u>"

freight	neighbor
height	weight

Adding Prefixes

When you add a prefix to a word, the spelling of the word itself does not change.

un + natural = unnatural	over + run = overrun
mis + spell = misspell	im + mobile = immobile
un + excused = unexcused	re + supply = resupply

Adding Suffixes

When adding the suffixes <u>-NESS</u> and <u>-LY</u>, the spelling of the word does not change.

dry + ness = dryness	mere + ly = merely
kind + ness = kindness	shy + ly = shyly

Exceptions: For words that end in <u>Y</u> not representing the long "<u>I</u>" sound, change the <u>Y</u> to <u>I</u> before adding <u>-NESS</u> or <u>-LY</u>.

happy + ness = happiness	ready + ly = readily

Drop the final E before adding a suffix that begins with a vowel.

hope + ing = hoping   live + able = livable
use + able = usable

Retain the final E after C or G if the suffix begins with A or O.

advantage + ous = advantageous   notice + able = noticeable
courage + ous = courageous   service + able = serviceable

Retain the final E before adding a suffix that begins with a consonant.

care + ful = careful   hope + ful = hopeful
Exceptions: argument, awful, ninth, wholly, wisdom

For words ending in Y preceded by a consonant, change the Y to I before adding a suffix. Retain the Y if it is preceded by a vowel.

funny + est = funniest   boy + ish = boyish
happy + ness = happiness   enjoy + ing = enjoying
merry + ment = merriment   stay + ing = staying
Exceptions: Retain the y in words such as *babyish, ladylike, studying.*

Double the final consonant before adding a suffix beginning with a vowel if both of the following two conditions exist: 1) the word has only one syllable *or* the accent is on the second syllable; and 2) if the word ends in a consonant preceded by a vowel.

control + ed = controlled   propel + er = propeller
occur + ence = occurrence   quit + ing = quitting
plan + ing = planning   refer + ed = referred

BUT
cancel + ed = cancelled (Accent not on last syllable, but final
    consonant is doubled)
prefer + able = preferable (Accent shifts to first syllable)

Add K before adding ING, ED or Y to words ending in a hard C.

picnic + ed = picnicked   mimic + ing = mimicking
panic + ed = panicked   traffic + ing = trafficking

Plurals

To form the plural of nouns, observe the following rules:

The most common way to form the plural of a noun is to add S.
  book, books   table, tables   desk, desks

The plural of nouns ending in S, SH, CH and X is formed by adding ES.
  box, boxes   church, churches   dress, dresses

To form the plural of nouns ending in Y *preceded by a consonant*, change the Y to I and add ES.
  army, armies   enemy, enemies   fly, flies

To form the plural of nouns ending in Y *preceded by a vowel*, add S.
  donkey, donkeys   key, keys   monkey, monkeys

To form the plural of most nouns ending in F or FE, add S. However, the plural of a few nouns ending in F or FE is formed by changing the F to V and adding either S or ES.

  chief, chiefs   dwarf, dwarfs
  BUT
  calf, calves   elf, elves
  hoof, hooves   knife, knives
  leaf, leaves   loaf, loaves

To form the plural of nouns ending in O *preceded by a vowel* add S. If the final O is preceded by a consonant, the plural is formed by adding S or ES.

  (O preceded by a vowel)
  rodeo, rodeos   radio, radios

  (O preceded by a consonant)
  domino, dominoes or dominos   tomato, tomatoes
  hero, heroes

All words ending in O that pertain to music, form the plural by adding S.

  alto, altos   piano, pianos
  crescendo, crescendos   solo, solos

To form the plural of compound nouns written as one word, add <u>ES</u> if the word ends in <u>S, SH, CH</u> or <u>X</u> and <u>S</u> if it ends in anything else.
   spoonful, spoonfuls   strongbox, strongboxes

The plural of hyphenated compound nouns consisting of a noun plus modifiers is formed by making the noun plural.
   mother-in-law, mothers-in-law   passer-by, passers-by

Some nouns are the same in the singular and plural.
   deer, sheep, species, trout

Many words of foreign origin have two plurals. Others have a plural that is irregular by English standards. When in doubt, check your dictionary.

Singular	*Plural*
alumna (feminine)	alumnae (feminine)
alumnus (masculine or mixed)	alumni (masculine or mixed)
curriculum	curriculums, curricula
appendix	appendixes, appendices
beau	beaus, beaux
focus	focuses, foci
memorandum	memorandums, memoranda
fungus	funguses, fungi
index	indexes, indices
analysis	analyses
basis	bases
crisis	crises
criterion	criteria

The plural of numbers, letters and symbols is formed by adding an *apostrophe* and <u>S</u>.
   two 5's,   three x's,   How many +'s are there in that equation?

The Research Paper

A research paper is a formal composition that includes information from a number of sources. It is essentially a summary of the information the writer has discovered about a particular subject.

Many research papers simply present the information the writer has found. Others attempt to draw a conclusion which persuades the reader to adopt a particular point of view. A paper on the origins of American jazz would probably be informational; one on ways in which the federal tax system could be reformed could proceed from the facts to a conclusion and then to a recommendation for a future course of action.

Strictly personal opinions are usually out of place in a research paper. As a result, the word "I" is seldom used. It is important in a research paper to "let the facts speak for themselves." You should let the authorities you cite carry the weight. It is much more convincing for a research paper to say, *"Thomas Jefferson* thought the taxing system should . . ."* than to say, *"I think the taxing system should . . ."*

If you wish to draw a persuasive conclusion in a research paper, you should generally present a series of facts in an "If . . ., then . . ." statement such as:

"If Jefferson's view that . . . can be applied today, and if the constitutional principle that . . . is still valid, then the tax system of the United States is not what the Founding Fathers intended."

This writer presents information from one of the Founding Fathers (the argument would probably be stronger if the writer had presented information from others as well); there are also appropriate facts from the U.S. Constitution. Then, in a conclusion, the writer brings those facts together into a summary statement. The careful reader would probably have picked up the differences between present practice and the intent of the Founding Fathers as they were presented throughout the paper. By stating the conclusion in the final paragraph, the author makes sure that no reader misses the point.

Parts of the Research Paper

1. Title Page

The title page includes at least the title of the paper and the author's name, both centered in the middle of the page. Often, the name of the course, the teacher's name, and the date are also included on three separate lines in the lower right-hand corner of the page (see Figure 1).

figure 1

USING EXISTING KNOWLEDGE AND TECHNOLOGY
TO DEAL WITH THE ENERGY DILEMMA

By

Susan Spangler

Introduction to Science
Mrs. Pomranka
April 6, 198—

2. The Abstract (optional)

An abstract is a brief summary of the content of the paper. It should state the central idea and main divisions of the paper as well as summarize any inferences made or comparisons drawn from the author's research. If the paper attempts to solve a problem or recommend a future course of action, the abstract should also state how the author arrived at the problem, how the research was done (reading, interviews, questionnaires, etc.), how the results were compiled, and how the conclusion was formulated.

3. Table of Contents

The Table of Contents lists the main divisions of the paper and their corresponding page numbers (see Figure 2).

4. List of Illustrations (if any)

(see Figure 3).

5. Introduction (optional)

The purpose of an introduction is to inform the reader of the intent or purpose of the paper and the extent of the research involved. If the paper covers a problem or a controversial issue, the problem should be clearly introduced, the necessary background given, a statement included about the method of research, and information given telling how the conclusions are derived.

Figure 2

TABLE OF CONTENTS

Figure 3

LIST OF ILLUSTRATIONS

6. Text

(This is the main body of the paper).

7. Appendixes (if any).

Supplementary or explanatory material not essential to the text but of importance should be included in the appendixes at the end of the paper.

8. Bibliography

The bibliography is a listing of all reference material used in preparing the paper. It includes published material such as books and magazines; it also includes such things as interviews, letters, and the like which may have been used but which are not commercially published. A later section provides specific information about the form to be used in the bibliography.

Choosing a Topic

Choosing a topic is the most important part of writing a research paper. If you choose an unsuitable topic or write on one which is too broad, your paper will not be successful.

Here are two suggestions which are very important to consider in choosing a topic. First, be sure to *select a topic which you find interesting*. If you write about something you have no interest in, you will probably not write well.

Then, be sure *the topic is in an area you would like to learn more about*. Having insurance against boredom is important for anyone writing any paper, but it is especially important in the case of a research paper, since you will spend a considerable amount of time with the topic.

Where do ideas for topics come from? For most writers, they come from one or more of at least three places:

1. Often topics come from *assignments given by teachers*. Usually a teacher will provide you with a broad area, however, and you will be expected to narrow the topic to something specific which you feel to be an important dimension of the area and something which is interesting to you.

2. Many times topics come from *your own experience*. For example, if you were concerned about the conservation of energy resources, you certainly could find a specific topic for research in that area. Sometimes, your interests and general topics assigned by a teacher coincide in strange ways. A student interested in engineering might respond to an assignment to write a research paper on Shakespeare's plays by writing about the stage machinery which performers of Shakespeare's time used.

3. Sometimes, especially as you read widely, you will find topics arising from *articles or books which you read*. If you keep your eyes open and search for topics when you are reading, you will find some excellent ideas. Most often, you will find the main thrust of the article provides an idea for a topic. But sometimes you will be struck by a single sentence or idea hidden in an article. If you are alert, always looking for ideas to write about, you will spot those hidden topics.

When you choose a topic, you should keep in mind the availability of materials that you will need for your research. Once you have an idea, go to your school, community, or home library and see if there is sufficient material to use as a basis for a paper. If you can't find at least ten sources which apply to your topic, you should probably look for another area. Use the card catalogue, the *Readers' Guide to Periodical Literature*, and other appropriate indexes to determine whether your library has enough material to provide you with a good base to work from.

Limiting the Topic

Once you find you have enough material, limit your topic. Imagine trying to write a paper on a topic such as "World History." You could literally write for a lifetime and never complete the work. You need to narrow that broad topic.

The key to limiting your topic is to select a subject for writing which you can cover *completely* in the time available to you. You must also consider the length of your paper. An illustration of the process of limiting a topic follows:

History
> U.S. History
>> The Depression Years
>>> Roosevelt's Anti-Depression Activities
>>> Government Work Programs
>>>> The Works Progress Administration (W.P.A)
>>>> Highways Built by the W.P.A.

An eventual title for a paper emerging from this process might be "The Impact of the W.P.A. on Transportation in the United States from 1935 to 1950." Included in the paper could be a description of W.P.A. sponsored activities, the costs of W.P.A. highway building programs, and the like. It would be possible in such a paper to develop a conclusion based on the benefits of the activity as it is related to its cost.

Taking Notes

Prepare a preliminary outline to guide you in note-taking.

In order to begin researching a topic in an organized way, you need to write some kind of outline that includes the topics on which you need information. Sometimes you will need to begin reading before such an outline can be written; at other times you will already know enough about your topic to anticipate the main sections of your paper.

Suppose you were going to write a research paper on the origin of modern-day blues music. Your tentative outline might look something like this:

1. The music of black Africa
2. The importation of black Africans to America and the treatment of black slaves.
3. Early black work songs, religious and gospel spirituals, and "plantation blues"
4. The emergence of urban blues in cities with high black populations
5. The music of early blues greats such as Louis Armstrong, Bessie Smith, and Billie Holliday
6. The influence of New Orleans ragtime and big band sounds on the blues
7. Progressive problems of black people and how these problems changed their music

Prepare a "heading card" for each topic of your outline.

A heading card is a single card, usually 3″ by 5″, which you use at the front of all note cards containing information on that particular area. An example of a heading card is shown below.

Heading Card

```
┌─────────────────────────────────────────────┐
│                                               │
│        1.    The Music of Black Africa        │
│                                               │
│                                               │
│                                               │
│                                               │
│                                               │
│                                               │
└─────────────────────────────────────────────┘
```

As you read, you may find that topics need to be added to your outline. As you add them, prepare heading cards for them as well.

Prepare a "bibliography card" for each source you use.

The moment you begin using a source (book, magazine, interview, letter) prepare a bibliography card for it. Use cards that are the same size as your heading cards.

The bibliography card serves two purposes: First, it provides a correct identification for each note you will take, and it saves you the effort of writing the complete source on each note card. Second, it provides a bibliography entry in correct form so that when the final draft of the paper is written, you need only arrange your "bib" cards in alphabetical order and copy them on the page.

If you were writing a research paper on energy conservation, you might use a book by Davis and Schubert entitled, *Alternate Natural Energy Sources in Building Design.* Your "bib" card would look like this:

Bibliography Card

Davis, Albert J. and Robert P. Schubert,
Alternate Natural Energy Sources in Building Design,
New York: Van Nostrand Reinhold Company, 1977.

Specific directions about how to prepare bibliographic entries are included in the "bibliography" section of this Handbook. Be sure to follow the directions very carefully. If your "bib" cards are carefully and accurately done, you will save yourself considerable time and trouble later on.

Prepare a note card for each potentially useful idea you encounter in your sources.

When you encounter something in your reading which you feel may be useful for your paper, either write it on a 3″ by 5″ notecard in your own words (paraphrase it) or copy it directly. If you copy it directly, enclose it in quotation marks. If you paraphrase the material, be sure you do not use the author's exact words.

Once you have written your note, write the author's last name, the publication date, and the page number(s) of the source at the top left of the card. At the top right, write the number of the topic (from your outline) to which the note refers. Here is an example of a notecard from Davis and Schubert's book, *Alternate Natural Energy Sources in Building Design:*

Note Card

Davis and Schubert, 1977, p. 42   #4

"There are three basic types of light. First there is <u>direct</u> sunlight, which originates from the southeast to southwest (high angle), and east to west (low angle). <u>Ground</u> light, a secondary source, is reflected from the earth's surface and varies in intensity in relationship to ground surface, angle toward the sun, and the slope of the ground. <u>Diffused</u> light or skylight is direct light diffused by the particles of the atmosphere."

You know several things from the form of the notecard: first, you know the source from which the material came; second, you know the page from which it came; third, you know that it is quoted directly (note that the material is enclosed in quotation marks); finally, you know which outline topic the quoted material refers to (**#4** refers to topic number 4 in the outline).

Notice that you do not write the entire bibliographical entry on each card, but only the author's name, date of publication, and page. You also do not write out the entire topic from the outline; rather, you simply identify the card according to the number of the topic from the outline.

When you have finished the notecard, place it immediately behind the header card for the appropriate outline topic. Most people like to place rubber bands around the cards to keep them together.

It is important that you use a fresh notecard for each idea you identify, so that you can have all cards for a single topic together and not have single cards which fit under several headings. Also, when you arrange your cards in the best order to help organize your paper, you will be able to shift ideas around as you shift cards. If you have many ideas on a single card, it becomes much more difficult to organize your paper. Most students get a pack of 100 3″ by 5″ notecards when they begin a research paper. Those following good procedures will frequently use all of the cards as they prepare a 10-12 page paper.

Writing the Paper

Review your outline.

As you have been taking notes, you have probably been modifying your outline. You have probably encountered new topics, and found that certain topics you originally felt important are no longer worth including. As you modified your outline during the notetaking stage, you probably modified the numbers on your notecards to conform to your changing outline. However, once you finish your notetaking, it is important to step back for a short time and look at the outline carefully. Ask yourself the following questions:

1. Do the main topics reflect the major ideas I want to present?
2. Are the topics reasonably independent of one another?
3. Are the topics arranged in the sequence that will be the most effective in presenting the information?
4. Do the topics lend themselves to an appropriate conclusion?

Based on your answers to the questions, modify your outline as necessary. You may find this to be a good time to add sub-categories to help you organize your materials even better. Some people like to develop very detailed outlines at this point; others go directly to the first draft of the paper.

The Thesis Statement.

Some writers like to write a single sentence which sums up where they intend to go with their research before the research effort gets underway. Most beginners like to let the major idea of the paper evolve as they become familiar with the sources they intend to use. Whatever your preference is, the first step in writing the first draft is to write a *single sentence* which sets the stage for what you will write in your paper. You may never use the precise sentence you write as your initial thesis sentence; in fact, you will probably revise it several times before you write your final draft. However, that single sentence is very important to you. It guides you as you organize your material and as you select which material to use.

A good thesis statement does at least two things: it tells the reader what your paper will be about, and it captures his or her interest. In the case of a research paper which intends to persuade, it also hints that the reader will be asked to accept the writer's conclusions. The following thesis statements may serve as examples:

1. The emphasis in the Constitution of the United States on the rights and responsibilities of the common person is due in large measure to Benjamin Franklin.
2. The world has a serious energy problem, but it can be solved through the intelligent use of existing knowledge and technology.
3. Jane Smith has the qualities Hamilton looked for in a governor.

Usually the thesis statement appears in the final draft of the paper at the end of the first paragraph; however, under some circumstances, it may not be explicitly stated until the end of the paper. A useful model for the research paper is the following:

First paragraph.

This sets the stage for the paper by catching the reader's attention; then it quickly moves to the thesis statement. The following is an example of an introductory paragraph:

The world's fossil fuels will be used up in less than one hundred years if consumption continues at present rates (Ernhardt, 1981, p. 18). Numerous high-technology solutions such as generation of electricity through panels in space with micro-waves transmitting the energy to earth have been proposed to solve the problem. Most solutions involve considerable governmental expenditure. What has been ignored by officials is the abundant supply of answers to the energy problem that we already have. The world has a serious energy problem, but it can be solved through the intelligent use of existing knowledge and technology.

The Text.

Once the first paragraph (with its thesis statement) has been written, organize your notecards according to the outline and begin to juggle them until they seem to fit an appropriate order within the topics. Then, using the notecards, begin writing, using the cards as guides. Often you will use only bits and pieces of the material on the cards; sometimes you will have to go back to the original source to get additional information (although if you have been careful in the notetaking process, this will rarely happen).

Sections of the paper should correspond to the topics of the outline, and you may wish to title those sections. Should you wish to do so, center the titles on the page and underline them. They should be included in the Table of Contents once you finish your final draft.

The Conclusion.

Usually research papers will have a conclusion. More often than not, the conclusion is a re-statement of the first paragraph and its thesis statement. The following is an example of a concluding paragraph:

> The intelligent use of the energy sources supplied by the wind, by the seas, and by the sun can eliminate the problem posed by rapidly diminishing fossil-fuel supplies. But rather than waiting for high technology to capture those energy sources, the common, ordinary citizen can make a common-sense application of techniques that go back to the cave dweller and thus delay the onset of a crisis in energy. Ultimate answers to the energy problem may involve complex technology, but immediate answers involve common sense and common people.

Conventions

Headings.

Most research papers use three levels of headings to sub-divide the content and to provide helpful cues to the reader.

A centered main heading
A flush-left side heading
An indented paragraph heading

Here are examples of the three headings:

METHODS OF RESEARCH
Library Research
Procedure
Written Results
Questionnaires
Writing the Questions
Procedure
Written Results

Proper Presentation of Numbers

When referring to numbers in a research paper, use *words* to express the following:

The numbers zero through nine
five others
We questioned *eight* doctors regarding their knowledge of the latest in cancer research.

Any number that begins a sentence

Sixty percent of those questioned answered, "yes".

One hundred forty students were given scholarships.

Use figures to express

Numbers 10 or greater

They tabulated a total of 48 responses.

Units of measurement or time

He was given 500-mg doses for 2 weeks.

Ages

Her daughter is 7 years old.

Times and Dates

8:25 A.M., January 29, 1988

Percentages

A total of 18% responded to the letter.

Ratios

The people voted 4:1 in favor of the bond issue.

Exact sums of money

Each person who completed the petition was paid $5.

Page numbers, figure or table numbers

Table 4 on page 26 shows the 1952 election results.

Numbers grouped for comparison within a single sentence

Of the 25 cases, 11 were settled out of court, 3 were settled in court, and 1 is still pending.

Commas in numbers

In figures of 1,000 or more, use commas between groups of three digits.

1,000 children 84,396 Libyans

Illustrative Material

Illustrative material such as tables, figures, charts, graphs, and photographs can increase understanding of the text in ways that words cannot. Just as "one picture is worth 1,000 words," one table or chart can show pages of written description at a glance, making it easy for the reader to assimilate and compare vital information.

- Figures, charts and graphs should be clear, properly labeled, and easy to read.
- Use heavy lines for vertical and horizontal axes clearly labelling the units in which they are measured.
- If possible, color-code each separate line placed on graphs.
- Number each figure, chart, or graph throughout the paper.
- If there are many figures within each chapter, number the figures by chapter (figure 3.8—the 8th figure in chapter 3).

Footnotes

There are three common kinds of footnotes, each serving a different purpose:

1. Content footnotes

Content footnotes explain or amplify the information in the paper. An example of a content footnote would be a reference to something in an appendix.[1]

[1]See appendix B for Solar Tables for North America.

> Most often, especially in short papers, you will place information such as this in parentheses at an appropriate point in the paper instead of putting it at the foot of the page. (See Appendix B for Solar Tables for North America.)

2. Reference footnotes

Reference footnotes are used to inform the reader about the source from which material was taken. Footnotes of this sort are used for all ideas taken from other sources, whether or not the sources are quoted directly. Avoid the mistake of footnoting only quoted material.

The most common way of indicating the source of referenced material is to use the following format: (Davis and Schubert, 1977, p. 42) immediately following the quoted material. The sequence of material is: a parenthesis, the name(s) of the author(s), the date of publication, the page(s) on which the material appeared, and a parenthesis. This reference appears in the text of the paper, not at the bottom of a page. Should the reader wish to find the specific article to which the reference refers, he or she should go to the bibliography, where a book entitled, *Alternate Natural Energy Sources in Building Design* appears under the authorship of Davis and Schubert.

3. An older system of footnoting

This system placed reference notes at the bottom of the page on which the quoted or referenced material appeared. This system was troublesome for a number of reasons: first, it required the reader to shift from the text to the bottom of the page, thus interrupting the flow of the reading; second, it was extremely difficult for a typist to allow a precise amount of space at the bottom of a page for anticipated footnotes; and finally, scholars who read research papers tend to be the ones who check footnotes, and they usually know the contributions of authors rather than the precise names of books or articles. Thus, they appreciate the appearance of the author's name in the text rather than at the bottom of the page.

The system advocated here is the one most widely accepted in scholarly writings today. It is also the most commonly accepted system in colleges and universities for research papers.

Bibliography

When writing a bibliography, observe the following details of form:

- Items should be arranged alphabetically according to the last names of authors.
  > If the source has more than one author, alphabetize it under the first author's last name. The names of co-authors are written first name first.
- It is not necessary to number the sources in a bibliography.
- Anonymous items such as encyclopedia articles are alphabetized by the first word of their titles, unless the first word is *the*, *a*, or *an*, in which case it is alphabetized according to the second word in the title.
- If an item occupies more than one line, the second line should be indented so that the author's name stands out on the page.
- Type bibliographical entries using single spacing leaving a double space between entries.

Follow the following format when compiling a bibliography:

Books
> Kotzwinkle, William, *Dr. Rat: A Wild Novel About the Ultimate Revolt of Mother Nature*, New York: Bantam Books, 1977.

Newspapers and Magazine Articles
> "GOP Unveils Tax Relief Ideas," *The Boulder Daily Camera*, March 22, 1979. (no author given)
> Attaway, Roy, "A Viking in the Keys," *Motor Boating and Sailing*, April 1979, pp. 67–70 ff. (*ff* means the article is continued later in the magazine.)

Encyclopedias
> "United States of America: Racial Composition," *Encyclopaedia Britannica*, vo. 22, Chicago: Encyclopaedia Britannica, Inc., 1966, pp. 18–19.

Interviews
> Davis, James S., Interview, Oct. 14, 1981.

A Glossary of Grammatical Terms

Sentence

A sentence is a string of words that makes good sense and is complete. The following strings of words are examples of sentences:

The elephant died.

Drop your packages off at the drugstore.

Every person at the celebration overate.

My dog chased the neighbor's cat into the street.

If a string of words that makes good sense is not complete, it is called a *sentence part*. The following are sentence parts:

On the chair next to the broken window

The carnival manager socked the

The man in the third row from the top of the balcony

Sometimes strings of words make no sense at all. In that case, they are called *non-sentences*. "Dribbled jumped the by and if the man" is a non-sentence.

Sentence Types

Most English sentences are statements or *declarative* sentences. The following are *declarative* sentences:

The book was large and difficult to carry.

Sammy is the nicest cat we've ever had.

The first baseman caught the fly to retire the side.

Another type of sentence is the question or *interrogative* sentence. The following sentences are *interrogative*:

Can you stop and pick me up?

Will John ever grow up?

A third type of English sentence is the command, often called the *imperative* sentence. The following are examples of *imperative* sentences:

Hit the deck.

Please go with me to the movies.

Enter the room quietly and take your places in your assigned seats.

Parts of the Sentence

A sentence consists of a *subject* and *predicate*. The subject is the part of the sentence something is said about; the predicate is the section which says something about the subject.

The Subject

The *subject* normally occurs at the beginning of the sentence. It contains the noun or pronoun which the predicate says something about. That noun or pronoun is called the *simple subject*. The subject is underlined in the following sentences, and the simple subject is enclosed in a box.

The boy ran fast.

The boy *who lives in the house next to mine* ran fast.

We noticed the boy who lives in the house next to mine running down the street.

Sometimes the subject is not at the beginning of the sentence.

Everywhere there was *laughter.*

The Predicate

The *predicate* usually occurs at the end of the sentence. It contains the main verb in the sentence and says something about the subject. In distinguishing between subjects and predicates, it is often useful to identify the verb first. Once that is done, finding the subject is usually quite simple.

In the following sentences the predicates have been underlined and the main verbs enclosed in boxes:

The boy *ran fast.*

The boy who lives in the house next to mine *ran fast.*

We *noticed the boy who lives in the house next to mine running down the street.*

Sometimes the predicate is not at the end of the sentence.

Everywhere there was *laughter.*

The Direct Object

The *direct object* is the noun or pronoun which receives the action of the verb. It is a part of the predicate. The direct objects in the following sentences are in italics:

The boy chased the *dog.* We saw *him.* He was chasing a *cat.*

The Indirect Object

The *indirect object* is a noun or pronoun which comes before the direct object in the sentence. It tells for whom or to whom the action of the verb is being done. Indirect objects in the following sentences are in italics:

Mary gave *Susan* a birthday card.
The donkey threw *Henry* a baseball.

Predicate Adjective

The *predicate adjective* is an adjective in the predicate which tells something about (modifies) the subject, and is joined to it by a linking verb such as the verb *to be*. The predicate adjectives in the following sentences are in italics:

The lake is *quiet* today.
The throat of the fire-eater became *sore* after yesterday's performance.
My mother's health seems *better* after her stay in the hospital.

Predicate Noun or Pronoun

A *predicate noun or pronoun* appears in the predicate. It is the same person or thing as the subject, and is joined to it by a linking verb such as the verb *to be*. The predicate nouns and pronouns in the following sentences are in italics:

My mother is the *Representative* from our congressional district.
Jim was the *candidate* who won the election.
It was the Jones *family* coming up our drive.
The culprit could be *she*.

Parts of Speech

Noun

A noun is the name of a person, place, thing, or idea. Here are some examples of nouns.

Henry gave his *brother* the *apples*.

Henry is a proper noun as all names are. It is the SUBJECT of the sentence. Proper nouns are capitalized.

Apples is a common noun and is the DIRECT OBJECT of the verb; it tells directly what was given.

Brother, another common noun, is the INDIRECT OBJECT of the verb; it tells to whom the apples were given.

Beauty is everywhere.

Beauty is an abstract noun and is the SUBJECT of the sentence.

Pronoun

A pronoun is a word that takes the place of a noun. In one of the preceding sentences, *he* can replace *Henry*, *him* can replace his *brother*, and *them* can replace *apples*.

Verb

A verb is a word which shows action or expresses a state of being.

When she *is* at home, they *visit* her.

Is expresses a state of being; it does not describe an action of any kind.

Visit is an action verb.

Adjective

An adjective is a word used to modify (more fully describe) a noun or pronoun.

The *full* moon peered over the *Chinese* junks.

Full is a common adjective modifiying the noun *moon*.

Chinese is a proper adjective modifying the noun *junks*. Since it is proper, it is capitalized.

Adverb

An adverb is a word used to modify (more fully describe) a verb, an adjective, or another adverb.

The *very* small child ran *extremely quickly.*

Very is an adverb, modifying the adjective *small.*

Quickly is an adverb, modifying the verb *ran.*

Extremely is an adverb, modifying the adverb *quickly.*

Function Words

Most of the words you use fit in the above five classes of words (parts of speech). These are called *content* words; they carry the majority of the meaning in sentences. Since certain pronouns replace and carry the content of nouns, they are *content* words.

Of course, content words aren't the only classes of words you use in speaking and writing English. Other words are called *function* words. They connect the content words according to the patterns of the English language. They include:

Pronouns

Sometimes pronouns are used to connect two sentences together and form one.

The man lives in Korea.

We met the man today.   (whom)

The man *whom* we met today lives in Korea.

Preposition

Words that connect nouns or pronouns to the rest of the sentence are called *prepositions*. The noun or pronoun is called the *object of the preposition*.

A friend *of* mine lives *in* Canada.

Conjunction

A *conjunction* is a word that connects two parts of a sentence. If the conjunction connects two parts that are similar in structure, it is called a *coordinating* conjunction.

Mary *and* Jim like ice cream, *but* I don't.

And connects two words. *But* connects two sentences.

If the conjunction connects two parts that are different in structure, it is called a *subordinating* conjunction.

Jeremy continued to fight *until* the bell rang.

Until connects a sentence (independent clause) with an adverb clause (dependent clause).

Articles

The, a, and *an* are articles. They always precede a noun and modify it. Thus, they are a kind of adjective. *The* is used when the noun it precedes refers to a specific object or idea.

The man left *the* dream of his boyhood behind.

A or *an* is used when the noun it precedes does not refer to a specific, but rather to a general object or idea.

An elephant can drink *a* gallon of water in seconds.

A and *an* refer to any or all elephants and to any and all gallons of water.

Interjection

An *interjection* is an exclamation that has no grammatical connection with the rest of the sentence. Many times interjections are used to show strong feeling. The following are examples of interjections:

Oh! Oh! There's a mouse in the house.

Please! Don't you know this is a library?

Alas, poor Yorick; I knew him well. (Shakespeare, *Hamlet*)

Multiple Classes

Words that you use in speaking or writing can fall into any number of the previous classes. For example, the word *up* can be used in the following sentences:

Preposition: The men's room is down the hall, *up* the stairs, and to the right.

Verb: Our neighbors *upped* the price of their house $3,000 last week.

Noun: "*Up*" was written on every sign around the hall.

Adjective: The *up* escalator stopped while we were between floors.

Adverb: Anyone going *up*?

The Prepositional Phrase

The *prepositional phrase* is a string of words which begins with a preposition and ends with a noun or pronoun. The noun or pronoun which ends the phrase is called the object of the preposition. The prepositional phrases in the following sentences are in italics:

The girl *with the baseball glove* is my sister.

My sister is the one *with the baseball glove*.

In the afternoon, we went *to the beach*.

On the other hand, we knew the burglar in the house would take the television set *near the family room*, the silverware *from the buffet*, and the coin collection *on my dresser*.

Prepositional phrases may be either adjectival (modifying a noun or pronoun) or adverbial (modifying a verb, adjective, or adverb).

The Clause

The Independent Clause

An *independent clause* is a string of words which could stand alone as a sentence. It is complete and makes good sense by itself, but it is a sentence that is connected to another independent clause or to a dependent clause. The following are examples of independent clauses:

I met a classmate, and *we went to the cafe for a soda*.

The man whom I expected to meet *wasn't there*.

I met a classmate whom I haven't seen in five years.

Dependent Clause

A *dependent clause* is not a complete string of words. It cannot stand alone as a sentence. The dependent clauses in the sentences below are in italics:

I met a classmate *whom I haven't seen in five years.*
The man *whom I expected to meet* wasn't there.

Verb Tense

Present tense verbs indicate action which is taking place at the present time:

The group *is going* to the film.
The singer also *plays* piano.
Ann *does play* the violin well.

Past tense verbs indicate action which took place at a previous time:

The group *went* to the film last period.   (past)
The birds *have returned* from the South.   (present perfect)
The rock band *had finished performing* when the star *appeared*.   (past perfect and past)

Future tense verbs indicate action which will take place at some time in the future:

The group *will go* to the film.   (future)
They *will have left* by the time you arrive.   (future perfect)

Voice of Verbs

Active Voice

The *active voice* verb makes the subject the chief actor, as in the following examples:

The dog chased the cat.
Henry ate his food quickly.
Sarah carried the whole load of firewood.

Passive Voice

The *passive voice* verb places the actor in the predicate, as in the following examples:

The cat was chased by the dog.
The food was eaten quickly by Henry.
The whole load of firewood was carried by Sarah.

Sometimes the passive voice is used when the actor is unknown:

The silver *was stolen*.

An error *has been found* in the ballot count.

Number of Verbs

Verbs may be either *singular* or *plural*. Singular verbs go with singular subjects as in the following sentences:

John (singular) chases (singular) deer out of the family garden nearly every night.

The students (plural) visit (plural) a neighboring school each year.

The book (singular) lies (singular) open on the desk.

Grammatical Relationships

Coordination

Coordination means that two equal things are connected in some way. The following sentences show coordinate relationships between elements:

The *boy* and his *father* walked to school.   (coordinate subjects)

The cat *lapped* the milk and *dripped* it on the floor.   (coordinate verbs)

The teacher thanked *Sandy* and *Martin*.   (coordinate direct objects)

The lady gave *him* and *me* candy bars.   (coordinate indirect objects)

Grandma spoiled Jim, and *Grandpa told her not to*.   (coordinate independent clauses)

They went *over the river* and *through the woods*.   (coordinate prepositional phrases)

The shark was *huge* and *ugly*.   (coordinate predicate adjectives)

Subordination

Subordination means that two unequal things are connected in some way. These sentences show subordination of one element to another:

When I get tired, I find it hard to get to sleep.   (dependent clause followed by an independent clause)

My teacher, *who has been teaching for ten years*, is an expert on language.   (dependent clause connected to an independent clause)

Modification

Modification means that a word, phrase, or clause makes the meaning of another element of the sentence more specific. The following sentences illustrate modification:

The *big* cat walked *quietly*.   (*Big* tells something about cat; *quietly* tells something about how the cat walked)

The man with the heavy coat left the movie.   (*With the heavy coat* tells which man left.)

In the beginning of the film, the hero finds a horse.   (*In the beginning of the film* tells when the hero finds the horse; it gives a time element to the verb, *finds.*)

Pronoun Antecedent

An antecedent is the word which a pronoun replaces. The following paragraph illustrates the relationship of pronouns and their antecedents:

Father turned on the news to watch the weather forecast. He (father) said that it (the forecast) warned of a major storm on its (the storm's) way. "Too bad," he (father) mumbled. "Looks like my (father's) golf match will be cancelled."

Pronoun Reference

Sometimes it is not clear what the antecedent of a pronoun is. For example, in the following sentence a reader could misunderstand the meaning because of an *ambiguous reference*.

The soldiers fought with the invaders until they were nearly destroyed.

Who was nearly destroyed? The soldiers? The invaders? Because the reader cannot be sure of the antecedent of the pronoun *they*, this sentence should be rewritten so that the antecedent is absolutely clear. Placing the pronoun very close to its antecedent usually eliminates the possibility of confusion.

THE BUSINESS LETTER

A business letter should include the following elements. Their numbers may be identified on the sample letter which appears on the facing page.

1. The Heading includes the street address; the city, state, and ZIP code; and the date. Always abbreviate the name of the state, since the recipient of your letter may write back to you, and he or she will want to use your return address on the envelope. The U.S. Post Office asks that names of states be abbreviated on envelopes to make sorting easier.

2. The Inside Address should be identical to the address on the envelope in which you send the letter. It should contain the name and address of the company or person to whom you are writing.

3. The Salutation will always include the name of the person included in the inside address. However, if you are writing to a company, not a specific individual, you have a small problem. Avoid the salutation, *Gentlemen.* That assumes an all-male company, something that almost never exists. If you address someone by title in the inside address (Executive Director, for example), you might write, *Dear Executive Director* or *Dear Director.* If you are writing to a firm and have no idea what area your letter should be directed to, simply wirte, *To Whom It May Concern* as your salutation. That is a bit formal, but if you are quite indefinite about the company, it may be best to be a bit formal in your whole letter. Whenever possible, include a specific name in your saluation.

4. The Body of the letter contains the message you wish to send. It should be clear and concise; it should reflect a business-like tone.

5. The Closing will normally be something like *Sincerely;* however, closings such as *Very truly yours, Respectfully,* and *Sincerely yours* are each appropriate. Capitalize only the first word of the closing.

6. The <u>Signature</u> should appear immediately below the closing, with the full name of the writer typed below it. Generally, one should leave four spaces between the closing and the typed name of the writer.

7. The <u>Envelope</u> should be addressed exactly as is the letter. The return address should be identical to the heading, except that the date is not included; the address should be identical to the letter's inside address.

The following is a list of U.S. Postal Service abbreviations for the fifty states, the District of Columbia, and the several trust territories of the United States. Use of these abbreviations speeds handling of the mail.

Alabama	AL		
Alaska	AK	Nebraska	NB
Arizona	AZ	Nevada	NV
Arkansas	AR	New Hampshire	NH
California	CA	New Jersey	NJ
Colorado	CO	New Mexico	NM
Connecticut	CT	New York	NY
Delaware	DE	North Carolina	NC
District of Columbia	DC	North Dakota	ND
Florida	FL	Ohio	OH
Georgia	GA	Oklahoma	OK
Guam	GU	Oregon	OR
Hawaii	HI	Pennsylvania	PA
Idaho	ID	Puerto Rico	PR
Illinois	IL		
Indiana	IN	Rhode Island	RI
Iowa	IA	South Carolina	SC
Kansas	KS	South DAkota	SD
Kentucky	KY	Tennessee	TN
Louisiana	LA	Texas	TX
Maine	ME	Utah	UT
Maryland	MD	Vermont	VT
Massachusetts	MA	Virgin Islands	VI
Michigan	MI	Virginia	VA
Minnesota	MN	Washington	WA
Mississippi	MS	West Virginia	WV
Missouri	MO	Wisconsin	WI
Montana	MT	Wyoming	WY

287 Beacon Street
① ⟶ Boston, MA 02215
January 3, 198–

②

Director of Public Relations
Denver Museum of Natural History
1295 Colfax Avenue
Denver, CO 80209

Dear Director:⟵ ③   ④

    Please send me a copy of your bulletin "Artifacts
of the Plains Indians of Colorado." I am enclosing a
money order for $3.50 which should cover the cost of
the publication. If there is a fee for handling and
mailing, please bill me.

    I would appreciate your prompt handling of this
request. I am writing a paper on the Plains Indians
and need the bulletin immediately.

⑤ ⟶ Sincerely,

⑥ ⟶ *Aaron Smith*

        Aaron Smith

⑦

Aaron Smith
287 Beacon Street
Boston, MA 02215

        Director of Public Relations
        Denver Museum of Natural History
        1295 Colfax Avenue
        Denver, CO 80209

A BRIEF GRAMMAR

Sentences

Most English sentences have subjects and predicates, and English speakers naturally expect to hear subjects and predicates when they hear the language spoken. Should a subject be omitted, they automatically supply one. For example, in this sentence

Get out of here!

The English speaker probably understands something like, "*You* get out of here."

The sentences below have been marked with a slash (/) to show the division between subject and predicate. The subject is in the first part of the sentence and the predicate in the last under normal circumstances.

Some dogs   /   have nasty habits.
No two dogs   /   behave in exactly the same way.
All dogs, including the so-called barkless hounds,   /   have voices.
(You)   /   Watch out!

Elements of the Sentence

There are three basic elements of the English sentence: the simple subject, the simple predicate or verb, and the complement.

Simple subject	Simple predicate or verb	Complement
Dogs	*like*	*humans.*
Newspapers	*spread*	the *news.*
The *pioneers*	*founded*	*Valley City.*
The *school*	*is*	*large.*
Henry	*seems*	*ill.*

A complement is not always necessary to complete the sentence's message; thus, some sentences do not have complements. The following sentences have no complements.

subject	verb
Most *dogs*	*bark.*
Susan	*is thinking.*

Word order.   The order in which words appear in an English sentence is very important in determining meaning. Read the following sentences to see how important word order is.

The lion ate Henry.
Henry ate the lion.

Simple subject.   The simple subject is the main *noun* or *pronoun* in the subject. Simple subjects are italicized in the following sentences.

The *man* with the heavy coat   /   is my father.
The vigorous young *colt*   /   is the son of the winner of the race.
He   /   ate the cookies.

Simple predicate.   The simple predicate is the main *verb* in the complete predicate. Sometimes the simple predicate contains more than one word. Simple predicates are italicized in the following sentences.

The man with the heavy coat   /   *is* my father.
The vigorous young colt   /   *is* the son of the winner of the race
He   /   *ate* the cookies.

Transitive verb.   Transitive verbs are simple predicates which take direct objects as their complements. Transitive verbs are italicized in the following sentences.

Henry *chased* the intruder.
The caterpillar *made* a cocoon.

Direct object.   The direct object is the most common complement. It receives the action of the verb. Direct objects are italicized in the following sentences.

Henry chased the *intruder*.
The caterpillar made a *cocoon*.

Indirect object.   The indirect object is a special complement which may appear only when a direct object is present. It indicates the person or thing for whom or to whom something is done. The indirect objects in the following sentences are italicized.

Sally gave a book.   Carrie showed her stamp collection.

Sally gave *Sandy* a book.   Carrie showed *Jim* her stamp collection.

Object complement.   The indirect object always precedes the direct object; the object complement follows it. In the following sentences, the object complement is italicized.

The voters elected Maria *treasurer*.

The results made Sam a former *politician*.

The couple kept their marriage a *secret* for ten days.

Linking verbs.   Linking verbs connect the subject with certain kinds of complements. Linking verbs are words such as am, are, is, were, was, be, being, been, seem, appear, become, smell, and taste. Linking verbs are italicized in the following sentences.

Marv *became* a dragon for the school play.

Sherril *is* the main character.

The play *is* really good.

The leading character *must be* terribly ambitious.

Predicate noun.   Predicate nouns are complements which follow linking verbs. The predicate nouns in the following sentences are italicized.

Marv became a *dragon* for the school play.

Sherril is the main *character*.

Predicate adjective.   Predicate adjectives are complements which also follow linking verbs. The predicate adjectives in the following sentences are italicized.

The play is really *good*.

The leading character must be terribly *ambitious*.

Basic Sentence Patterns

There are six basic sentence patterns in English. These patterns are the common ones, those which every native speaker of English understands naturally. These patterns reflect the order in which the elements of the sentence appear; thus, they contribute much to meaning.

Subject, Verb, Direct Object Pattern.   This pattern is the most common of the sentence structures in English. In it, the subject acts through the transitive verb on the direct object. The following sentences illustrate this pattern.

subject	verb	direct object
Our *dog*	*ate*	the *cake.*
He	*chased*	the neighbor's *cat.*

<u>Subject, Verb Pattern.</u>   This pattern has no complements. The verb is called an *intransitive complete verb* because it is complete, not requiring complements. The following sentences illustrate this pattern.

subject	verb
Dogs	*bark.*
Birds	*fly.*
Henry	*sits* in the garden every night.

<u>Subject, Linking Verb, Predicate Noun Pattern.</u>   In this pattern, the noun after the linking verb means the same as the subject. The following sentences illustrate this pattern.

subject	linking verb	predicate noun
The Mississippi	*is*	a *river.*
Elephants	*can be*	good *workers.*

<u>Subject, Linking Verb, Predicate Adjective Pattern.</u>   In this pattern is much like the Subject, Linking Verb, Predicate Noun pattern except that the word in the predicate is an adjective. It tells something about the subject, rather than being another word for it. The following sentences are examples of this pattern.

subject	linking verb	predicate adjective
Candice	*is*	*ill* today.
Little *brothers*	*can be*	*troublesome.*
Defensive *backs*	usually *are*	strong *runners.*

<u>Subject, Verb, Indirect Object, Direct Object Pattern.</u>   This pattern introduces a receiver of the direct object. The following sentences illustrate this pattern.

subject	verb	indirect object	direct object
Consuela	*gave*	her *family*	the *money.*
Mary's *mother*	*showed*	*everyone*	her baby *pictures.*
The *pitcher*	*threw*	the second *baseman*	the *ball.*

Notice that each of these sentences can be rewritten to place the indirect object in a prepositional phrase following the direct object.

subject	*verb*	direct object	phrase
Consuela	*gave*	the *money*	to her family.
Mary's *mother*	*showed*	her baby *pictures*	to everyone.
The *pitcher*	*threw*	the *ball*	to the second base-man.

Subject, Verb, Direct Object, Object Complement Pattern.   This pattern is the least common of those listed. The object complement follows the direct object and is a noun which means the same as the direct object. The following sentences illustrate this pattern.

subject	verb	direct object	object complement
The *couple*	*named*	their *baby*	*Harrington Spencer III.*
The *class*	*elected*	*Dennis*	*treasurer.*

Notice that in each instance you can connect the direct object and the object complement with "is." (Their baby *is* Harrington Spencer, III. Dennis *is* treasurer.)

Variations on the Sentence Patterns
There are a number of variations on the basic sentence patterns. These variations usually involve a shifting of the elements of the sentence, the addition of words, or the omission of words.

Questions.   Basic patterns are formed into questions in several ways. Notice the basic patterns below and the ways in which they have been changed to make questions.

Subject, Verb, Direct Object Pattern
Our dog ate the cake.
Did our dog eat the cake?

Subject, Verb Pattern
Dogs bark.
Do dogs bark?

Subject, Linking Verb, Predicate Noun Pattern.
The Mississippi is a river.
Is the Mississippi a river?

Subject, Linking Verb, Predicate Adjective Pattern
Candice is ill today.
Is Candice ill today?

Subject, Verb, Indirect Object, Direct Object Pattern
Consuela gave her family the money.
Did Consuela give her family the money?

Subject, Verb, Direct Object, Object Complement Pattern
The couple named their baby Harrington Spencer III.
Did the douple name their baby Harrington Spencer III?

Negatives.   The following examples illustrate some of the many ways that negatives may be made in English.

Samantha has slept much this week.	(positive statement)
Samantha hasn't slept much this week.	(negative through *n't*)
Samantha has not slept much this week.	(negative through *not*)
Samantha needs sleep.	(positive statement)
Samantha needs no sleep.	(negative through *no*)
Samantha needs little sleep.	(negative by diminution)
Samantha needs hardly any sleep.	(negative by diminution)
Samantha needs scarely any sleep.	(negative by diminution)
Samantha is kind.	(positive statement)
Samantha is unkind.	(negative by prefix)
Samantha is not kind.	(negative through *not*)

There are many other ways to form the negative in English; they usually involve shifting meaning by using different words.

Commands or Requests.   Requests and commands normally do not have directly stated subjects. English speakers usually understand the subject, however, even when it is unstated. If there is any question about the identity of the person to whom the command or request is directed, the listener normally asks the speaker to name the subject. The following are examples of requests and commands.

Please polish the car this morning.
Close the door when you leave.
Hit the deck!

Passive Voice.   Only Subject, Verb, Direct Object patterns may be changed to passive voice. This operation permits the Direct Object to function as the Subject of the sentence. In the examples below, the first sentence is in active voice; the second is in passive voice.

Active: The alligator ate the duck.
Passive: The duck was eaten by the alligator.
Active: The president opened the meeting with a bang of her gavel.
Passive: The meeting was opened by the president with a bang of her gavel.

Sentence Expansion

English would be a rather unexciting language if its speakers could only use the six basic sentence patterns without embellishment. In actual practice, one might think of the basic sentence patterns as a kind of framework on which the sentences of the language are formed. As one adds to that framework, the language fills out just as a building might take shape around its wooden or metal framework.

Modification.   One of the most common ways to expand sentences is through modification. Look at the following ways in which modification may take place in sentences.

Single-word Modifiers.   Words that modify (more fully explain or describe) nouns are called *adjectives*. Look at the following sentence-combining problems to see how basic sentence patterns are expanded through the addition of adjectives.

Basic sentence: The car blocked the street.
Add modifiers from: The car was dirty.
                       The car was old.
                       The street was busy.

Expanded sentence: The *dirty old* car blocked the *busy* street. *Dirty, old*, and *busy* are adjectives. *Dirty* and *old* modify *car* (they tell us more about *car*); *busy* modifies *street*.

Words that modify verbs, adjectives, or other adverbs are called *adverbs*. The adverbs in the following sentences appear in italics. Notice how they make the meaning of the verb more specific by explaying *how, when,* or *under what conditions.*

I won *easily*.   (explains how I won)
I won *yesterday*.   (tells when I won)
I won *handily*.   (tells under what conditions I won)

Notice how easily adverbs may be moved around the sentence.

Yesterday I won the golf tournament.

I won the golf tournament *yesterday.*

I *easily* won the golf tournament.

I won the golf tournament *easily.*

Immediately I felt better.

I *immediately* felt better.

I felt better *immediately.*

In all modification, the basic sentence pattern remains. Adjectives and adverbs are added to make the meaning of the sentence more precise.

<u>Phrase Modifiers.</u>   Phrases (groups of words usually beginning with prepositions such as *of, in, between, among,* or *with*) that modify nouns are called *adjective phrases.* The adjective phrases in the following sentences are printed in italics.

The girl *in the car* shouted.

They built a cabin *in the mountains.*

The dog bit the man *with torn pants.*

The house *between the oaks* is ours.

The blade *of the knife* is very sharp.

We love our little house *among the pines.*

Phrases that modify verbs, adjectives, or adverbs are called *adverb phrases.* As with single-word adverbs, they often tell *how, when,* or *under what conditions.* They also may be placed in many different parts of the sentence. Adverb phrases in the following sentences are italicized.

We eat breakfast *in the morning.*

We eat breakfast *in five minutes.*

We eat breakfast *in the kitchen.*

We eat breakfast *with our friends.*

We eat breakfast *with Grandma's old silver.*

Notice how easily adverb phrases can be shifted to different places in the sentence.

In the morning, we eat breakfast.

We eat breakfast *in the morning.*

There is little change in meaning when adverb phrases are shifted within sentences. Emphasis, however, changes a good deal. In the examples above, the first sentence (In the morning, we eat breakfast.) suggests that you will tell a listener what you do at other times of the day in later sentences. We might expect you to say, "Then, we have lunch at noon," or something like that in your second sentence.

The second example suggests something else could follow, although not necessarily so. One might follow "We eat breakfast in the morning" with "Some people sleep so long they have to wait until noon for their breakfast."

<u>Participial phrases</u> are phrases that begin with participles (verb forms) and modify nouns. The participial phrases in the following sentences have been printed in italics.

> *Going full speed,* the biker collided with a telephone pole.
> A little boy *carrying a large bag* slipped on the ice.
> The man *sitting there* is my uncle.

<u>Clause Modifiers.</u>   Clauses are groups of words that have subjects and predicates. Those that can stand by themselves, without the addition or deletion of words or phrases, are the same as sentences. They are called *independent clauses*. Those that cannot stand by themselves but must be included in the context of a sentence are called *dependent clauses*. It is the dependent clause which can serve as a modifier.

<u>Adjective clauses</u> are dependent clauses that modify nouns. Look at the following sentence-combining problem which produces an adjective clause.

Base sentence:	Vandals destroyed the house
Add modifier:	Vandals lived in our neighborhood (who)
Expanded Sentence:	Vandals <u>who lived in our neighborhood</u> destroyed the house.

Notice how "who lived in our neighborhood," a dependent clause, modifies the noun *vandals*.

Adjective clauses usually follow the noun they modify, just as adjective phrases do.

<u>Adverb clauses</u> are dependent clauses that modify verbs, adjectives, or adverbs. The following example illustrates the formation of an adverb clause.

Add modifier:	A storm had raged throughout the night. (After)

Basic sentence:	We woke up to a yard full of fallen trees.
Expanded sentence:	After a storm had raged throughout the night, we woke up to a yard full of fallen trees.
Or	We woke up to a yard full of fallen trees after a storm had raged throughout the night.

Adverb clauses begin with *subordinating conjunctions*, words such as *after, when, until, because,* and *if.* Adjective clauses begin with relative pronouns—*who, which,* and *that.*

Joining. Basic sentence patterns can be joined together quite simply. The simplest way is through the use of a *coordinating conjunction* (*and, but, or,* or *nor*).

    I like apples.
    My sister likes plums. (, but)
    Result: I like apples, but my sister likes plums.

Two sentences may also be joined by using a semi-colon (;), thus avoiding the use of the coordinating conjunction.

    I like apples.
    My sister likes plums. (;)
    Result: I like apples; my sister likes plums.

Sentences that have similar subjects may be joined by stating the subject only once and incorporating the remaining words into the new sentence.

    The angry elephant jerked the rope off the stake.
    , The angry elephant turned toward the stands. (,)
    , and The angry elephant charged at the surprised spectators. (, and)
    Result: The angry elephant jerked the rope off the stake, turned towards the stands, and charged the surprised spectators.

Sentences that have similar predicates may be joined by stating the different subjects and then stating the predicate only once.

    Jim checked his watch.
    , Charlie checked his watch. (,)
    , and Kevin checked his watch. (, and)
    Result: Jim, Charlie, and Kevin checked their watches.

Words

Nouns

Nouns are naming words; they normally name persons, places, or things.

Kinds of nouns

<u>Concrete nouns</u> name things that can be observed with one or more of the senses. Words such as table, city, apple, and girl are concrete nouns.

<u>Abstract nouns</u> name things that usually cannot be observed with the senses. Words such as hostility, love, anxiety, and concern are abstract nouns.

<u>Proper nouns</u> include all nouns that specifically name people, places, or things. Words such as Sandra, Mt. McKinley, Broadway Avenue, and *The Washington Post* are proper nouns.

<u>Common nouns</u> include all nouns not included in the category of proper nouns.

<u>Collective nouns</u> are common nouns that refer to groups or collections of persons, places, or things. Examples are crowd, gathering, and family.

Functions of nouns.

<u>Subject of a sentence.</u>   Nouns are commonly used as simple subjects of sentences. The nouns used in this way are printed in italics in the sentences which follow.

   The *man* is nearly seven feet tall.
   Whether we like it or not, that *team* is going to win.

<u>Direct Object of a verb.</u>   Examples of nouns used in this way follow:

   Thoreau wrote *essays* in the nineteenth century.
   The jury made a *decision*.

<u>Predicate Noun.</u>   Examples of nouns used in this way follow.

   Texas is the largest *state*.
   The overcharge was really a *tax*.

<u>Indirect Object.</u>   Nouns used in this way appear in the following sentences.

   The French offered *the United States* soldiers.
   Henry gave *Lucy* a locket.

Objective Complement.   Nouns used in this way appear in the
following sentences.

The judge appointed him *bailiff*.
The people elected him *chairman*.

Object of a Preposition.   The examples that follow are prepositional
phrases (a preposition followed by a noun or pronoun, together with any
modifiers). Nouns acting as objects of prepositions are printed in italics.

in the *house*
near an open *field*
outside the *law*

Possessive.   Singular nouns show possession as in the following
examples.

Henry's automobile
Carolina's apples
the *law's* variety
the *crowd's* anger

Forming plurals of nouns.

The following rules may be helpful in determining the plural forms of
nouns.

Most nouns form their plurals by adding *s*. Some notable exceptions
are listed in the following items.

1. Nouns which end in *s, z, x, ch,* and *sh* form their plurals by add-
    ing *es*.
    Examples   lens, lenses; fox, foxes; wrench, wrenches; wish,
    wishes.
2. Most nouns ending in *f* or *fe* change the *f* to *v* and add *s* or *es*.
    Examples: knife, knives; calf, calves.
3. Some nouns have similar singular and plural forms.
    Examples: deer, sheep.
4. Hyphenated compound nouns (nouns which contain more than one
    word) usually form their plurals by making the first part of the word
    plural.
    Examples: Secretaries-of-State, mothers-in-law.
5. Nouns ending in *y* preceded by a consonant change *y* to *i* and add *es*
    to form the plural.
    Examples: fairy, fairies; cherry, cherries; spy, spies.

6. Nouns ending in *y* preceded by a vowel form their plurals by adding *s*.

   Examples: monkey, monkeys; alley, alleys.

7. Some nouns form their plurals by changing the entire word.

   Examples: man, men; woman, women; mouse, mice.

8. Nouns ending in *o* preceded by a vowel form their plurals by adding *s*.

   Examples: radio, radios; studio, studios.

9. Nouns ending in *o* preceded by a consonant form their plurals by adding *es*.

   Examples: potato, potatoes; hero, heroes. There are several exceptions to this rule, however. Some are: piano, pianos; solo, solos; soprano, sopranos.

10. Nouns with Greek roots ending in *-sis* form their plurals by changing the i to e.

    Examples: analysis, analyses; hypothesis, hypotheses.

11. Some nouns keep their foreign forms.

    Examples: datum, data.

Pronouns

Pronouns are words used in place of nouns. They may be classified as personal, relative, demonstrative, reflexive, or indefinite.

Personal pronouns refer to persons. They are classified according to person, case, and number. The following chart illustrates this classification.

	First person Singular	First person Plural	Second person Singular	Second person Plural	Third person Singular	Third person Plural
Nominative Case	I	we	you	you	he, she, it	they
Objective Case	me	us	you	you	him, her, it	them
Possessive Case	my, mine	our, ours	your, yours	your, yours	his, her, its, her	their, theirs

Nominative case is used for subjects and predicate pronouns. Possessive case is used whenever ownership is expressed. Objective case is used for direct objects, indirect objects, and objects of prepositions.

Relative pronouns take the places of nouns as well as joining dependent clauses to the remainder of sentences. The relative pronouns are *who*, *which*, *what*, *that*, and *whom*. Examples of the use of relative pronouns in sentences are as follows:

The fellow *whom* I saw in the store is following us.
Those *who* step forward will get $8,000.

Demonstrative pronouns point out some definite person, place, or thing.
Examples: *This* scarf is mine, *that* one is yours.
These seats are taken; *those* are not.

Reflexive pronouns are formed by adding *self* or *selves* to the personal pronouns. They may be used in the following ways.

Direct object: He likes *himself* too much.
Indirect object: He bought *himself* a candy bar.
Predicate pronoun: The ducks are not *themselves* this morning.
Object of a preposition: Play by *yourself* for a while.

Indefinite pronouns are words like none, something, nothing, anything, and everything. They do not require antecedents, since they stand for things that are non-specific.

Verbs

The verb is the chief function word in the predicate. It establishes a connection between the subject and the complements that follow, or it serves to complete the sentence's action.

Transitive verbs are verbs that express action and that take direct objects. The following sentences contain transitive verbs (printed in italics).

Karl *hit* the fence.
While we all looked on, Daphne *tied* the score.

Each of the above sentences is in the *active voice*, that is, the direct object receives the action (expressed by the verb) of the subject.

The *passive voice*, on the other hand, involves shuffling the sentence around. The following are the same sentences expressed in passive voice.

The fence *was hit* by Karl.
While we all looked on, the score *was tied* by Daphne.

<u>Intransitive verbs</u> either show no action at all or limit their action to the subject. The following sentences illustrate the *intransitive complete verb.*

  The dogs *are barking* tonight.

  The pianist certainly *plays* well.

Contrast the last sentence with this same verb used as a transitive verb. Note the presence of the direct object in the changed sentence.

  The pianist certainly plays *Bach* well.

  Bach is the direct object in the sentence; thus the verb *plays* is now transitive.

<u>Intransitive linking verbs</u> connect the subject to either a predicate adjective or a predicate noun or pronoun. Linking verbs are usually forms of the verb *be* (*is, are, was, been,* etc.), although others such as *seems, became, appear, feel, smell, taste,* and *sound* may also be used. The following sentences illustrate the use of the intransitive linking verb.

  Henry is certainly a good basketball *player.* (*Henry* and *player* are connected by the linking verb *is.*)

  Henry seems better today. (*Henry* and the adjective *better* are connected by the linking verb *seems.*)

  The previously tame *tiger became* a *monster* in thirty seconds. (The subject, *tiger,* and the predicate noun, *monster,* are connected by the linking verb, *became.*)

Forms of Verbs

Verbs take two forms, regular and irregular. One of the reasons children or persons just learning English make errors such as "I holded the puppy" is that they are attempting to make the verb *hold* a regular verb. If it were regular, one would say, "I am holding the puppy," "I holded the puppy," "I have holded the puppy," and "I will hold the puppy." As you can see, when the same thing is done with a truly regular verb ("I am carrying the puppy," "I carried the puppy," "I have carried the puppy," and "I will carry the puppy"), *hold* is *not* a regular verb.

<u>Regular verbs</u> have four forms. The first, called the *infinitive form,* is the basic word from which all forms are created. The second is the *singular* form; it is used with singular subjects. Its regular form is made by adding *-s* or *-es* to the infinitive form. The third is the *past* form, used to express action which has occured in the past. Its form is created by adding *-ed* to the infinitive. The final form is the *present participle* form, made by adding *-ing* to the infinitive.

The following table shows the four basic forms of regular verbs.

infinitive	singular	past	present participle
carry	carries	carried	carrying
stop	stops	stopped	stopping
walk	walks	walked	walking
move	moves	moved	moving
hiss	hisses	hissed	hissing

Note the irregularities in spelling. Rules governing the spelling of regular verb forms are stated above. However, exceptions include the following.

1. When the infinitive form ends in *y* preceded by a consonant, as in *carry*, the *y* is changed to *i* and *-ed* is added to form the past.   (carried)
2. When the infinitive form ends in *s*, *x*, *ch*, or *sh*, as in *hiss*, add *-es* rather than the normal *-s*.   (hisses)
3. When the infinitive form ends in *e* as in *move*, add only *-d* to form the past and drop the *e* when adding *-ing* to form the present participle.   (moved, moving)
4. When the infinitive is only one syllable and it ends with a consonant preceded by a single vowel, as in *stop*, double the final consonant when adding *-ed* and *-ing*.   (stopped, stopping)

Irregular verbs do not appear to make their forms according to any systematic formula as do regular verbs. The following list illustrates the considerable number of irregular verbs. It also shows how common they are in ordinary usage.

infinitive	singular	plural	past	past participle	present participle
be	is, am	are	was, were	been	being
begin	begins	begin	began	begun	beginning
bite	bites	bite	bit	bitten	biting
choose	chooses	choose	chose	chosen	choosing
do	does	do	did	done	doing
feel	feels	feel	felt	felt	feeling
forget	forgets	forget	forgot	forgotten	forgetting
freeze	freezes	freeze	forze	frozen	freezing
get	gets	get	got	gotten	getting
have	has	have	had	had	having

infinitive	singular	plural	past	past participle	present participle
hold	holds	hold	held	held	holding
know	knows	know	knew	known	knowing
lie (recline)	lie	lie	lay	lain	lying
write	writes	write	wrote	written	writing
swim	swims	swim	swam	swum	swimming
go	goes	go	went	gone	going
make	makes	make	made	made	making
run	runs	run	ran	run	running
say	says	say	said	said	saying
sit	sits	sit	sat	sat	sitting
hurt	hurts	hurt	hurt	hurt	hurting
teach	teaches	teach	taught	taught	teaching
wear	wears	wear	wore	worn	wearing
thrust	thrusts	thrust	thrust	thrust	thrusting
think	thinks	think	thought	thought	thinking

Functions of verb forms

<u>The infinitive form</u> is used in the present tense and with the pronouns *I* and *you*. It may also be used with helping verbs such as *can, may, should, could, shall,* and *will.*

   I *will begin* at the beginning.
   I *feel* as good as new.
   The man *will choose* the fabric for the uniforms.

<u>The singular form</u> is used with singular nouns and certain pronouns, in the present tense.

   The detective *knows* the truth.
   She *swims* well enough to win the tournament.
   Horace *runs* the forty in twenty-seconds.

<u>The plural form</u> is used with plural subjects to express present tense.

   The members of the class always *forget* to close the door.
   They *hold* their new puppies so carefully.

<u>The past form</u> indicates past tense with either singular or plural subjects.

   He *chose* to go skiing.
   They *chose* to go skiing.

The past participle form uses the helping verb *had*, as well as related forms such as *should have, must have, might have, could have, should have,* and *will have.*

We *had begun* our trip by eight o'clock.
We *should have felt* relieved to be getting out of there.
We *had run* as far and as fast as we could.
We *could have worn* warmer clothes.

The present participle form uses helping verbs such as *am, is, are, was,* and *were.* It expresses action which is continuing, is anticipated, or had been happening.

The champion *is swimming* around the pool.
The children *were freezing* to death.
I *am getting* out of here.
They *are holding* the puppy.

Adjectives

Adjectives modify nouns in one of two ways; 1. they describe the noun or 2. they limit it.

Descriptive adjectives are the more common type, and are reflected in the following sentences.

The *tired old* man straightened his *aching* back and smiled.
It was a *solid* victory, and the team was *happy.*

In the second sentence, the adjective *happy* is a predicate adjective. It modifies the subject, *team,* just as if the sentence had begun, "The happy team . . ."

Limiting adjectives are of three types.
1. Numeral adjectives show how many or in what order things are considered.

    There are *three* types of limiting adjectives.
    The *first* item concerns the condition of the classroom.
2. Demonstrative adjectives indicate "which one" or point out specifics.

    This book should have been returned to the library.
    Both criminals were guilty.
3. Indefinite adjectives express an indefiniteness about a noun. They serve a writer by permitting the expression of a non-specific quantity or quality.

    Some students want the lunchroom closed.
    However, *many* want it to remain open.

All descriptive adjectives and some limiting adjectives have the potential for expressing comparison. The table below illustrates this quality.

adjective base	comparative form	superlative form
old	older	oldest
young	younger	youngest
fat	fatter	fattest
kind	kinder	kindest

Adjectives of one syllable normally form their comparative and superlative forms by adding *-er* for the comparative and *-est* for the superlative. However, those with two or more syllables often form their comparatives by adding the words *more* or *less* the words *most* or *least* being used for the superlative form.

adjective base	comparative form	superlative form
dependable	more dependable	most dependable
careful	more careful	most careful
foolish	less foolish	least foolish
careless	less careless	least careless

Some adjectives form their comparatives and superlatives on irregular bases. Following are some examples.

adjective base	comparative form	superlative form
good	better	best
bad	worse	worst
many	more	most
little	less	least

The comparative form of an adjective is used when one is comparing two things.

My father is *older* than yours.

That runner is certainly *faster* today than the last time I saw her.

I am even *more tired* today than I was yesterday.

The superlative is used when comparing more than two things.

My father is the *oldest* person in the room.

That time must be the *fastest* she has attained.

I am the *most tired* today that I have ever been.

Adverbs

Adverbs, like adjectives, modify other words. Adverbs modify verbs, adjectives, and adverbs. They can help a writer express time, place, manner, degree, and cause.

Time is expressed by adverbs such as *now* and *today* for present; *soon* and *tomorrow* for future; *before* and *yesterday* for past. Duration of time is shown by the adverbs *always* and *never*; frequency is shown by adverbs such as *frequently* and *sometimes*.

Place is expressed by adverbs such as *above* for position; *forward* for motion toward; *away* for motion from.

Manner is expressed by adverbs such as *quickly, slowly, better,* and *worse.*

Degree is expressed by adverbs such as *little, more, very,* and *almost.*

Cause is expressed by adverbs such as *consequently, then,* and *why.*

The following examples illustrate adverbs used in these ways.
    Today we're going to the country.   (present time)
    Soon we'll go to the country.   (future time)
    Yesterday we went to the country.   (past time)
    We're *always* going to the country.   (duration)
    Sometimes we go to the country.   (frequency)
    The picture is *above* your favorite.   (position)
    Move the picture *forward* just a bit.   (motion toward)
    Get that cat *away* from me!   (motion from)
    Let's get this over *quickly*.   (manner)
    Move it just a *little* to the right.   (degree)
    If we don't want to get fired, *then* we'll have to work hard-
      er.   (cause)

Many adverbs end in *-ly,* and are easy to identify. However, some adjectives also end in *-ly,* thus creating a problem. Also, there are many adverbs which do not end in that suffix.
    It is probably best to think of adverbs as answering questions like "When?", "Where?", "How long?", "How often?" and "How much?" Look at the following sentences.
    adjective   We all need *daily* bread.
    adverb   We all need bread *daily*.

Note how *daily* in the first sentence modifies bread. It functions as *wheat* in *wheat bread*. In the second sentence, however, *daily* functions as an adverb in that it answers the question, "when?" Therefore, it modifies the verb *need*. It tells the reader when the bread is needed.

Some adverbs which are commonly used but which do not end in *-ly* are the following.

almost	here	never	straight
already	instead	now	then
back	late	often	there

Prepositions

Prepositions are used with a noun or pronoun to make a phrase called a prepositional phrase. Such a phrase acts as an adjective or adverb in a sentence.

The following is a list of commonly used prepositions.

about	at	but (except)	into	through
above	before	by	near	to
across	behind	down	of	toward
after	below	during	on	under
against	beneath	for	out	underneath
along	beside	from	outside	until
among	between	in	over	up
around	beyond	inside	past	with

The following sentences illustrate the use of prepositions.

The man *with the Western hat* is a singer.   (adjective phrase)

We always eat *on Grandma's best china*.   (adverb phrase)

The rope *around the tree* keeps insects *from the leaves*.   (adjective phrase; adverb phrase)

INDEX

Art Credits

Photo Credits